Crime and Punishment in America

ALMANAC

Crime and Punishment in America

ALMANAC

VOLUME 1

Richard C. Hanes and Sharon M. Hanes
Sarah Hermsen, Project Editor

U·X·L
An imprint of Thomson Gale,
a part of The Thomson Corporation

THOMSON

GALE

Detroit • New York • San Francisco • San Diego • New Haven, Conn. • Waterville, Maine • London • Munich

Crime and Punishment in America: Almanac
Richard C. Hanes and Sharon M. Hanes

Project Editor
Sarah Hermsen

Rights Acquisitions and Management
Ann Taylor

Imaging and Multimedia
Dean Dauphinais, Lezlie Light, Dan Newell

Product Design
Michelle Dimercurio

Composition
Evi Seoud

Manufacturing
Rita Wimberley

Library of Congress Cataloging-in-Publication Data
Hanes, Richard Clay, 1946–Crime and punishment in America. Almanac / Richard C. Hanes and Sharon M. Hanes ; Sarah Hermsen, project editor.
    p. cm. — (Crime and punishment in America reference library)
    Includes bibliographical references and index.
    ISBN 0-7876-9163-1 (set hardcover : alk. paper) — ISBN 0- 7876-9164-X (v. 1) — ISBN 0-7876-9165-8 (v. 2)
    1. Criminal justice, Administration of—United States—History. 2. Crime—United States—History. 3. Punishment—United States—History. I. Hanes, Sharon M. II. Hermsen, Sarah. III. Title. IV. Series.
HV9950.H39 2005
364.973'09—dc22
        2004017067

Contents

Volume 1

Volume 2

Reader's Guide

Crimes are forbidden acts considered harmful or dangerous. They fall outside society's rules of proper behavior. Some acts—such as murder, robbery, and rape—violate the behavioral codes of almost every society. Other acts may be considered crimes in one culture but not in another. In criminal law both society and the individual victim, when there is one, are considered harmed by crimes. Each crime threatens some aspect of society; for example, white-collar crime—business-related crimes such as fraud or embezzlement—threatens the economy, and the illegal dumping of waste threatens the quality of the environment. For this reason, a victim's approval is not necessary for the government to prosecute a crime and punish the offender.

Over the past four centuries, crime and punishment in America have steadily changed as society has changed. Some types of behavior considered criminal in colonial times, such as idleness and heresy, have ceased to be treated as crimes, while other behaviors, such as computer hacking and toxic-waste dumping, have since been added to the list of prohibited acts. Technological advances have improved the abilities of criminals to commit crimes and avoid detection, but such advances have also aided law enforcement officials in their work. The rise of the automobile in the early twentieth century resulted in an increase in interstate crime and faster getaways for the criminals, but with their new patrol cars police were able to respond more readily to calls for help. At the end of the twentieth century, advances in telecommunications introduced new methods of breaking the law but also gave law enforcement officials many new ways to catch criminals and expanded crime-fighting to an international stage.

In a democratic society, the rules of behavior that maintain social order come from citizens, not from a church or from a royal head of state such as a king. These rules are set through judicial decisions, legal history, and cultural tradition. Rules are also established by legislatures, or law-making bodies, acting through democratic principles by passing laws of government based on the beliefs, opinions, and desires of the citizens. The rules and consequent punishments for violations are organized in sets and written down. Those who break the codes of criminal law in the United States are subject to the U.S. criminal justice system—arrest by law enforcement authorities, court trial, and punishment.

As English colonists established settlements in the New World beginning in the early seventeenth century, they brought English common law with them. This law included the well-known process of accusation, arrest, decision to prosecute or to dismiss, trial, judgment, and punishment. However, in colonial America rigid social order had to be maintained for survival of the first settlements and the colonists had to modify the English legal system to accommodate their unique situation in the New World. For example, there were often too few people residing in a given area for jury trials to be practical. In addition, many areas lacked a person with the proper law training to serve as a judge. Often an officer of the colony or a respected member of the community made legal decisions. Another difference between English courts and the developing American legal system involved the death penalty—the punishment of death to those convicted of serious crimes. American criminal courts applied the death penalty to fewer crimes than English courts. Colonists were also more respectful of individual civil liberties, believing the accused had a legal right to fairness.

With independence from England following the American Revolution (1775–83), a new American criminal justice system came into being. The common-law crime system gradually gave way to statutory criminal law. In contrast to common law, in statutory law acts are deemed criminal when the legislative body responds to a changing society's needs and passes a law prohibiting some activity or behavior. During the nineteenth century other basic changes in criminal justice arrived, such as professional policing and penitentiaries, or prisons.

Although fairness in the criminal justice system is a trait traditionally valued by American citizens, it has not always been evident. Throughout much of American history political power was held by one segment of society—white Protestant males. As a result black Americans, immigrant minorities, women, and other segments of society felt the full weight of law for much of American history. For example in the early twentieth century women could be arrested for voting and blacks could be convicted and executed simply because they were accused of a crime, regardless of the evidence available. The march for equality before the law and fairness in criminal justice procedures as guaranteed by the U.S. Constitution made steady progress through the late twentieth century.

The criminal justice system today is composed of many parts and numerous players. Legislatures, usually under pressure from society, make laws defining crime. Police and detectives apprehend offenders. Courts, prosecutors, defense lawyers, and judges determine the offenders' guilt. Prison wardens and guards, probation officers, and parole board members carry out the sentences. Criminal justice can be found in many varied settings, ranging from street community policing on bicycles to high-tech forensic laboratories; from isolation cells in a maximum-security prison to the historic chamber of the U.S. Supreme Court.

For an action to be considered a crime, not only does a loss or injury have to occur, but there must typically be a proven willful "intent" to commit the act. A harmful action that is an accident and did not occur from irresponsible behavior is not usually considered a crime. Crimes defined in the codes of law are either felonies or misdemeanors. Felonies are major crimes resulting in prison sentences of longer than one year. For certain felonies, namely murder cases, and in certain states, the punishment might be the death penalty, also known as capital punishment. Other felonies include robbery and rape. Misdemeanors are minor crimes punishable by fines or short periods of time, up to one year, in a local jail. Misdemeanors are sometimes called "petty" crimes, including such acts of petty theft as stealing a lawnmower from a shed or a compact disc player from a car.

Academics search for reasons why social deviance grew during the twentieth century. Criminologists and other professionals attempted to find the causes of crime in the hope of finding a cure for crime. Even though crime can be highly predictable—despite a seeming randomness at times—progress has been slow in isolating the causes.

Even less clear than the root cause of crime is the effect of the justice system on criminal activity. Crime seems to increase even as efforts to combat crime are intensified. Crime impacts millions of people, and the prevention, control, prosecution, rehabilitation, and punishment of criminals result in extraordinary expenses—not to mention the losses resulting from the crimes themselves. By the end of the twentieth century, operation of the criminal justice system at federal, state, and local levels cost $130 billion a year in addition to the $20 billion a year in losses to crime. On the other hand, industries related to crime and punishment create thousands of jobs, and the various forms of crime-related entertainment bring in many millions of dollars.

Features

Crime and Punishment in America: Almanac presents a comprehensive overview of the development of the American justice system. The two-volume set covers in twenty-five chapters various topics including violent crime, crimes against property, cyber crime, terrorism, environmental crime, organized crime, public order crime, school violence, and white-collar crime, from the first European settlements of the seventeenth century to the early twenty-first century. The *Almanac* also describes elements of the criminal justice system including courts, policing, forensic science, corrections, military justice, American Indian criminal justice systems, and juvenile justice. Additional chapters address the influences of moral and religious values as well as the media on crime and punishment. Each chapter contains sidebars highlighting people and events of special interest as well as a list of additional sources students can go to for more information. More than 160 black-and-white photographs illustrate the material. Each volume begins with a timeline of important events in the history of crime and punishment; a "Words to Know" section that introduces students to difficult or unfamiliar terms, and a "Research and Activity Ideas" section. The two volumes conclude with a general bibliography and a subject index so students can easily find the people, places, and events discussed throughout *Crime and Punishment in America: Almanac*.

Crime and Punishment in America Reference Library

Crime and Punishment in America: Almanac is only one component of the three-part Crime and Punishment in America Reference Library. The set includes two other titles:

Crime and Punishment in America: Biographies (one volume) presents the life stories of twenty-six individuals who have played key roles in the history of crime and punishment. People from all walks of life are included. Some held prominent national roles in developing or influencing the U.S. criminal justice system; others were defendants in key court trials that contributed significantly to the field. Profiled are well-known figures such as former Federal Bureau of Investigation (FBI) director J. Edgar Hoover, authors Charles Dickens and Truman Capote, Supreme Court justice Felix Frankfurter, domestic terrorists Ted Kaczynski and Timothy McVeigh, and social reformer Jane Addams. A number of lesser-known individuals are included as well, such as early female lawyers Belva Ann Lockwood and Arabella Mansfield, criminal defendants Daniel McNaughtan and Ernest Miranda, New York City police chief George Washington Walling, and political radical Emma Goldman.

Crime and Punishment in America: Primary Sources (one volume) tells the story of the criminal justice system in the words of the people who shaped the field and the laws that contributed to its development. Eighteen excerpted documents touch on a wide range of topics related to crime and punishment. Included are excerpts from colonial and federal laws, such as the Harrison Narcotic Drug Act of 1914; the Magna Carta; trial transcripts; newspaper accounts; government documents; various publications, including "The Al

Qaeda Training Manual" and Charles Dickens's *American Notes*; and notable speeches.

A cumulative index of all three titles in the Crime and Punishment in America Reference Library is also available.

Comments and Suggestions

We welcome your comments on *Crime and Punishment in America: Almanac* and suggestions for other topics to consider. Please write to: Editor, *Crime and Punishment in America: Almanac*, U•X•L, 27500 Drake Road, Farmington Hills, Michigan 48331-3535; call toll-free: 1-800-877-4253; fax to 248-699-8097; or send e-mail via http://www.gale.com.

Timeline of Events

1215   King John signs the Magna Carta in England, recognizing certain fundamental liberties and rights of landowners.

1609   English and other European colonists begin settling the East Coast of North America, adapting the English common-law criminal justice system to the New World. One such adaptation is establishing the position of sheriff.

1611   The colony of Virginia issues "Lawes Divine, Morall and Martiall" to maintain a strict control over the settlement's residents during its infancy.

1692   A series of witchcraft trials occurs in Massachusetts, leading to the conviction and execution of several supposed witches.

1740s   Slave patrols are established in the southern colonies to monitor slave activities. Such patrols are considered a forerunner of policing.

1775   The American Revolution (1775–83) erupts, driven partly by the colonists' desire to increase fairness and obtain legal protections in the criminal justice system.

1787 The U.S. Constitution is adopted, establishing a new national governmental system that includes a Supreme Court and gives Congress authority to make laws and establish other federal courts as needed.

1787 The first prison reform organization is established in Philadelphia, the Philadelphia Society for Alleviating the Miseries of Public Prisons, promoting rehabilitation over punishment.

1789 Congress passes the Judiciary Act, establishing the Supreme Court and various levels of federal courts, such as district and appellate (where district court decisions are appealed or reviewed) courts, and identifies their jurisdictions (the geographic area over which a court has legal authority). The act also created the U.S. attorney, attorney general, and marshal offices.

1790 Congress passes the Crimes Act, outlining seventeen federal crimes.

1790 Philadelphia opens the Walnut Street Jail, introducing a four-tier prisoner system based on type of offender. The system includes isolation for some prisoners.

1791 The first ten amendments to the U.S. Constitution, known collectively as the Bill of Rights, are adopted. The amendments contain several sections concerning crime and punishment, including freedom from unreasonable search and seizure, freedom from self-incrimination, the right to legal counsel, and freedom from cruel and unusual punishment.

1794 The Pennsylvania legislature becomes the first in the United States to define the crime of first-degree murder and eliminates the death penalty for all crimes other than first-degree murder.

1819 The state of New York opens the Auburn maximum security prison for men, an institution that becomes the model for prison-industry programs.

1829 Sir Robert Peele establishes a professional police force in London, England, becoming a model for future policing developments in U.S. cities.

1829 Pennsylvania opens the Eastern State Penitentiary, also known as Cherry Hill, which becomes the model for the Separate System, in which inmates are placed in solitary confinement around the clock.

1835 New York becomes the first state to stop public executions.

1844 New York City establishes the first city police force to address the rising crime rate.

1846 Michigan becomes the first state to abolish the death penalty.

1850 Allan Pinkerton establishes a private detective agency, known as the Pinkerton National Detective Agency, to provide security services for railroads and others.

1865 Congress creates the Secret Service in the U.S. Treasury Department to combat counterfeiting of U.S. currency.

1890 Congress passes the Sherman Antitrust Act to stop price fixing and to break up business monopolies.

August 6, 1890 William Kemmler becomes the first prisoner executed by the electric chair at the Auburn Prison in New York.

1899 Illinois creates the nation's first juvenile court system.

1905 Pennsylvania creates the nation's first state police force.

1906 Congress passes the Pure Food and Drug Act, requiring companies to label the contents of foods, particularly addictive ingredients. Congress also bans the importation of opium.

1908 The Bureau of Investigation is created in the U.S. Department of Justice to conduct investigations. It becomes the Federal Bureau of Investigation (FBI) in 1935.

1910 Congress passes the Mann Act, which prohibits taking women across state lines to engage in prostitution.

1914 The U.S. Supreme Court in *Weeks v. United States* rules that evidence illegally obtained by a federal law enforcement officer cannot be used in a federal criminal trial.

1914 Congress passes the Harrison Act requiring anyone who produces, sells, or distributes opium, morphine, heroin, or cocaine to register with the Treasury Department and pay taxes. The Harrison Act becomes the model for future drug legislation.

1915 Alice Stebbins Wells establishes the International Association of Policewomen, which later becomes the International Association of Women Police.

1920s Adoption of the police car revolutionizes policing, increasing responsiveness but reducing contact between police and citizens.

1920 The Eighteenth Amendment to the U.S. Constitution goes into effect prohibiting the production, sale, and transportation of alcoholic beverages.

1923 August Vollmer establishes the nation's first modern crime laboratory in Los Angeles.

1924 J. Edgar Hoover becomes head of the Bureau of Investigation and builds it into a model professional police organization.

1925 Congress passes the Federal Probation Act, giving federal courts the legal authority to use probation in sentencing.

1927 The first women's federal prison is established in West Virginia.

1929 President Herbert Hoover becomes the first U.S. president to identify crime as a key national issue in his inaugural address. Hoover appoints George Wickersham as head of the National Commission on Law Observance and Enforcement to examine all aspects of the U.S. criminal justice system. The commission issues fourteen reports by 1931.

1930 The Bureau of Investigation begins the Uniform Crime Reporting (UCR) program, the first national crime statistics system.

1932 Congress responds to the kidnapping and murder of the infant son of famous aviator Charles Lindbergh by passing the Lindbergh Act, making it a federal crime to transport kidnap victims across state lines.

1932 The U.S. Supreme Court rules in one of the Scottsboro cases, *Powell v. Alabama,* that states must provide defense lawyers for those defendants who are charged with capital crimes and who are too poor to afford lawyers. In 1938 the Court extends this requirement to all defendants facing possible incarceration. In 1963 the Court rules that all indigent defendants are entitled to free legal counsel.

December 1933 Prohibition ends with the adoption of the Twenty-first Amendment to the Constitution, which repeals the Eighteenth Amendment.

1935 Congress passes the Ashurst-Summers Act, prohibiting the interstate transportation of goods produced in prisons. This act essentially ends prison industries, a key part of prison life since the early nineteenth century.

1937 The American Bar Association recommends that all motion picture and still cameras be banned from courtrooms. Congress adopts the recommendation in 1944, banning radio broadcasting, cameras, and, in 1962, television from federal courtrooms.

1939 Indiana passes the first law prohibiting driving while intoxicated.

1939 Criminologist Edwin Sutherland introduces the concept of white-collar crime.

1941 The American Society of Criminology, originally called the National Association of College Police Officials, is founded.

1941 Hervey Cleckley publishes *The Mask of Sanity,* which introduces the idea of psychopathic behavioral disorders contributing to criminal activity.

1946 The United Nations identifies genocide as a war crime under international law.

1950s The rise in popularity of television introduces law enforcement shows such as *Dragnet.*

1950 The congressional Kefauver Commission begins a two-year investigation of organized crime.

1951 Congress enacts the Uniform Code of Military Justice (UCMJ) for military services.

1961 The U.S. Supreme Court in its *Mapp v. Ohio* ruling establishes the criteria for preventing illegal searches and seizures.

1962 A federal court rules that prisons cannot restrict inmates from practicing the Islamic religion.

1966 The U.S. Supreme Court rules in *Miranda v. Arizona* that criminal suspects must be advised of their legal rights before interrogation. This rule becomes known as the Miranda warning.

1966 Author Truman Capote introduces the first true-crime book when *In Cold Blood* is published. The book later becomes a popular Hollywood movie.

1968 As part of President Lyndon B. Johnson's war on crime, Congress establishes the Law Enforcement Assistance Administration (LEAA) to provide funding assistance to states for fighting crime.

1970 Congress passes the Racketeer Influenced and Corrupt Organizations (RICO) Act, giving law enforcement greater legal power to combat organized crime.

1972 The FBI opens its new academy in Quantico, Virginia, and adds the Behavioral Science Unit.

1972 The Bureau of Justice Statistics begins the National Crime Victimization Survey (NCVS), collecting data on both attempted and successful crimes.

1972 Congress passes the Juvenile Delinquency Prevention Act, establishing general rules for state juvenile justice systems, including the separation of juveniles from adults during custody and incarceration.

1972 The U.S. Supreme Court in *Furman v. Georgia* declares that the manner in which most states apply death penalty sentencing decisions violates the Constitution's protection from cruel and unusual punishment. In 1976, with *Gregg v. Georgia,* the Supreme Court upholds a new process for deciding on the death penalty using a separate sentencing trial.

1975 The National Organization for Victim Assistance (NOVA) is established to coordinate the victims' rights movement.

1976   Congress passes the Resource Conservation and Recovery Act (RCRA), making it a crime to dispose of waste in a way that could cause harm to public health and the environment.

1978   Congress passes the Foreign Intelligence Surveillance Act to increase law enforcement's counterterrorism capabilities, including greater surveillance authority.

1978   Ted Kaczynski, known as the Unabomber, begins an eighteen-year period of domestic terrorism by mailing bombs to various targeted individuals. He is arrested in 1996 after killing three people and injuring twenty-three others with his explosive devices.

1980s   White-collar crime captures headlines as scandal erupts around a number of savings and loans corporations.

1980   The victims' rights group Mothers against Drunk Driving (MADD) is formed to lobby Congress and states for tougher laws.

1980   Wisconsin is the first state to pass a crime victims' bill of rights.

1982   The Broken Windows theory is introduced, emphasizing that community disorder breeds criminal activity. This theory leads to a reorientation of policing, focusing on petty crimes in order to curb major crimes. Foot patrols take the place of car patrols as community policing techniques are adopted around the nation.

1982   Texas becomes the first in the nation to execute a prisoner by lethal injection, which becomes the primary method of execution in the United States.

1982   Congress passes the Victim and Witness Protection Act to provide protection for victims involved in the criminal justice system as well as for witnesses and informants of federal crimes.

1984   Congress passes the first law addressing computer-related crime, the Computer Fraud and Abuse Act, which prohibits interference with computer systems involved in interstate communications and economic trade.

1986   The War on Drugs begins with passage of the Anti-Drug Abuse Act that leads to a major increase in arrests, court cases, and prison population. The act also makes money laundering a federal crime.

1988   Gang violence continues to escalate in the nation's cities as Los Angeles County reports 452 gang-related deaths for the year.

1989   The U.S. Supreme Court rules that execution of offenders as young as sixteen years of age does not violate the Constitution's Eighth Amendment barring cruel and unusual punishment.

1990   Congress passes the Victims' Rights and Restitution Act, confirming that victims had a right to compensation and use of federal services offering help to crime victims.

1990   California passes the first law criminalizing stalking. Other states soon follow.

1992   The acquittal of Los Angeles police officers who had been videotaped beating black motorist Rodney King triggers extensive rioting for several days in the city, leaving some sixty people dead, twenty-three hundred injured, and six thousand arrested.

1993   Islamic terrorists set off a car bomb in the underground parking garage of New York's World Trade Center, killing six people and injuring one thousand.

1994   In its "get tough on crime" push, Congress passes the Violent Crime Control and Law Enforcement Act, which increases the number of federal capital crimes from two to fifty-eight, provides $4 billion for new prison construction, adds 100,000 new police officers in police departments across the nation, and adopts a "three-strikes" sentencing guideline for repeat offenders committing federal crimes.

1994   Congress passes the Violence against Women Act, providing funding for assistance to women who are the victims of crime.

1995   The murder trial of former football star O. J. Simpson is televised around the world, drawing attention to the U.S. criminal justice system, particularly forensic science.

June 1995 In a domestic terrorist attack, Timothy McVeigh bombs the federal building in Oklahoma City, Oklahoma, killing 168 people. McVeigh is executed by lethal injection in 2001, the first person convicted of a federal crime to be executed in thirty-eight years.

1996 Congress passes the Communication Decency Act to regulate obscene material on the Internet. Courts rule it unconstitutional, a violation of free speech protections.

1996 Congress passes the Antiterrorism and Effective Death Penalty Act, enhancing law enforcement capabilities in terrorism cases and banning U.S. citizens and companies from doing business with or supporting organizations designated as foreign terrorist organizations by the U.S. State Department.

1998 Congress passes the Identity Theft and Assumption Deterrence Act, making identity theft a federal crime.

1998 Congress passes the Digital Millennium Copyright Act, protecting video and computer game manufacturers from Internet sales of pirated software.

May 1998 Having murdered his parents the day before, high school student Kip Kinkel, enters the cafeteria of Thurston High School in Springfield, Oregon, and opens fire, killing two students and wounding twenty-six others. He is convicted in 1999 of the four murders and of twenty-six counts of attempted murder.

October 1998 Ecoterrorists set fire to a Vail, Colorado, resort, causing extensive damage. The perpetrators allege that the resort damaged wildlife habitats.

2000 Congress passes the Religious Land Use and Institutionalized Persons Act, recognizing a prisoner's right to practice religion while incarcerated.

September 11, 2001 Terrorists of Middle Eastern origin crash three hijacked airliners into New York's World Trade Center and the Pentagon in Washington, D.C. A fourth hijacked airliner crashes in rural Pennsylvania on its way to a target. Almost 3,000 people are killed in the attacks.

October 2001 Congress passes the USA Patriot Act, giving law enforcement officials more power to combat the threat of terrorism.

2002 Criminal investigation of the bankruptcy of Enron, one of the nation's largest corporations, begins, leading to several convictions over the next few years on securities fraud violations.

March 2003 The U.S. Department of Homeland Security begins operation to combat terrorist threats.

Words to Know

A

Adjudication: The process of resolving an issue through a court decision.

Aggravated assault: An attack by one person upon another with intent to inflict severe bodily injury, usually by using a weapon.

AMBER Alert: (America's Missing: Broadcast Emergency Response) A national communications network for alerting the public immediately after the abduction of a youth under eighteen years of age has been reported and when the child is considered in danger. The alerts bring in the assistance of the local public in spotting the missing child or his or her abductor.

Appellate: Courts that do not hear original cases but review lower trial court decisions to determine if proper legal procedures were followed. Appeals are heard in front of a panel of judges without a jury.

Arraignment: A part of the criminal justice process during which the formal charges are read to the defendant. The defendant is advised of his or her rights, enters a plea of guilty or not guilty, and has bail and a trial date set.

Arson: Any intentional or malicious burning or attempt to burn a house, public building, motor vehicle or aircraft, or some other personal property of another person.

Assault: An attack that may or may not involve physical contact. Intentionally frightening a person or shouting threats could be considered assault.

B

Bail: Money paid for the temporary release of an arrested person and to guarantee that the accused will appear for trial.

Beyond reasonable doubt: A phrase referring to the need to determine a defendant's guilt with certainty. This level of certainty is required for criminal convictions.

Bill of Rights: The first ten amendments to the U.S. Constitution, adopted in 1791. The Bill of Rights includes various protections of civil liberties in the criminal justice system, including protection from cruel punishment, unreasonable search, and self-incrimination.

Biohazard: Any biological material that has the potential to cause harm to human beings or to the environment.

Black market: The illegal sale of goods in violation of government regulations, such as selling illegal liquor at very high prices.

Blasphemy: A colonial-era crime of showing a lack of reverence toward God.

Bootlegger: A person who illegally transports liquor.

Bullying: Behavior such as teasing and threats, exclusion from social activities, and more physical intimidation; a common form of behavior among juveniles.

Burglary: Forcefully entering a home to commit a crime.

C

Capital punishment: The execution of a criminal offender; also known as the death penalty.

Capitalism: An economic system in which private business and markets determine the prices, distribution, and production of goods largely without government intervention.

Child abuse: Causing physical or emotional harm to a child.

Child labor laws: Laws restricting the type of work children can do and the number of hours they can work. These laws are designed to protect children from dangerous, unsanitary factory and farm conditions and from long hours of work at low pay. Such laws also enable them to pursue an education.

Child neglect: A failure to provide a child's basic needs, including adequate food or shelter.

Child pornography: A felony criminal offense often involving photographing and videotaping nude children or children being sexually abused.

Chop shop: A place where stolen cars are taken apart and the parts individually sold.

Civil disobedience: Challenging rules of public behavior in a nonviolent manner.

Civil law: Laws regulating ordinary private matters, in contrast to criminal law.

Civil liberties: Certain basic protections from government interference offered by the U.S. Constitution, such as freedom from self-incrimination and freedom from unreasonable searches.

Common law: A legal system in use for several centuries in England that provides a set of judicial rules "commonly" applied to resolve similar disputes. Common law is built on a history of judge's decisions rather than relying on codes, or laws, passed by a legislature. The decisions are written down and compiled annually in legal volumes available for judges to refer to.

Communism: A political and economic system where a single party controls all aspects of citizens' lives and private ownership of property is banned.

Community-based corrections: Facilities, often located in neighborhoods, that allow convicted offenders to maintain normal family relationships and friendships while receiving rehabilitation services such as counseling, work training, and job placement.

Constable: A colonial policing figure who delivered warrants, supervised the volunteer night watchmen, and carried out the routine local government functions of the community.

Copyright: The legal right of an author, publisher, composer, or other person who creates a work to exclusively print, publish, distribute, or perform the work in public.

Coroner: A public official who investigates deaths that have not clearly resulted from natural causes.

Counterterrorism: A coordinated effort among many government agencies to fight and stop terrorism.

Court-martial: A court consisting of military personnel trying a case of another military person accused of violating military law.

Crime: A socially harmful act that is prohibited and punishable by criminal law.

Crime syndicate: A group of people who work together in an illegal business activity.

Criminal justice system: The loose collection of public agencies including the police, courts, and prison officials responsible for catching and arresting suspected criminals, determining their guilt, and imposing the sentence.

Criminology: The scientific study of criminal behavior to aid in preventing and solving crimes.

Cycle of violence: The tendency of people abused during childhood to commit abuse or other crimes as adults.

D

Defendant: A person accused of a crime.

Defense attorney: A lawyer who represents a defendant to provide him or her the best possible defense from the time of arrest through sentencing and, later, appeals of the case. The defense attorney is responsible for seeing that the constitutional rights of the defendant are protected.

Delinquents: Juveniles who commit acts considered adult crimes.

Democracy: A system of government that allows multiple political parties, the members of which are elected to various government offices by popular vote of the people.

Desertion: The military crime of abandoning a military post or assignment without approval.

Disposition: The legal term for a sentence in the criminal justice system; sentences may range from fines to imprisonment in a large, tightly guarded correctional facility.

Dissident: A person with opposing political views to those in power or the government.

DNA: DNA is deoxyribonucleic acid, the substance that chromosomes are made of. Chromosomes, long connected double strands of DNA that have a structure resembling a twisted ladder, contain an individual's genetic code, which is unique to every person (except identical twins, who share the same genetic code).

Double jeopardy: A rule stating that a person cannot be tried for the same offense twice.

Drug cartel: An organized crime group that grows and sells narcotics.

Drug trafficking: The buying or selling of illegal drugs.

E

Ecoterrorism: Terrorist activities that target businesses or other organizations that are thought to be damaging the environment. The term can also refer to terrorist actions designed to harm the environment of a political enemy.

Embezzlement: The stealing of money or property by a trusted employee or other person.

Encryption: The use of secret codes that can be translated into meaningful communications only by authorized persons who have knowledge of the code.

Environmental crime: To commit an act with intent to harm ecological or biological systems for the purpose of personal or corporate gain; actions that violate environmental protection laws.

Espionage: Spies acquiring information about the activities of another country.

Exclusionary rule: Evidence obtained illegally by the police cannot be used—will be excluded from consideration—in a court of law.

Extortion: Threats to commit violence or other types of harm with the intent of obtaining money or property from another person or group.

F

Felony: A serious crime that can lead to imprisonment or execution.

First-degree murder: A deliberate and planned killing; or, a murder in connection with the commission of another felony crime such as robbery or rape.

Forensic science: The application of a wide range of scientific knowledge within a court of law. Forensic science is used to analyze a crime scene, including weapon identification, fingerprinting, document analysis, chemical identification, and trace analysis of hair and fibers.

Forgery: The signing of a false name on a legal document such as a check, and the cashing of such a check at a store or bank using false identification.

Fraud: Intentionally deceiving another for personal economic benefit.

G

Grand jury: A group of citizens chosen from the community who determine in a hearing closed to the public if there is sufficient evidence to justify indictment of the accused and a trial. Only prosecutors present evidence in grand jury hearings, not attorneys representing the defendant.

Grand larceny: Theft of money or property of great value.

H

Habitual offender: A criminal who repeatedly commits crimes, often of various types.

Hacker: Someone who gains unauthorized access to a specific computer network system and reads or copies secret or private information.

Halfway house: Rigidly controlled rehabilitation homes for offenders who have been released early from prison or are on parole. Halfway houses were created to relieve prison overcrowding. Services can include counseling, treatment, and education programs, or halfway houses can simply be a place to live under supervision.

Hate crime: A violent attack against a person or group because of race, ethnicity, religion, or gender.

Hazardous waste: Any solid or liquid substance that because of its quantity, concentration, or physical or chemical properties may cause serious harm to humans or the environment when it is improperly transported, treated, stored, or disposed of.

Heresy: Holding a belief that conflicts with church doctrine. In some societies, during certain eras—such as colonial America—heresy has been prosecuted as a crime.

Hung jury: A circumstance wherein a jury cannot agree on a verdict; in such cases the defendant may face a retrial.

I

Identity theft: The theft of an individual's identifying information—including credit card numbers, social security number, or driver's license number—to allow a criminal to use another person's identity in making purchases or for other unauthorized activities.

Impartial jury: The notion that the members of jury will regard all evidence presented with an open mind.

Incarceration: Confining a person in jail or prison.

Indictment: A written accusation of criminal charges against a person.

Insider trading: Buying and selling securities based on reliable business information not available to the general public.

Insubordination: A military crime involving the disobeying of an authority, such as a military commander.

Intake worker: A person trained to work with youthful offenders, such as a probation officer.

Intellectual property (IP) theft: The theft of material that is copyrighted, the theft of trade secrets, and violations of trademarks.

Involuntary manslaughter: A homicide resulting from negligence or lack of regard for safety.

J

Jail: A facility operated by a city or county for short-term detention of defendants awaiting trial or those convicted of misdemeanors.

Jim Crow: State and local laws in the United States that enforced legal segregation in the first half of the twentieth century, keeping races separated in every aspect of life from schools to restrooms and water fountains. Such laws were particularly common in the South.

Jurisdiction: The geographic area or type of crime over which certain branches of law enforcement or courts have legal authority.

Juvenile courts: A special court system that has jurisdiction over children accused of criminal conduct, over youthful victims of abuse or neglect, and over young people who violate rules that apply only to juveniles.

L

Labor racketeering: The existence of a criminal organization that works its way into a position of power in a labor union in order to steal from the union's retirement and health funds.

Landmark decision: A ruling by the U.S. Supreme Court that sets an important precedent for future cases and can influence daily operating procedures of police, courts, and corrections.

Larceny: Theft of property, either with or without the use of force.

Loan sharking: Charging very high interest rates on loans.

M

Mafia: A crime organization originating in Sicily, Italy, that is thought to control racketeering in the United States.

Magistrate: In colonial times the magistrate was the key judicial official in local courts, often a key member of the community. In modern times, a magistrate is an official with limited judicial authority who issues arrest and search warrants, sets bail, conducts pretrial hearings, and hears misdemeanor cases.

Mail fraud: Using the mail system to make false offers to or otherwise defraud recipients.

Malice: The intent to inflict serious bodily harm.

Mandatory sentence: A specific penalty required by law upon conviction for a specific offense.

Manslaughter: A homicide not involving malice, or the intent to inflict serious harm.

Martial law: A legal system through which the military exerts police power in place of civilian rule in politically unstable areas to protect safety and property.

Mass murderer: A person who kills many people in a single crime episode.

Mediation: A process for resolving disputes in which both the victim and offender must agree to meet and attempt to settle their dispute in a face-to-face manner, under the guidance of a neutral party.

Midnight dumping: The illegal disposal of hazardous wastes under cover of darkness in a remote area.

Miranda rights: The rights of a defendant to obtain legal counsel and refrain from self-incrimination.

Misdemeanor: A minor crime usually punishable by brief jail time or a fine.

Mistrial: A circumstance whereby a trial is discontinued because of a serious mistake or misconduct on the part of attorneys, court officials, or jury members.

Money laundering: To make the tracking of crime profits very difficult by placing money gained from crime into legitimate financial institutions, often banks outside the United States; placing such money into accounts of bogus companies; or mixing such funds with legally obtained money in the bank accounts of legitimate companies owned or operated by organized crime groups.

Moral values: The commonly accepted standards of what is right and wrong.

Multiple homicide: A crime in which a person kills more than one person on a single occasion.

Murder: Killing another person with malicious intent.

N

Narcotic: Habit-forming drugs that relieve pain or cause sleep, including heroin and opium.

Neighborhood watch: A crime prevention program in which residents watch out for suspicious activity in their neighborhoods and notify the police if they spot criminal activity.

O

Obscene: Material that has no socially redeeming value and is considered offensive according to community standards of decency.

Organized crime: People or groups joined together to profit from illegal businesses.

Organized labor: A collective effort by workers and labor organizations in general to seek better working conditions.

P

Page-jacking: A fake Web site using the same key words or Web site descriptions as a legitimate site with the intention of misdirecting Internet traffic to another site such as a pornography site.

Paraphilia: Sexual behavior considered bizarre or abnormal, such as voyeurism (spying on others for sexual pleasure) or pedophilia (sexual desire involving children).

***Parens patriae*:** The concept that the government has the right to become the parent of children in need—to save them from terrible living conditions or protect them from criminal influences.

Parole: The release of an inmate before the end of his or her sentence.

Pedophilia: Receiving sexual pleasure from activities that focus on children as sex objects.

Penitentiary or prison: A state or federal facility for holding inmates convicted of a felony.

Perjury: Intentionally making a false statement or lying while under oath during a court appearance.

Petition: Requesting to be heard by the courts on some dispute.

Petty larceny: Theft of small amounts of money.

Pillory: A form of colonial-period punishment consisting of a wooden frame that has holes for heads and hands.

Plea bargain: A guilty plea offered by the defendant in return for reduced charges, a lighter sentence, or some other consideration.

Pollutant: A man-made waste that contaminates the environment.

Pornography: Materials such as magazines, books, pictures, and videos that show nudity and sexual acts.

Prejudice: A judgment or opinion formed without sufficient information.

Preponderance of evidence: A sufficient amount of evidence to indicate the guilt of the accused. The term also refers to the level of evidence used in civil cases and juvenile courts.

Price-fixing: Governments or companies artificially setting the price for particular goods rather than letting the market determine pricing.

Probable cause: Sufficient evidence to support an arrest.

Probation: A criminal sentence other than jail or prison time for persons convicted of less serious crimes; those sentenced with probation are usually placed under court supervision for a specific period of time.

Prohibition: Prohibiting the production, sale, transport, and possession of alcoholic beverages resulting from the adoption of the Eighteenth Amendment to the U.S. Constitution in 1919 and the resulting Volstead Act of 1920; this amendment was repealed by the Twenty-first Amendment to the Constitution in December in 1933.

Property crimes: Theft where no force or threat of force is directed toward an individual; such crimes are usually driven by the prospect of financial gain.

Prosecutor: Public officials who represent the government in criminal cases. Prosecutors are often known as district attorneys or prosecuting attorneys in federal courts and are commonly elected or appointed to their positions.

Prostitution: A person offering sexual acts in return for payments, generally payments of money.

Public defender: A state-employed attorney who provides free legal counsel to defendants too poor to hire a lawyer.

Public order crime: Behavior that is banned because it threatens the general well-being of a community or society.

R

Racism: To be prejudiced against people of a different race.

Racketeering: The act of participating in a continuing pattern of criminal behavior.

Rape: Having sexual relations by force or the threat of force.

Rehabilitation: Providing treatment to an offender to prevent further criminal behavior.

Restitution: Compensation or payment by an offender to a victim; restitution may involve community service work rather than incarceration or payments.

Restraining trade: An effort to inhibit business competition through illegal means, such as fixing prices of goods and services artificially low.

Robbery: Taking money or property by force or the threat of force.

S

Sabotage: To destroy military or industrial facilities.

Second-degree murder: An unplanned or accidental killing through a desire to cause serious bodily harm.

Securities: Stocks or bonds.

Securities fraud: An individual or organization falsely manipulating the market price of a stock or commodity by deliberately providing misleading information to investors.

Self-incrimination: Offering damaging information about oneself during a trial or hearing; a person cannot be made to testify against him or herself and has the right to remain silent during a trial or interrogation.

Serial killer: A person who kills multiple people over a period of time.

Shield laws: Legislation prohibiting rape victims from being questioned about their prior sexual history unless specific need for the information is identified.

Shoplifting: A common form of petty larceny; taking merchandise from a store without paying for it.

Slave patrols: Groups of white volunteers assembled in the 1740s to police the black slave populations with the intent of protecting white citizens from slaves, suppressing slave uprisings, and capturing runaway slaves. Slave patrols are considered an early form of organized policing.

Sociopathic: A personality disorder characterized by antisocial, often destructive, behavior with little show of emotion.

Sovereignty: A government largely free from outside political control.

Speakeasy: A place where alcoholic beverages were illegally sold during Prohibition.

Stalking: The act of repeatedly following or spying on another person or making unwanted communications or threats.

Status offenses: Rules that apply only to juveniles such as unapproved absence from school (truancy), running away from home, alcohol and tobacco use, and refusing to obey parents.

Statutory rape: Rape without force involving an adult and teenager under the age of consent who has apparently agreed to the act; it is a crime because it is established by statute, or law.

Stranger violence: A crime in which the victim has had no previous contact with his or her attacker.

Strike: A work stoppage intended to force an employer to meet worker demands.

Subversive: Political radicals working secretly to overthrow a government.

Supermax prisons: Short for super-maximum-security prisons. Supermax prisons are designed to keep the most violent or disruptive inmates separated from other prisoners and correction staff, often in a special area within an existing prison.

T

Temperance: The use of alcoholic beverages in moderation or abstinence from all alcohol.

Terrorism: The planned use of force or violence, normally against innocent civilians, to make a statement about a cause. Terrorist attacks are staged for maximum surprise, shock, and destruction to influence individuals, groups, or governments to give in to certain demands.

Three-strikes laws: Laws that dictate that a criminal convicted of his or her third felony must remain in prison for an extended period of time, sometimes for life.

Toxicity: The degree to which a substance is poisonous.

Toxicology: The study of toxic or poisonous substances that can cause harm or death to any individual who takes them, depending on the amount ingested.

Trace evidence: Microscopic or larger materials, commonly hairs or fibers, transferred from person to person or object to object during a crime; examples include human or animal hair as well as wood, clothing, or carpet fibers.

Treason: An attempt to overthrow one's own government.

True crime: Stories in books, magazines, or films or on television programs that are based on actual crimes.

Trusts: Organizations formed by combining several major industries together to stifle competition and run smaller companies out of business.

V

Victim compensation: Payment of funds to help victims survive the financial losses caused by crimes against them.

Victimization: The physical, emotional, and financial harm victims suffer from crime, including violent crime, property crime, and business corruption.

Victimless crime: Crimes often between two persons who agree to the activity, leaving no immediate victims to file charges; such crimes are considered crimes against society and are defined by law or statute.

Victims' rights: A guarantee that victims of crime be treated with dignity and fairness by police, prosecutors, and other officials and be protected from threats and harm; victims may be notified about the progress of their case and informed of upcoming court dates such as parole hearings.

Vigilantes: A group of citizens assembled on their own initiative to maintain order.

Violent crime: Crimes against the person including murder, robbery, aggravated assault, rape, sniper attacks, crimes of hate, and stalking.

Virus: A computer program that disrupts or destroys existing computer systems by destroying computer files. Viruses often cost companies and individuals millions of dollars in downtime.

W

Warrant: An order issued by a judge or magistrate to make an arrest, seize property, or make a search.

White-collar crime: A person using a position of authority and responsibility in a legitimate business organization to commit crimes of fraud and deceit for his or her personal financial gain.

Work release: The release of selected inmates from a prison or community residential center for work during the day, returning at night.

Research and Activity Ideas

The following research and activity ideas are intended to offer suggestions for complementing crime and punishment studies, to trigger additional ideas for enhancing learning, and to provide cross-disciplinary projects for Internet, library, and classroom use.

Crime Statistics: The following annual publications can be found either online or in the reference section of local libraries: the Federal Bureau of Investigation's Uniform Crime Reporting Program (UCR) yearly report (http://www.fbi.gov/ucr/ucr.htm) or the National Crime Victimization Survey (NCVS), an ongoing study by the U.S. Bureau of the Census and the Bureau of Justice Statistics, an agency in the U.S. Department of Justice (http://www.ojp.usdoj.gov/bjs/cvict.htm). Divide the class into two groups and assign one statistic publication to each. Members of the groups should explore and analyze the statistics and report to the class on what they've found.

Three-Strikes Laws: As a class, research the three-strikes law in your state or a nearby state. Have a debate on the pros and cons of having such a law. Each student make a pro-con chart listing arguments for each side.

Neighborhood Watch Programs: Research neighborhood watch programs in your community. Students who live in a neighborhood with a program should interview its organizers and learn what is expected of participants in the program.

Map of Correction Facilities: Using a map of your state and some pushpins, locate federal, state, and county correction facilities. Explain to others the different roles of the facilities in housing convicted offenders.

Causes of Crime: Create a visual diagram illustrating the leading causes of crime. Place the word "crime" at the center of the diagram and surround it with words or pictures that convey the various causes.

Types of Crime: Create a visual diagram illustrating the various types of violent crimes, crimes against property, and public order crimes (such as substance abuse, prostitution, and pornography). Place the word "crime" in a circle at the center of the diagram, surround it with three more circles representing each general crime category, and then surround each category circle with words that describe the types of crime within that category. Be sure you can explain terms that many people find confusing. For example, what is the difference between murder and manslaughter? What are the definitions of robbery, burglary, and larceny? What does aggravated assault mean?

Newspaper Reports: Scan your community's newspaper for stories about crimes committed in your locality. Place them into a specific crime category—violent, property, public order, white collar, environmental, or cyber crime. For a well-publicized crime, attempt to follow court proceedings for as long as possible.

AMBER Alert: Research the history of AMBER Alerts. Learn the specifics needed to call an AMBER Alert in your state. How is the public notified of an alert and what should each individual do when they hear an alert called? Research actual AMBER Alerts in your state and find out their success rates or outcomes.

White-Collar Crime: Divide the class into eight groups and assign each group to learn about one type of white-collar fraud: healthcare, government, financial institution, loan, telemarketing, insurance, stock market (securities), and corporate fraud. Find actual high-profile examples of fraud cases. Each group then explains the specific type of white-collar fraud so the rest of the class can readily understand what is involved.

Car Theft Poster: Explore the Web site of the National Insurance Crime Bureau (NICB) at http://www.nicb.org for information on car theft. Create an informational poster on some aspects of car theft, such as illustrating where areas of car theft are likely to occur, the types of cars most often stolen, or ways to prevent car theft.

Organized Crime: In 2002 the FBI reported that U.S. organized crime activities brought in between $50 and $90 billion dollars, more income than any major national industry. The stories of real-life mobsters and street gangs have always captivated the American public. While throughout the twentieth century Americans thought organized crime meant only the American Mafia, by the twenty-first century street gangs had become dangerous and profitable organized crime groups. Many foreign organized crime groups also operate in the United States. Research one of the legendary American Mafia families—Colombo, Bonanno, Genovese, Lucchese, or Gambino. Alternatively, research a street gang—Hell's Angels, Bloods, Crips, Green Light Gangs, Gangster Disciples, or Latin Kings. Finally, examine a foreign crime unit operating in the United States—Japanese Yakuza, Chinese Triads, Hong Kong Triads, Russian Mafia, South American drug cartels, or Mexican Mafia.

Driving Under the Influence (DUI): Research and report on your state's DUI laws. Explore three organizations either through local chapters or through the Internet: Mothers against Drunk Driving (MADD; http://www.madd.org); Students against Destructive Decisions (SADD, http://www.nat-sadd. org); and Remove Intoxicated Drivers (RID, http://www.crisny. org/not-for-profit/ridusa).

National Institute on Drug Abuse: The National Institute on Drug Abuse (NIDA), a department of the National Institutes of Health, keeps up-to-date information on eighth through twelfth graders' alcohol and drug use. Go to their Web site, http://www.nida.nih.gov/Infofax/HSYouthtrends. html, and report to the class on the various trends.

School Violence: Research and then have a class discussion regarding the many possible causes that might push a young person to shoot his teachers and classmates. Be sure to include bullying and what your school is doing to combat bullying.

Death Penalty: Study all sides of the death penalty issue and check to see if the death penalty is legal in your state. Divide into two groups and have a debate on the use of the death penalty. Each student make a pro-con chart listing arguments for each side.

Juvenile Justice System: Explore the juvenile justice system in your state. Locate a nearby facility for youthful offenders. Make an appointment and interview an official at the facility. An administrator, juvenile probation officer, counselor, or clergy all would have available information for you to take back to the class. Also, check up-to-date juvenile justice statistics at the Web site for the National Center for Juvenile Justice, http://www.ncjj.org.

Environmental Crime: Using your favorite Internet search engine, identify recent environmental crimes prosecuted in your state. Also, explore cases at the U.S. Environmental Protection Agency's Criminal Enforcement division's Web site, http://www.epa.gov/compliance/criminal/index.html. What are the dominant types of environmental offenses? Do not confuse environmental crime with environmental terrorism such as setting gas-guzzling vehicles on fire or tree-sitting to prevent logging.

Careers: Find out what the qualifications are in your state or locality for becoming a law enforcement officer. Look into the departments of city police, sheriffs, and state police. Learn how their duties differ. Also check into the careers of probation officers and correctional facilities officers. Is there an FBI office in your state and, if so, where is it located? There are fifty-six FBI field officers spread across the United States, plus a number of small offices. What are the qualifications to become an FBI agent? How long is the training and where is the training facility?

Cyber Crime: Discover the latest information about cyberspace offenses from the Federal Bureau of Investigation's (FBI) Cyber Educational Letter at http://www.fbi.gov/cyberinvest/cyberedletter.htm.

Forensic Science: Every year the Federal Bureau of Investigation (FBI) publishes the *FBI Laboratory* yearbook, which is also available online. Within the publication the FBI explains each unit in its forensic laboratory. Research one type of forensic service in detail such as latent prints (finger-, palm-, and footprints), firearms and toolmark identification, documents, trace evidence, and so on. Find out where the nearest forensic laboratory is in relation to your community. What services does it provide? If possible, schedule a tour for the class.

Terrorism (part 1): The U.S. Congress requires the U.S. State Department to provide an annual assessment of significant terrorist actions in foreign countries. U.S. law also requires the report to describe how countries cooperate with the United States to apprehend, convict, and punish terrorists who attack U.S. citizens or interests. The report also addresses other countries' attempts to prevent future terrorist acts. This report, called "Patterns of Global Terrorism," is issued every year, and can be found at the U.S. State Department website (http://www.state.gov/s/ct/rls/pgtrpt). Go to this site and find the latest report. This report reflects the official State Department's words on the latest attempts to halt terrorism. Pull out the most important points and report to the class.

Terrorism (part 2): Each year the Secretary of State designates certain foreign organizations as terrorist organizations and puts them on the Foreign Terrorist Organization List (FTO). Find this updated list at the U.S. State Department's Office of Counterterrorism website (http://www.state.gov/s/ct/rls/fs/2003/12389.htm). Detailed information on each listed group may be found on the Center for Defense Information (CDI) website at http://www.cdi.org/terrorism/terrorist-groups.cfm. Choose several groups from countries that you are interested in and research them as fully as resources will allow. What is their goal, where do they operate, and what terror tactics have they used? Report to your class.

Crime and Punishment in America

ALMANAC

Colonial Period

Religious beliefs played heavily in legal thinking of the early colonial period, a period dating from 1607 to the end of the American Revolution (1775–83; a war fought between Great Britain and the American colonies in which the colonies won their independence). The modern American criminal justice system has its roots in the legal concepts carried by early English settlers to the New World. Drawn from the English legal system the colonists knew back home, colonial law evolved substantially through the next three centuries from the time of the first settlements up to the Revolutionary War. Following the war, independence from England allowed a distinctly new American legal system shaped by the experiences of the early colonists.

European settlement of North America

In 1492 the explorer Christopher Columbus (1451–1506) arrived from Spain to what Europeans referred to as the New World. Some seventy years of exploration of the North American continent by various European adventurers followed before settlements began. Explorers discovered the New World

Pilgrims signing the Mayflower Compact, an agreement to provide just and equal laws in their settlement. *(© Bettmann/Corbis)*

was inhabited by many American Indian societies with various legal systems that had developed over thousands of years.

Despite finding existing societies in the New World, Europeans considered Indian culture inferior to their own heritage and decided to create their own settlements. In 1565 Spain created the first permanent European settlement at St. Augustine on coastal land that later became part of Florida. Through the next century, however, most colonists who arrived from Europe to settle the eastern coast of North America were from England. Others came from France, Germany, Holland, and Ireland. Sir Walter Raleigh (c. 1554–1618), with the permission of Queen Elizabeth I (ruled 1558–1603), attempted settlement of the first British colony in 1585 on Roanoke Island off the coast of what would become North Carolina. Known as the "Lost Colony," the Roanoke settlement proved unsuccessful as the colonists vanished without a trace. Their fate remains a mystery to this day.

The curious disappearance of the Roanoke colony did not prevent enthusiasm for colonization of the New World. News of a continent with unlimited opportunities spread throughout Europe. A population growth spurt in the late 1500s and early 1600s had left many in crowded European cities without jobs or land. Religious intolerance and persecution (being treated badly because of one's religious beliefs) was also common. Thousands of Europeans looked to a new beginning across the Atlantic Ocean.

The first half of the seventeenth century saw the establishment of many permanent European settlements in the New World. The British royalty, eager to gain control over any valuable natural resources that might be found, began granting charters (documents granting certain rights to a person, corporation, or group of people) for establishing colonies in the New World. The charters went to companies run by adventurous merchants who recruited settlers. King James I (ruled 1603–25) chartered the Virginia Company of London in 1606.

Jamestown and Plymouth

In 1607 about one hundred settlers sent by the Virginia Company arrived at Jamestown, the first permanent British settlement. It later grew into the Virginia colony. The English merchants who organized the Jamestown colonists expected prosperity or wealth from the venture. They were particularly interested in sources of gold. Not finding great fortune and treasures, the colonists began growing tobacco by 1612 for shipment back to England. Tobacco provided a steady economic base for the young settlement. In 1619 the colonists formed their first representative legislature (body of persons authorized to make and change laws) called the House of Burgesses.

Another settlement occurred in 1620 when the Puritans, English Protestants who opposed the Church of England, traveled across the Atlantic Ocean on the *Mayflower*. They landed in New England and established the Plymouth settlement. Also known as Pilgrims, they came to America seeking religious freedom rather than economic gain. Before leaving the ship, the Pilgrims created the Mayflower Compact, an agreement to provide "just and equal laws" in their settlement. They agreed to abide by rules for the general good of all.

Half of the Pilgrims died during the harsh winter of 1620–21 but the Plymouth colony managed to survive. Settlers spread out to establish New Hampshire in 1623. In 1630 approximately one thousand Puritans set sail from England in eleven boats for the New World where they established more strict religious communities including the new settlement of Boston. Connecticut was established in 1633 and Rhode Island in 1636. By 1642 Plymouth had grown into the Massachusetts Bay Colony with twelve thousand inhabitants. In addition to family farms, small industries developed around fishing, lumber, and crafts.

Only a few years after the settlement of Plymouth, more colonists, including non-English settlers, arrived a short distance down the coast. In 1624 Dutch colonists from Holland established New Amsterdam on what would become Manhattan Island. They expanded settlement up the Hudson River Valley, later part of New York State. Further down the coast the Calverts of Roman Catholic faith, who had fled religious persecution in England, founded Maryland in 1632. Protestants also arrived in Maryland, and in 1649 Maryland established the first religious toleration act to grant religious freedom in the colony.

Other non-English colonists arrived during this period, including the Swedish in 1638 who established New Sweden, later the location of Delaware. The more numerous English acquired the New Netherlands and New Sweden settlements in 1664 under a charter held by James, Duke of York, brother of King Charles II. New Amsterdam, renamed New York City after the Duke, became a shipping and trade center.

Multiplying colonies

Establishment of colonies continued into the second half of the seventeenth century. In 1663 the British king issued charters for settling lands south of Virginia. The southern charters eventually lead to the establishment of North Carolina and South Carolina in 1712 and Georgia in 1733. The economies of these three colonies varied from small farms and fur trading in North Carolina to large farms, called plantations, owned by wealthy landowners in South Carolina and Georgia. On the larger farms rice and indigo (plants that yield dark blue dye) were major cash crops. Because of the large size of these plantations, the colonists needed more manpower to work the land. They began importing black Africans as slaves to plant, tend, and harvest the crops. Because slavery was banned in England, new laws had to be created to make slavery legal and acceptable in the colonies. New laws, known as "black codes," also dealt with such problems as how to buy, sell, and inherit slaves.

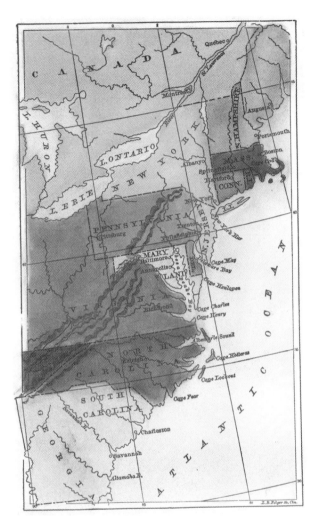

A map of the original thirteen American colonies.
(© Bettmann/Corbis)

Back to the north of Virginia, William Penn, a Quaker, founded Pennsylvania in 1681. Quakers are a Christian group that formed in England in the mid-1600s who oppose all wars and practice religious tolerance, or acceptance of differences. Penn sought to create a colony, like Maryland, where Quakers and people of other faiths could enjoy religious freedom.

Quaker colonies had laws emphasizing harmony and were in favor of solving disagreements peacefully. Remarkably, the Quakers lived in peace with the Indians for the next seventy years.

Despite the many kinds of people living in the colonies, the English speakers and their society dominated and their concepts of law and order became widely accepted. By the mid-1700s the English settlers had formed the original thirteen colonies, each with its own governor and legislature, but all under control of the British king. The thirteen colonies were Virginia, Massachusetts, Connecticut, Rhode Island, New Hampshire, New York, New Jersey, Delaware, Maryland, Pennsylvania, North Carolina, South Carolina, and Georgia.

The once small population of the thirteen colonies grew to some three million people by the time of the American Revolution. By 1783, however, 96 percent of the colonists still lived in rural areas. The uncertain nature of their daily struggle to carve out a life in the New World shaped colonial law. Throughout the colonial period, newly created laws focused on rules of behavior to help assure survival of the colonies by offering hope and stability.

Factors influencing early colonial law

Though the arriving colonists had familiarity with complex European legal traditions, there were few trained lawyers or law books available, so they had only basic ideas of the English common law system. The new setting of the colonies, so different from civilized England, called for new solutions to new problems. Several factors influenced changes in English law, including the fragile frontier existence, an American society distinct from that of England, and later the establishment of slavery.

Fragile frontier existence

Perhaps the most important factor in the fragility of frontier life was trying to establish a way of life in the isolation and desperate condition of the settlements. The first European settlements along the East Coast of North America were tiny and isolated. Of the original 105 settlers in Jamestown, only 38 survived the first seven months from May to December in 1607. The area around Jamestown was marshy and proved to

This drawing shows a fort built by the first English settlers on their arrival at Jamestown, Virginia, in 1607 as protection against American Indians. *(AP/Wide World Photos)*

be poor farmland. It was also a breeding ground for malaria-carrying mosquitoes. The survivors slowly spread out onto surrounding lands but the harsh winter of 1609–10, known as the "starving time," again nearly wiped out the struggling Virginia settlements.

Adding to this delicate existence were numerous American Indian tribes. The Indian peoples greatly outnumbered the early European settlers and the colonists were nervous and suspicious of them. Relations with the Indians deteriorated quickly as the English treated them with little or no respect. Soon the settlers endured not only disease and starvation but hostile Indian attacks.

Given their isolation and vulnerability, the colonists developed their own strict ways of maintaining order so as to protect themselves and allow their small settlements to grow. They used their knowledge of a common law system to come up with new laws. The first colonial legal code, titled "Lawes Divine, Morall and Martiall," was drafted by the Virginia Company in London and sent to the Virginia Colony in 1611. The laws were harsh and military-like, reflecting the serious problems of the settlement. The English wanted to avoid another disaster like the "Lost Colony" of Roanoke twenty years earlier. Their strict behavior codes and hard work, however, paid off. The colonies grew and the communities became more established, able to support its citizens. Other colonial laws followed but were not as severe as the "Lawes Divine."

A new social order

Another factor influencing the development of colonial law was a New World social order very different from the one found in England. The legal system in England was built around the aristocracy (wealthy landowners). No aristocratic social order existed in early colonial society. In most settlements, religion was the driving factor in place of money. Colonial laws were created to reflect these religious beliefs instead of being based on land ownership.

Many early settlers who left England were fleeing religious persecution, or mistreatment. These included the Puritans in New England, the Quakers in Pennsylvania, and the Roman Catholics in Maryland. The fresh start in the New World presented an opportunity to build new societies based on godly ways; what colonists considered good and right in the sight of God dictated their laws. The most important concern was maintaining an orderly, religious life in their small communities. Obedience to those in power, inspired by religious teachings, was most important to the order and survival of each settlement.

Differences from the English criminal justice system

As the first settlements became established, one major difference from the English criminal justice system occurred with the colonial courts. Over several centuries England had developed many kinds of special courts to hear various types of cases. Given the small populations of the North American settlements, the colonial court systems and their proceedings were much simpler and more informal. At first some colonies had too few people to even hold grand juries (groups of citizens gathered to determine if enough evidence exists to have

English Common Law

The legal system most familiar to seventeenth century colonists was English common law. English common law had been in use for several centuries in England before the New World's settlement. Common law provides a set of rules "commonly" used to solve problems. It is built on a history of judges' decisions rather than relying on lawmaking codes, or laws. In England the decisions that contributed to a common law tradition were written down and compiled annually in legal volumes available for judges to study. Common law developed a reputation for fairness in the courts as well as the protection of individual rights and private property.

Common law distinguished two basic types of crimes, the very serious called felonies and the less serious called misdemeanors. For the more serious crimes, evidence concerning the crime was first heard by a grand jury consisting of citizens from the community. The grand jury decided whether enough evidence existed. If so, an indictment (official charges) was issued charging the person with a crime and leading to a court trial before a regular jury. The judge and jury would then hear the arguments presented by both sides and offer a verdict.

Early English common law had some distinctive qualities. Unlike modern law, no district attorneys or public prosecutors brought court cases against the accused. It was up to the victim of the crime to bring the case to the court and pay for it. As a result, only people of means (having money or property) could pursue prosecutions. Under such a system, many citizens could not afford to press charges against someone who victimized them.

a trial). It would be years before the colonial criminal system became more formal and complicated like those of later years.

Colonial justice was different from the English legal system in other ways besides the organization of the courts. Early colonial courts had no "professionals," like judges and lawyers. Since the English legal system had been developing for centuries, it had highly trained judges and lawyers who were wealthy citizens of English society. They had no desire to travel and resettle in the New World, so the men running the colonial courts usually had no legal training and were merely respected persons within the community. Since they had no legal training, there was little difference between ordinary citizens of the community and those attempting to manage public law within the courts.

Salem Witchcraft Trials

Trials of the early colonial justice systems often dramatically reflected how different the world of the colonists was from American society in later centuries. The Salem Witchcraft Trials of 1692 is perhaps the most infamous event to highlight these differences. Belief in magic and witchcraft was widespread in the 1600s. Witchcraft, which people believed represented direct human contact with the devil, was one of the most serious crimes in the early colonies. A series of misfortunes—fires, epidemics, costly battles with Indians—affected Massachusetts colonists in the 1670s, 1680s, and early 1690s. The settlers began looking for what was causing such misery.

When a number of persons began exhibiting odd behavior described as screaming, trances, and seizures, the people decided they were cursed or under the spell of witches. Settlers would also explain the sudden death of livestock to witch curses. They believed witches were responsible for bringing God's wrath upon their settlements. An effort to rid the region of these supposed witches led to 154 trials through-

out Massachusetts beginning in the spring of 1692. Because of a large number of trials in the village of Salem, they became known as the Salem Witchcraft Trials.

Based on testimony by respected citizens who claimed to have been placed under spells and tortured by visions created by accused, a number of the men and women on trial for witchcraft were convicted. Nineteen of those convicted were executed, including thirteen women. Ten of the executions took place in Salem. Four others died in prison, and one person was crushed to death by rocks for refusing to respond during questioning.

After several months of trials citizens grew uncomfortable with what was unfolding in their communities. The special witchcraft trials were finally halted in late October. In addition, new laws were passed more precisely defining "witchcraft behavior" and what kinds of conduct were subject to arrest and prosecution. Although a few accusations continued, most were dismissed. Witchcraft trials disappeared in the early 1700s.

Colonial courts

Though the colonies in the earliest times were led by strong, assertive individuals, they were clearly not dictatorships. The common people were free to use the courts to fix problems and they did so often. The courts were open and available to everyone; they were the place to relieve community tensions and solve disputes between the colonists. Often the opportunity to talk about a complaint was enough

A woman, standing trial for being a suspected witch, lashes out in anger at her accusers. *(© Bettmann/Corbis)*

to satisfy the victim without the court actually reaching a verdict.

Local courts and magistrates

While the colonies were different and changes occurred independently through the next century, some basic traits in the court system were widely shared. The major figure in the colonial court system was the magistrate (a local official with limited power), often called justice of the peace or, simply, judge. This person mostly dealt with petty (minor) crimes in his local area. The local trial courts in the colonies were commonly called county courts. Judges overseeing these courts were not professionals but usually religious or political leaders. Some colonies also had higher courts to hear appeals from the county courts. As communities grew larger they developed special courts to hear certain kinds of cases. Occasionally appeals from these various courts would be taken back to England's courts.

Rarely did colonial courts use juries or lawyers. In early colonial times it was difficult to assemble a jury in many areas since the settlements were so small and far apart. Juries mostly served only when the death penalty was involved. For petty crimes, a magistrate heard the case and decided the verdict. Such local courts heard thousands of cases.

Magistrates were fully in charge of the colonial court proceedings. These early colonial justices firmly believed their main role was to enforce God's plan. Their aim was to force a confession from the accused and make them repent (apologize for) their sins. The goal was not necessarily punishment, but confession and bringing order back to the society. If a defendant requested a jury, he or she was viewed as disrespectful of the judge's authority. Many defendants favored not having a jury as they preferred to rely on the mercy of a judge who was often more interested in seeing that the accused give in to his authority than to provide justice.

As the seventeenth century progressed and populations in the thirteen colonies grew, the legal system became more similar to the English court system. Use of juries, dating back to medieval England, increased in the colonies as did the number of lawyers. By the eighteenth century the jury trial was common. By 1730 the defendants were allowed to have defense lawyers.

The legal process

The local criminal process in early colonial times usually went as follows: when the magistrate heard that a possible crime had been committed, he sent the marshal or a deputy to bring in the suspect. The magistrate questioned the accused, often in the magistrate's personal home with other magistrates or deputies present. No lawyers were involved. Based on his findings, the magistrate either dismissed the case or scheduled a trial. Usually the defendant was allowed to go free until his trial with no bail (money held to make sure the defendant showed up for trial) required. These were small communities

Centre Street Magistrates Court in New York City circa 1900.
(© Photo Collection Alexander Alland, Sr./Corbis)

with few places for the accused to go or hide. Records show that defendants rarely failed to appear for trial.

Without juries and lawyers, the colonial trials moved quickly as witnesses gave their testimony. Since the magistrate who was to rule in the case was the same who ruled as to whether the person should stand trial, the verdicts were almost always guilty. Trials mostly gave defendants an opportunity to publicly admit guilt and repent so they could resume their roles in society. Order was thus restored. The trial and repentance also served to publicly reinforce rules of conduct and to discourage others from breaking the rules. In such intimate communities, the colonial justice system provided social drama and entertainment. The trials were often well attended by community residents.

Policing the Colonies

In the seventeenth century there was no professional police force. Ordinary citizens generally volunteered to enforce orderly conduct. Some communities such as the Dutch settlements in New York and in Boston tried paying "watchmen" in the mid-1600s to look after the behavior of their citizens, but the programs were dropped due to expenses. Nightwatchmen patrolled the streets looking for fires and disturbances. Constables, on duty during the day, apprehended offenders and enforced local ordinances (laws). The early colonial policing system proved loose and unreliable.

As the colonies became more established and populated, the governor in each colony began appointing sheriffs to enforce laws. The sheriff, running the jails, selecting juries, and managing prisoners, served as the top government agent in the county. Usually the community helped the sheriff to capture suspects. Sometimes a posse, a group of people assembled by a sheriff or other county official to help maintain order, was organized. A coroner (a public official who determined the cause of death when someone died unnaturally) was also appointed to look into violent or unexplained deaths, and to organize special juries to rule on cause of death cases.

Criminal law

Colonial laws emphasized the survival of the settlement by keeping social order. Survival relied on positive contributions from every individual. Given the strong religious beliefs of settlements, colonial law was most concerned with repentance and the return of the defendant back into community life. The colonists also believed in individual liberty (freedom), as first expressed in the 1215 English document, the Magna Carta. Though the Magna Carta had actually established very limited rights, by the 1600s it was believed to define a wide range of individual freedoms. With survival plus individual liberty in mind, magistrates and community leaders set about defining crime.

Colonists, particularly those in the Puritan settlements of New England, considered sin as crime and crime as sin. Since the criminal justice system was a part of the existing religious order of the community, all offenses were against God and society. Laws in the Puritan regions were filled with religious messages. The 1648 *Laws and Liberties of Massachusetts,* for example, often quoted biblical passages.

Puritans on their way to church. Puritans had strict punishments against any deviation from the strict laws of their religion.
(© Bettmann/Corbis)

Colonists considered lying, idleness (not working), drunkenness, various sexual offenses, and even general bad behavior as crime. Playing certain games in the Puritan colonies, such as shuffleboard or cards, was a crime. Those who flirted could face fines and warnings. Punishment for these lesser offenses was similar to parents punishing their children. Many of the early colonial laws were aimed at keeping the servants, slaves, and youth in line. The courts used shame, scorn, and humiliation to teach lessons for misbehavior. More severe crimes led to whipping and placing the guilty in wooden frames that had holes for heads and hands, called the pillory.

Heresy (holding a belief that conflicts with church teachings) was a major crime that could lead to the most severe sentence—banishment (being forced to leave the colony). A banished individual caught returning to the settlement could be put to death. Another major crime was blasphemy (showing a lack of respect toward God). Blasphemers could be sentenced to a whipping, to the pillory, have a hole made in their tongue with a red-hot iron, or stand for a period of time on the gallows (a wooden structure built for hangings) with a rope around their neck. Other laws punished colonists for not properly observing the Sabbath (Sunday, observed as a day of rest and worship by most Christians) and skipping religious services. Some colonial laws even banned traveling on Sundays. Various forms of these Sunday laws existed in all colonies.

During the early colonial period settlers believed in the supernatural, or unexplained occurrences. The world was full of omens, signs, and marks representing the invisible world. As a result, witchcraft was considered one of the most serious crimes. It was believed that people who practiced witchcraft and had made pacts with the devil.

Punishment

Like court proceedings, punishment in colonial America was a public event intended to discourage other individuals from committing crimes against the social order. Whipping, the most common form of punishment, generally attracted an audience. Whipping posts were located next to the courthouse so punishment could be carried out quickly following the trial. The goal was repentance of the convicted along with swift lessons for the whole audience.

Besides whipping, branding, cutting off ears, and placing people in the pillory were common publicly administered punishments that set examples for others. As described in noted author Nathaniel Hawthorne's novel *The Scarlet Letter* (1850), men and women convicted of certain crimes had to wear letters such as a capital A on their clothing in clear view for conviction of adultery (a married person having sexual relations with someone other than his or her spouse) or a B branded on their forehead for burglary. Banishment was a more extreme punishment.

Though less prevalent than the other forms of punishment, hangings also occurred in public places. The convicted were expected to publicly confess while standing on the gallows just prior to their hanging. Many of those attending considered the hangings to be deep spiritual experiences. Executions were far less common in the colonies than in England. An exception was execution for the crime of adultery in

Pillory, shown here circa 1657, was one of several forms of humiliating punishment that was carried out throughout early colonial times.
(© Bettmann/Corbis)

Massachusetts that lasted until the mid-1600s. Murder and rape (forcing someone to have sexual relations) were the main capital offenses as well as repeat offenders in other serious crimes. Use of the death penalty varied among the colonies and was more commonly used in the southern colonies, particularly when applied to slaves in the eighteenth century.

With the colonial courts acting as an arm of the church, in some instances both the courts and the church handed out punishment. For example, for unmarried men and women caught having sexual relations, the court could have them whipped, fined, or placed in stocks. Women bearing illegitimate children (born when the woman was not married) were often whipped. In addition to the court punishment, the church scolded defendants, denied certain privileges, or

The Colonial Criminal in the Seventeenth Century

Colonial criminals were almost all men. Men were accused of 95 percent of violent crimes and 74 percent of thefts, or an overall 80 percent of the serious crimes. Witchcraft was one of the few crimes where women were the majority of the accused. Another female-related crime was infanticide, in which women killed their newborn children. Those in the lower ranks of the colonial social order, such as laborers, apprentices, the poor, and slaves, received most of the punishment courts handed out.

issued the ultimate punishment—excommunication (taking away the rights to church membership).

Bonding

Courts did not use probation (sentencing an individual to commit no crimes for a period of time instead of going to jail) as punishment. Colonies did, however, make wide use of bonds in the place of probation. Courts required people who were regarded as troublemakers to put up money (security) to guarantee future good behavior. Those punished with whipping or fines also had to post money to guarantee no further troubles. Bonds were also posted to guarantee appearances at trials as in New York. In some places such as Virginia some members of the community posted money for the accused. The bond system worked well in the small communities where everyone minded (or paid attention to) everyone else's business.

Imprisonment

Taking away a person's liberty or freedom was not a common way of punishing criminals in the colonial period. In New York the courts handed out only nineteen prison sentences between 1691 and 1776. With such a small population people were too valuable to local economies to put them away. The colonists also had little money to build prisons and feed prisoners. Prisons were not established until much later in the nineteenth century. Colonial jails primarily held people awaiting trial or who owed money to others (debtors). Debtors were free to leave during the day and work to pay off their debts and then return for the night. Workhouses also existed for the homeless, unemployed, and impoverished (poor). They were expected to learn the work ethic during their stay.

Controlling slaves

Controlling slaves was a primary concern of the criminal justice system in the colonial South. Slave owners and overseers policed slave society. The whip was a symbol of authority and used frequently. Whipping was administered swiftly, usually on the plantation, and was often severe. If death resulted, the overseer was normally not charged with murder unless the situation was extreme. Slaves were considered property, and the courts did not expect that a master would intentionally destroy his own property.

Eighteenth century developments

The influence of religion on criminal justice steadily decreased through the 1700s. Towns grew and their populations became more diverse. Social and technological change brought new issues in addition to moral concerns. The criminal justice system shifted from moral crimes (sin) to crimes against property such as stealing or trespassing.

Another example of eighteenth century change was the increasing importance of the "due process" concept in American courts, a concept not embraced in England. Due process means to protect the rights of the accused and not issue a verdict or penalties without using fair lawful procedures (innocent until proven guilty). The concept decreased the power of the judge and the government in controlling the courts. It required fair trials, arrests, and punishment.

Colonies also added district attorney positions. A district attorney is a lawyer who prosecutes crimes on behalf of the community. No such position existed in England where it was up to the victim to pursue the case and pay for prosecution. Since it usually cost too much money for colonists to pay for prosecutions themselves, the popular notion emerged that it was a government or public responsibility to prosecute criminals. This change in the legal system demonstrated how the colonial system helped common people who were the victims of crime. The use of juries also increased. The duties of professional lawyers, however, were still limited to advising the accuser or defendant. Lawyers did not argue cases before the judge or jury.

One unusual aspect of the colonial criminal justice system was dropped as time passed. A tradition from the Middle Ages gave those who could read lighter sentences than those who could not read. By the late 1700s this rule was eliminated from the colonial legal system.

Toward an American legal system

New ideas about criminal justice continued to be defined in American colonial law through the eighteenth century as the colonial and English societies grew apart. For example, the king was considered the source of all English law. The colonies did not agree, considering God the source of justice. The Revolutionary War greatly affected the criminal justice system because America's new independence from England ended the influence of royalty. In the 1780s the Founding Fathers of the nation adopted the republican (a form of government where citizens hold the supreme power) ideal that people were the source of law. As a result, new individual rights were built into the emerging American legal system.

For More Information

Books

Abbot, W. W. *The Colonial Origins of the United States, 1607–1763.* New York: Wiley, 1975.

Butler, Jon. *Becoming America: The Revolution Before 1776.* Cambridge, MA: Harvard University Press, 2000.

Ferling, John. *A Leap in the Dark: The Struggle to Create the American Republic.* New York: Oxford University Press, 2003.

Hoffer, Peter C. *Law and People in Colonial America.* Baltimore: Johns Hopkins University Press, 1998.

McFarlane, Anthony. *The British in the Americas, 1480–1815.* New York: Longman, 1994.

Reiss, Oscar. *Blacks in Colonial America.* Jefferson, NC: McFarland & Company, 1997.

Taylor, Alan. *American Colonies.* New York: Viking, 2001.

Web Sites

Colonial Williamsburg. http://www.history.org/history (accessed on August 20, 2004).

History of Jamestown. The Association for the Preservation of Virginia Antiquities. http://www.apva.org/history (accessed on August 20, 2004).

"Puritan Studies on the Web." *Le Projet Albion.* http://puritanism.online.fr (accessed on August 20, 2004).

"Virtual Tour of Plimoth Plantation." *America's Homepage.* The Plymouth Area Chamber of Commerce. http://pilgrims.net/plimothplantation/vtour/ (accessed on August 20, 2004).

The Early Years of American Law

From the time of the American Revolution (1775–83) until the early part of the twentieth century, pieces of the American criminal justice system gradually came together to include courts, professional policing, and prisons at the federal and state levels. A criminal justice system is the collection of public agencies including the police, courts, and prison officials responsible for apprehending (catching and arresting), determining the guilt, and imposing the sentence of criminal offenders.

During the colonial period prior to the American Revolution (1775–83), no distinctive American legal system existed. Criminal codes, punishments, and courts varied from colony to colony. By the mid-1700s a reform movement was underway to create a more unified American legal system. The Revolution greatly sped up the reform process. The colonists' victory over Britain brought independence and a new justice system that provided both protection and rights for its citizens. The first several decades following the Revolution were an experimental period in criminal justice as court decisions and legislation formed the foundation for a modern criminal justice system.

VIRGINIA BILL *of* RIGHTS

DRAWN ORIGINALLY BY GEORGE MASON AND
ADOPTED BY THE CONVENTION OF DELEGATES

June 12, 1776.

A Declaration of Rights made by the Representatives of the good People of Virginia, assembled in full and free Convention; which Rights do pertain to them, and their Posterity, as the Basis and Foundation of Government.

I.

That all Men are by Nature equally free and independent, and have certain inherent Rights, of which, when they enter into a State of Society, they cannot, by any Compact, deprive or divest their Posterity; namely, the Enjoyment of Life and Liberty, with the Means of acquiring and possessing Property, and pursuing and obtaining Happiness and Safety.

II.

That all Power is vested in, and consequently derived from, the People; that Magistrates are their Trustees and Servants, and at all Times amenable to them.

III.

That Government is, or ought to be, instituted for the common Benefit, Protection, and Security, of the People, Nation, or Community; of all the various Modes and Forms of Government that is best, which is capable of producing the greatest Degree of Happiness and Safety, and is most effectually secured against the Danger of Mal-administration; and that, whenever any Government shall be found inadequate or contrary to these Purposes, a Majority of the Community hath an indubitable, unalienable, and indefeasible Right, to reform, alter, or abolish it, in such Manner as shall be judged most conducive to the public Weal.

IV.

That no Man, or Set of Men, are entitled to exclusive or separate Emoluments or Privileges from the Community, but in Consideration of public Services; which, not being descendible, neither ought the Offices of Magistrate, Legislator, or Judge, to be hereditary.

V.

That the legislative and executive Powers of the State should be separate and distinct from the Judicative; and, that the Members of the two first may be restrained from Oppression, by feeling and participating the Burthens of the People, they should, at fixed Periods, be reduced to a private Station, return into that Body from which they were originally taken, and the Vacancies be supplied by frequent, certain, and regular Elections, in which all, or any Part of the former Members, to be again eligible, or ineligible, as the Laws shall direct.

That

Virginia's 1776 declaration of rights served as a model for the U.S. Bill of Rights, added to the U.S. Constitution in 1791. *(© Bettmann/Corbis)*

Colonial freedom

By the 1750s the American colonists enjoyed the situation within which they found themselves. Distant from British rule, they had grown accustomed to a personal, political, and economic independence unheard of back in England for commoners. The colonies basically consisted of small agricultural settlements whose residents steadily converted woodlands to croplands. Plenty of land was at hand to claim and develop though much to the detriment (harm) of the existing American Indian populations who were shoved aside. Most families had enough land to satisfactorily support themselves, while in England as well as the rest of Europe, laborers and farmers had little freedom or property. Small farmers in European countries were largely tenant farmers, meaning they had to rent their land from wealthy landowners.

British officials were quite aware of the freedom and independence the colonists were growing accustomed to. They looked on it as a threat to traditional British social order they hoped to maintain in their worldwide colonial empire. Emigration (moving from one country to another) from Britain to the colonies was steadily increasing. Over a twenty-year period from 1754 to 1775 the colonial population grew from 1.5 to 2.5 million people, a 67 percent increase. British leaders feared the colonies were attracting so many common laborers away from England that soon wages for workers who stayed in England might have to rise. A trend of fewer workers earning higher wages could not only affect productivity but Britain's competitive edge in the world market.

Britain's push for greater control

British leaders decided something needed to be done to tighten their control over the colonists and discourage emigration. One way to accomplish these goals was to raise taxes in the colonies. This would make the colonies less attractive to possible emigrants and the existing colonists would be more obedient to the king.

Raising taxes would also help relieve Britain's war debt after successfully defeating the French in America in the costly French and Indian War (1756–63). The victory finally gave Britain more complete control over North America ending a struggle with France that had begun in the late 1600s. As soon

Riots broke out after the passage of the Stamp Act in March 1765. The act required Americans to purchase stamps to place on official documents such as deeds, mortgages, licenses of various sorts, and even publications such as newspapers. *(The Library of Congress)*

as the war was over, Britain began imposing various taxes. These included the highly unpopular Stamp Act in March 1765. The act required Americans to purchase stamps to place on official documents such as deeds, mortgages, licenses of various sorts, and even publications such as newspapers. Colonial leaders rebelled and declared the act unjust. Colonial resistance forced Britain to repeal (cancel or undo) the act the following year, but the bitterness remained.

The colonists were just as determined to hang on to their unique independence including their evolving court systems. Most colonists did not, however, want a violent confrontation such as a war. They wanted to enjoy their independence while taking advantage of the trade benefits available as members of the British Empire—such as trade with other British colonies around the world.

While many colonists took pride in being part of the great British Empire, the Stamp Act had become a symbol of the British threat to their independence. Colonists feared the royal colonial governors and their top officials would become an elite social class as the common taxpayers became poor laborers and farmers just like in England. The elite would use the criminal justice system to maintain control over the commoners, who would be at the king's mercy in criminal court proceedings. It was possible the newfound personal liberties and property ownership of the colonists could be lost forever.

The colonists believed that if they resisted the new taxes, Britain would simply back off and leave them alone. British officials, however, firmly believed the colonists were no match for the highly trained British troops if any open rebellion should occur. After all, the British had just defeated France, another European power. Therefore they were determined to press for tightened control over the American colonies.

A new start

On the eve of the open hostilities with Britain that led to the American Revolutionary War, the colonists formed the Continental Congress that began meeting in Philadelphia in 1774. For the next fifteen years the Continental Congress laid the foundation for their nation including a newly emerging judicial system. Yet while war raged, the existing colonial legal systems mostly came to a halt. The top priority of the colonists was to win the war. One crime of major interest to the colonists, treason, was prosecuted throughout the war. Treason is the attempt to overthrow one's own government by assisting another country. Charges of treason were brought against those colonists remaining loyal (called loyalists) to Britain. The colonists applied a broad definition of treason to the loyalists' actions. If loyalists provided any support to the British, colonists assumed authority to seize their property. Though treason became more specifically defined in the U.S. Constitution, it remained the most serious of crimes in the new democratic republic.

The colonists fought a difficult, bloody battle for their freedom. With victory in 1783, the successful rebellion resulted in political independence and the creation of a new federal legal system. In addition, ratification of the U.S. Constitution in 1787 transformed the thirteen colonies into a confederation or union of thirteen states.

A new criminal court system

In observance of the Constitution, the nation's founders added a new federal criminal court system on top of the thirteen individual state judicial systems. The Constitution itself, however, said very little about criminal law. Criminal law is the set of rules that identifies behavior prohibited by a government to protect the health and safety of its citizens and the punishments for violations of these rules. Each state still had the most responsibility for crime and punishment in the United States, which has continued into the twenty-first century.

Thomas Jefferson holds up the Declaration of Independence in front of the Continental Congress. *(The Library of Congress)*

The Constitution called for a U.S. Supreme Court and gave Congress the authority to create other federal courts. The U.S. Congress, meeting in its first session in Philadelphia, passed the Judiciary Act in 1789 establishing the Supreme Court and various levels of federal courts, such as district and appellate (where district court decisions are appealed or reviewed) courts, and identified their jurisdictions (the geographic area over which a court has legal authority). The act also created the U.S. attorney, attorney general, and marshal offices.

Under authority of the new Constitution, Congress passed the Crimes Act of 1790. It was a general bill identifying seventeen crimes against the federal government. In addition to treason these federal crimes included murder within a federal installation such as a fort or on the high seas, forgery (the deceitful creation or altering) of federal documents, piracy, assault on a federal official, and perjury (intentionally making a false statement or lying during a court appearance while under oath) in a federal court. Criminal trials in federal courts were also to be before juries.

The Bill of Rights

The main purpose of federal criminal justice came with adoption of ten amendments to the Constitution, known as the Bill of Rights, in December 1791. The colonists were quite familiar with injustices often involving violation of an individual's civil liberties after living under the rule of a British king. Many had wanted the Constitution to speak out more forcefully to protect civil liberties, including criminal justice procedures. Otherwise, they feared they would lose freedoms to a strong national government in the same way they had lost some rights to a king. The founders agreed to strengthen the Constitution's safeguards against the loss of individual liberties and the result was the Bill of Rights.

Unlike the Constitution, much of the Bill of Rights addressed criminal justice issues, carrying forward the judicial reform sought before the war. The amendments called for fair legal procedures including fair trials. One way of accomplishing this was to greatly reduce discretion (range of power) of the judges. English law had combined king's mercy (discretion of the courts) with terror posed by the extremely harsh legal codes to control society and keep nobility and large landowners in charge.

American reformers called for something far different. The basic right to have a lawyer was written into the Bill of Rights. The Fourth Amendment called for the right of people to be safe from unreasonable searches and the seizure of property. Warrants for arrest and search had to be based on sufficient (enough) evidence to support an arrest, known as probable cause. The Fifth Amendment called for grand juries (a panel of citizens called together to determine if sufficient evidence exists to charge a person with a crime), stated that a person could not be tried for the same offense twice, known as double jeopardy, and that a person could not be made to testify against him or herself and had the right to remain silent in a trial. The Sixth Amendment called for speedy, public trials using impartial or fair juries. The Eighth Amendment banned excessive bails (money a defendant pays a court to be released while waiting for a trial) and cruel and unusual punishment.

Though sweeping in nature, the Bill of Rights applied only to the federal criminal justice system, not to state governments. The states were quite varied in their criminal justice procedures and safety measures. Virginia actually passed a set of fundamental rights in the Virginia Declaration of Rights of 1776 that served as a model for the Bill of Rights. Other states adopted many of the provisions of the Bill of Rights into their own constitutions after 1791.

One outcome of a republican (where a nation's citizens hold the supreme power) form of criminal justice at the federal level was that more reliance was placed on written laws rather than a judge's rulings. All federal crimes and punishment would be clearly spelled out. Federal courts could not prosecute defendants for actions not specifically written down in the federal penal codes.

In English common law some crimes, such as murder, were not specifically written. Everyone simply knew that murder and some other offenses were crimes. Judges were free to invent new common law crimes as time passed and new issues came before the court. The American reformers ended the unwritten common law system in the New World. The new federal courts always operated under a set of written laws. State criminal justice systems throughout the nineteenth and twentieth centuries, however, slowly moved away from common law practices.

A change in America's way of life

Growth of criminal law through the nineteenth century was greatly influenced by major economic and social changes in the country. By the early nineteenth century, the nation's larger communities changed from farming to urban or city industrial centers. American capitalism (an economic system made up of businesses supported by monetary investments, or capital) was taking shape. This kind of production and sale of goods is largely free of government interference. The major transformation from farming to an industrial economy first began in the New England region in the 1780s immediately following the Revolution. The new economy slowly dominated parts of the East over the next twenty years.

With this economic change, society changed. In an agricultural, or farm-based, society, daily life had been guided by longstanding traditions centered around the community. The new industrial society was much more individualistic, often impersonal, and mobile with people constantly moving to where jobs were available. The change also brought a sharper growth of individual income or earnings, something not seen in colonial times.

With increased earnings came greater ownership of property. New laws were needed to protect against property crimes such as theft. From a criminal justice standpoint, the new industry-based society put pressure on government to create different laws and to change how criminals were punished.

Changes in criminal punishment

Due to the growth in population and the "cruel and unusual" punishment clause in the Bill of Rights' Eighth Amendment—death, torture, and public humiliation, all common in early colonial days—were gradually falling out of public favor through the 1700s. By the end of the eighteenth century many criminal justice reformers opposed the death penalty and other forms of physical punishment such as whippings and brandings. Reformers claimed these punishments were contrary (opposite) to the newly adopted Eighth Amendment that prohibited cruel and unusual punishment.

While many people believed these extreme forms of public punishment had been effective in small communities, their effectiveness declined as cities grew and became less personal. Hangings at the time of the Revolution were public spectacles drawing in some cases thousands of onlookers. Reformers argued such public violent deaths probably promoted bad behavior more than discouraged it—by exposing the public to violence. Reformers believed locking up criminals for long periods of time was more humane (caring) and effective as to prevent future crimes. At the time, however, the jails used to lock up convicts were small and primitive.

In 1790 Philadelphia opened a sixteen-cell house called the Walnut Street Jail. *(Hulton Archive/Getty Images)*

Growth of prisons

Not surprisingly, the Quakers in Pennsylvania, known for their humaneness, took an early lead in replacing incarceration (confinement in prison or jail) for execution. The 1776 Pennsylvania constitution included construction of buildings, "houses," to punish criminals. Though focused on putting the inmates to hard labor, they still maintained some degree of public humiliation by allowing the public at times to view the prisoners at work.

Philadelphia became the center for criminal reform in the nation in 1787 when the first prison reform organization was formed, the Philadelphia Society for Alleviating the Miseries of Public Prisons. The society supported treating a prisoner's problems (known as rehabilitation) over physical punishment. In 1790 Philadelphia opened a sixteen-cell house called the Walnut Street Jail. A jail warden assigned prisoners to one of four categories of offender. Prisoners entered solitary confinement supplied with a Bible to speed their rehabilitation.

Changes in punishment came in other states as well. In 1805 when the Massachusetts State Prison opened, the state eliminated whipping, branding, and use of the pillory (a wooden frame that has holes for heads and hands). A movement to build state prisons, or penitentiaries, grew through the 1820s and 1830s. This allowed more and more states to replace various forms of physical punishment with imprisonment in penitentiaries.

Opinions of the new American prison systems varied. French travelers Gustave de Beaumont (1802–1866) and Alexis de Tocqueville (1805–1859) favored the harsh system they observed. Others such as famous British novelist Charles Dickens (1812–1870) who visited the Philadelphia prison in the early 1840s found the experience horrifying.

While state prisons experimented with different kinds of incarceration, local and county jails remained more primitive. Many, particularly in rural areas, were poorly run and filthy.

Decrease in executions

Associated with the growth of state prisons was reducing the crimes calling for capital punishment (death penalty). In 1794 the Pennsylvania legislature passed a bill recognizing the difference between first-degree murder (a deliberate and planned act to kill) that received the death penalty, and second-degree murder (an unplanned or accidental killing) that called for imprisonment. It was the first law of its kind calling for different levels of punishment for different kinds of murder.

Other states followed in reducing the number of capital crimes. In 1835 New York became the first state to stop public executions and by 1841 the state reduced the death penalty to only three crimes: murder, treason, and some forms of arson. In 1846 Michigan was the first state to abolish the death penalty altogether. Wisconsin and Rhode Island soon followed.

Punishments were now performed in private, away from a public crowd, and new forms of punishment appeared. For example, one striking aspect about many prisons in the early nineteenth century was that strict silence among inmates was maintained. Prisoners were not allowed to speak. Those who visited the prisons, such as Beaumont and Tocqueville, found the total silence very eerie. Considered too stressful, by the 1850s the demand for silence was dropped by the prisons.

Auburn Prison, in New York, was notorious for its variety of tortures and punishments. *(© Corbis)*

Two types of prisons

States had little money available to maintain the new prisons. Therefore, a general goal in the early 1800s was to make the new prisons economically self-sufficient by having inmates produce goods. This goal was not without controversy. Businesses considered the prison industries unfair competition. However, the prison industries were particularly useful during the American Civil War (1861–65) producing uniforms, shoes, and other clothing.

Two different prison systems arose at first. Most states followed a New York prison model called the Auburn plan. It was named after the Auburn Prison opened in 1821 as a maximum-security facility. Inmates were locked in separate cells at night but worked in groups during the day. Pennsylvania had another system in which inmates were placed in solitary confinement, or by themselves with little or no contact with anyone else, around the clock. Each cell had running water, a heater, and an individual exercise area. Not only was this type of prison more expensive, but many considered the isolation too cruel. The Pennsylvania plan did not allow inmates to work or make money for the prison, so the Auburn system was more widely used.

Punishment in the South

Prisons were also developing in the South. Arkansas established its state prison in 1839. Yet the South, which remained largely rural, continued to punish inmates with whipping and public shaming. Whipping was the main means of controlling slaves since placing them in jail or prison would keep them from working for their owners. After slavery ended in 1865, prison populations in the South became predominately black. While Northern prisons resembled factories, prisoners in the South were put to work in the fields. To some observers, the prisons looked much like plantations.

Probation and parole

Along with growth of prison systems new measures, such as probation and parole, were introduced. Probation is imposing a criminal sentence other than jail or prison time for persons convicted of less serious crimes. The convicted person would be under court supervision but otherwise free. The person might be restricted from travel or other daily activities and had to check in with a court-appointed official to evaluate his or her progress. Probation had its beginnings in Boston in the 1850s. The more common use of probation, to sentence less serious crimes committed by both adults and juveniles, did not arrive until around 1900.

Parole is a decision to release an inmate before the end of his or her sentence. It was first introduced in New York in 1876, but it would not become widely used until the 1930s when tough economic times cut funding for prisons.

Professional policing

Another major development in the criminal justice system in the early nineteenth century was the growth of professional police departments. Following the Revolutionary War many communities began electing constables and sheriffs. For several decades, however, many towns still relied on volunteer watchmen to patrol the streets. On the western frontier, policing was performed by the U.S. Army or federal marshals. Because of the still largely rural character of the nation immediately following the war, property and personal crime rates were low. Volunteer watchmen could serve the community needs. As the national economy changed and towns grew in the early nineteenth century, the public grew increasingly concerned over rising crime rates such as theft.

Despite the growth of state prison systems through the 1830s, crime rates continued to increase. Unruly or wild behavior increased and riots broke out in the 1830s and 1840s. Often violence was targeted at special social groups such as blacks and Catholics.

In 1829 Sir Robert Peel (1788–1850) created a London police force to address rising crime rates in England related to the growth of urban industrial or manufacturing areas. The force consisted of paid, full-time police complete with uniforms and strict discipline. This force, known as "bobbies" (derived from Peel's first name), became a model for policing in the United States.

The first U.S. city to establish a police force was naturally the most heavily populated: New York. The city faced growing slums, fighting over ethnic differences, and rising crime. The city replaced the mostly volunteer watchmen with a paid police force in 1844. Refusing to adopt uniforms for fear of a citizen backlash or negative reaction, the police wore copper badges on their chests. The badges led to the slang term "coppers," and the shorter "cops."

Other cities were feeling similar pressures. Fourteen people were killed in one anti-Catholic riot in Philadelphia in 1844. Philadelphia created a professional police force the following year. Other city police forces followed: New Orleans and Cincinnati in 1852; Boston in 1854; Chicago in 1855; and Baltimore in 1857. Like the London bobbies, the American departments adopted uniforms by the mid-nineteenth century and rules to enforce increased discipline. American police discipline still did not approach the level of the London police. The more rural areas of the young country continued to rely on volunteers. Groups organized to fight crime without the approval of the sheriff or county lawmen, known as vigilantes, were active in controlling crime in some areas

One of the most famous U.S. marshals was Wyatt Earp, second from left in the bottom row. *(AP/Wide World Photos)*

like San Francisco, before it formed a city police force in the 1850s.

Federal policing through the first half of the nineteenth century was conducted by U.S. marshals, whose primary concern was counterfeiting. It was estimated that one-third of the new U.S. currency between 1815 and 1860 was counterfeit or fake. Congress finally created the Secret Service agency under the secretary of treasury in 1865 to target counterfeiting and free the marshals to tackle other crimes.

Women and minorities were limited to a small role in the growth of professional policing. The first full-time paid policewoman was Alice Stebbins Wells in 1910 for the Los

Angeles Police Department. Until then women were only allowed to work in jails, normally tending to female inmates, but also doing chores such as cooking. In addition, black Americans made up less than 3 percent of the urban police forces in 1900. They were usually assigned to patrol black communities.

Extending protection to black Americans

At the conclusion of the Revolution the northern states abolished slavery but in the South it remained a major part of the plantation economy. While many in the North sought to ban slavery, Southerners considered slaves as property, to be bought and sold. Slave masters could punish slaves as they saw fit; whipping was the most common form of punishment.

The threat of slavery expanding into new U.S. territories raised the issue of slavery to a new level. The U.S. Supreme Court in *Dred Scott* (1857) ruled that neither slaves nor freed blacks were entitled to U.S. citizenship or the protection citizenship provided under the criminal justice system. It was becoming clear that war was the only means to resolve this legal question.

Following the Union's victory in the Civil War, the states ratified the Thirteenth Amendment to the Constitution in 1865 making slavery a federal crime. In response, Southern states passed Black Codes in 1865 and 1866. The Black Codes were state laws denying basic freedoms to the newly freed slaves. Blacks still could not legally own property, sign contracts, testify against whites in court, or travel freely. In reaction, the Fourteenth Amendment was ratified by the states in 1868. The amendment made all people born in the United States citizens of both the United States and the state in which they were born. It gave black Americans the same legal protections as whites, such as the right to fair treatment in criminal justice procedures.

The Supreme Court, however, was slow in recognizing these Fourteenth Amendment rights. Minorities would not see the benefits of the Fourteenth Amendment until later in the twentieth century when courts became less concerned about protecting economic interests and more focused on civil liberties.

New demands on criminal justice

In the late nineteenth and early twentieth centuries crime rates rose as society experienced further changes. National economic depressions, large waves of immigrants from Asia and eastern and southern Europe, further growth of industrial centers, and violent labor outbreaks strained society and the criminal justice system. As local law enforcement had difficulty keeping up, states created state police forces. Through the 1920s almost thirty states created police organizations with some modeled after the military-like Pennsylvania State Police created in 1905.

During this time Congress also added new federal crimes, including criminal activities occurring in two or more states. The White Slave Traffic Act (Mann Act) in 1910 banned the transportation of women across state lines for immoral purposes. The National Motor Vehicle Theft Act of 1919 made it a federal crime to take stolen vehicles across state lines. By far the largest impact on the existing criminal justice systems was passage of the Volstead Act of 1920 banning the sale of alcoholic beverages. Through the 1920s the act produced a major crime wave as Americans obtained alcohol however they could. Respect for law enforcement decreased, and prison populations dramatically increased.

Based on these pressures, the criminal justice system was ready for major improvements, which began in the 1930s and eventually led to the modern legal system of the twenty-first century.

For More Information

Books

American Correctional Association. *The American Prison from the Beginning: A Pictorial History.* College Park, MD: American Correctional Association, 1983.

Foner, Eric. *The Story of American Freedom.* New York: W. W. Norton, 1998.

Friedman, Lawrence M. *Crime and Punishment in American History.* New York: Basic Books, 1993.

Hirsch, Adam Jay. *The Rise of the Penitentiary: Prisons and Punishment in Early America.* New Haven, CT: Yale University Press, 1992.

Huggins, Nathan I. *Black Odyssey: The Afro-American Ordeal in Slavery.* New York: Pantheon Books, 1977.

Web Sites

"LAPD Had the Nation's First Police Woman." *Los Angeles Almanac.* http://www.losangelesalmanac.com/topics/Crime/cr73b.htm (accessed on August 20, 2004).

Modern Criminal Justice

In early 1929 newly elected Herbert Hoover (1874–1964; served 1929–33) became the first U.S. president to mention crime as a major issue in his inauguration speech. A crime wave caused by bootleggers (persons who illegally made and sold alcohol) and gangsters swept America in the 1920s, thanks in large part to the introduction of Prohibition. Prohibition made it illegal to make, sell, or possess alcoholic beverages, which created a huge demand for obtaining and producing it illegally.

Respect for the criminal justice system, consisting of police, courts, and prisons, greatly declined as the public and criminals dodged the alcohol ban in every way possible. Law enforcement seemed very unskilled in enforcing the new law. As the crime spree continued through the decade, it became more violent and improvements in law enforcement gained greater public support.

From the 1930s into the twenty-first century, the federal government played an active role in criminal justice. Still, the states shouldered most criminal justice responsibility for the major crimes of murder, armed robbery, rape, theft, larceny,

Government officials break into barrels of illegal liquor, emptying the contents onto the street. Prohibition dramatically increased criminal activity—mainly the illegal distribution and purchase of alcohol. *(The Library of Congress)*

and arson. As crime rates rose in the twentieth century, the federal government increased funding for local and state law enforcement, set national crime policy, and kept national statistics. Crime concerns dramatically grew as society changed and new technologies were introduced through the twentieth century.

Criminal justice prior to the 1930s

Throughout the nineteenth century, criminal justice was overwhelmingly the responsibility of states, not the federal government. Before the era of automobiles and airplanes, travel across state lines was limited and slow. State jurisdictions (geographic areas over which states have legal authority) functioned well since few criminals crossed state lines. The federal government's responsibilities were restricted to a limited number of identified crimes, such as treason (seeking to overthrow the government), perjury (making false statements under oath) in a federal court, forgery (making a copy for illegal purpose) of federal documents, illegal immigration (foreign citizens coming into the country), smuggling (secretly bringing something into the country against the law), and violations of federal business regulations.

Federal police enforcement was limited to the District of Columbia, U.S. territories that had not become states, national parks and U.S. military posts, and the high seas. From 1888 to 1889 federal district courts heard fewer than fifteen thousand cases, a very small number compared to criminal cases heard before state and local courts.

Given the limited involvement of the federal government in criminal justice, no federal prisons existed before the 1890s and U.S. marshals handled mostly federal policing responsibilities. Those convicted of federal crimes were sent to state or local jails. In 1891 three federal prisons were approved by Congress. As a result, Ft. Leavenworth in Kansas opened in 1895 followed by facilities in Atlanta and western Washington. The policing powers of the federal government began growing as well. In 1908 the U.S. Department of Justice created the Bureau of Investigation (BOI) to lead in the investigation of federal crimes. It consisted at first of only eight unarmed agents.

In the early twentieth century, federal justice responsibilities expanded to include various types of activities from tax fraud (to deceive another for illegal gain) to criminal activity that crossed state lines. Tax fraud became an issue when federal income tax was introduced in 1913. Criminal activity that crossed state lines usually consisted of a violation of the Mann Act of 1910, which prohibited taking women across state lines to engage in prostitution (selling sexual services for pay) or violation of the National Motor Vehicle Theft Act of 1919, which made it a federal crime to take a stolen vehicle across state lines.

Following World War I (1914–18; war in which Great Britain, France, the United States, and their allies defeated Germany, Austria-Hungary, and their allies) federal concern turned to the control of suspects who engaged in political actions considered dangerous by the government. These activists were called radicals. The Red Scare (a time of extreme fear of communist influence) brought passage of the Espionage Act in 1917 and the Sedition Act of 1918. The acts sought to control aliens (immigrants who held citizenship in foreign countries) and political groups such as anarchists (those who wished to overthrow the government). The Justice Department carried out a series of raids, known as the Palmer Raids, on suspected foreign radicals in 1919 and 1920. U.S. attorney general A. Mitchell Palmer (1872–1936) placed a young man named J. Edgar Hoover (1895–1972) in charge of organizing the raids. Hoover would go on to be the director of the Federal Bureau of Investigation (FBI).

During the 1920s, Prohibition dramatically increased criminal activities, which not only violated federal laws but state laws as well. Some 22,000 liquor cases were brought before the courts in one twelve month period in the early 1920s. Organized crime (people or groups united to profit from crime) grew tremendously as it supplied thirsty Americans with alcohol. In combating liquor violations, police expanded their use of wiretapping (tapping telephones) and more aggressive search and seizure measures. The rising number of convictions created the need for more prisons. In the mid-1920s the federal government added more prisons, including the first federal women's prison, the Federal Industrial Institution for Women at Alderson, West Virginia, in 1927.

By the late 1920s the criminal justice system at federal, state, and local levels was in need of better coordination and increased professionalism. The task of fighting crime had outgrown the local police and court systems. It was clearly time for expansion and modernization.

Modernizing criminal justice

Concerns over the rising crime rate led to the need for more accurate information on growing crime trends. In late 1929 the Bureau of Investigation began the Uniform Crime Reporting (UCR) Program. The UCR provided nationwide statistics on seven key crimes—murder and manslaughter, rape, robbery, aggravated assault, larceny (theft of property), burglary, and motor vehicle theft. In 1979 arson was added. The UCR became the most used criminal statistics source in the nation into the twenty-first century.

In 1929 President Herbert Hoover created the National Commission on Law Observance and Enforcement, chaired by U.S. Attorney General George Wickersham (1858–1936). Known as the Wickersham Commission, the group was charged with evaluating the criminal justice system, including police behavior, the condition of prisons, and the causes of crime. Issued in 1931, the findings of the fourteen commission reports did not support the existing system.

The commission found many of the police departments in the nation were corrupt, poorly operated, and poorly trained. The report also criticized the newly expanded prison system for not trying hard enough to rehabilitate or help its inmates. The reports provided specific recommendations on how to improve criminal justice in America, some of which were gradually adopted.

J. Edgar Hoover, hired by the BOI in 1917, became its director in 1924. Hoover, along with others including Los Angeles police chief August Vollmer (1876–1955), responded to the call for greater professionalism in law enforcement. At the federal level, Hoover turned the BOI into a highly trained law enforcement organization. He established the first fingerprint database and changed the name from BOI to the Federal Bureau of Investigation (FBI) in 1935.

As time passed, Congress gave the FBI more responsibility for fighting crime. After Prohibition ended in 1933 and it was no longer illegal to make or sell alcohol, crime groups switched

J. Edgar Hoover, who became the director of the Bureau of Investigation in 1924, pointing to a crime map of the United States. *(AP/Wide World Photos)*

to gambling, extortion (to take money or property through threats or bodily harm), and vice (prostitution). In addition, fear of radical politics began to capture the attention of President Franklin D. Roosevelt (1882–1945; served 1933–45) as World War II (1939–45; war in which Great Britain, France, the Soviet Union, the United States, and their allied forces defeated Germany, Italy, and Japan) drew near in the late 1930s. He assigned J. Edgar Hoover and the FBI to monitor rebellious activity in the United States.

Hoover dominated the world of federal crime law enforcement through his forty-eight years of leadership until his death in 1972. Throughout the twentieth century, the FBI remained at the forefront of technological innovations, including forensic science, fingerprinting, and blood work analysis.

At the local level, August Vollmer, the police chief of Los Angeles, contributed a great deal to the advancement of law enforcement. In Los Angeles in 1923, Vollmer established a modern crime laboratory. He introduced the use of patrol cars, motorcycles, and bicycles for patrol officers. Vollmer set up fingerprint and handwriting systems and a way of filing information about how crimes were committed. Innovative and visionary, Vollmer created a police school where criminology, the study of criminal behavior, was taught. Following Vollmer's lead, police departments nationwide improved training, introduced new technologies, and developed new investigative procedures.

Further expansion of federal criminal justice

Two major factors made the growth of federal criminal justice an absolute necessity: the increased use of automobiles and commercial airlines by both the public and criminals. It was now easy to cross state boundaries. While planes, trains, and automobiles flowed freely across state lines, state law enforcement did not. By the 1930s interstate crime had become a key focus of federal responsibility.

Congress passed the Lindbergh Act of 1932 after the kidnapping and murder of the baby son of American aviator Charles Lindbergh (1902–1974). The act made it a federal crime to take people across state lines against their will. The person arrested and charged with the Lindbergh crime, Bruno Hauptmann, was convicted and executed.

During the Great Depression (1929–41), a period of severe economic hardship in the United States and much of the world, President Franklin D. Roosevelt introduced the New Deal, a collection of federal programs designed to provide jobs and bring economic relief to those most affected by the hard times. As a result, federal government grew dramatically and expanded its power in many areas, including law enforcement.

In 1933 it became a federal crime to flee across state lines to avoid arrest or to avoid testimony in criminal court cases. Congress passed laws establishing more actions as federal crimes in 1934. These included robbing a national bank,

Rows of tightly packed cots in a Louisiana state penitentiary in 1957, representative of the national prison overcrowding problem of the time. *(AP/Wide World Photos)*

extortion using telephones or telegraphs (to send fast messages called telegrams), and taking stolen goods worth more than $5,000 across state lines.

A growing prison population

With more criminal laws and improved policing, prison populations grew as well. Since the states were primarily responsible for criminal justice, most people convicted of crimes during the twentieth century were held in state prisons. In 1910 there were almost 67,000 prisoners in state prisons; in 1940 this figure rose to over 146,000. According to the Bureau of Justice Statistics produced by the U.S. Department of Justice, prison populations began to swell again by 1980 as longer sentences, often mandatory sentences set by state and federal law, were handed out by courts. In 1980 before the government's war on drugs began, there were over 503,000 inmates in state and federal prisons and local jails. By 2002, sixteen years after the war on drugs began, that figure rose to just over two million. New prisons were built to hold the growing population of inmates; in 1998 and 1999 alone 162 new prisons were under construction while another 675 facilities were remodeled. By 2001 daily operating expenses for state prisons reached $38 billion a year.

In an effort to lower prison expenses in the 1980s and 1990s, states began using outside companies to provide prison services. By the early twenty-first century private prisons (those not owned by the state) were operating in about thirty states, primarily in the South and West. Other facilities previously run by state agencies, such as drug treatment centers and halfway houses (residences where individuals can readjust to life after being released from prison), were also being operated by private companies.

In addition to state prisons, a dramatic growth in the number of federal inmates took place as well. In 1915, before Prohibition, there were only three thousand federal prisoners. By 1930, after a decade of Prohibition, there were thirteen thousand prisoners. To cope with the growing number of federal prisoners, Congress created the Bureau of Federal Prisons in 1930 and the bureau quickly added facilities, including Alcatraz in San Francisco, a prison that later became notorious for its harsh treatment of prisoners and reputation of being inescapable. Alcatraz began operation in 1934.

The number of prisoners continued to increase, climbing to twenty thousand in 1940 and twenty-five thousand in 1980 just before President Ronald Reagan's (1911–; served 1981–89) war on drugs that added thousands more. By 1985 the figure rose to almost forty thousand. Over fifty thousand were housed in almost fifty federal facilities operated by the Federal Bureau of Prisons by the end of the 1980s.

The U.S. prison population still remained high at the beginning of the twenty-first century. By 2000 two million inmates filled the nation's prisons and jails. Two-thirds were in state and federal prisons; the rest were in local city and county jails. Half of state inmates were convicted of violent crimes while the other half for property, drug, and other crimes. The majority of inmates were minorities, uneducated, and poor. Of industrial nations, the United States was second only to Russia in the percentage of its citizens held in prisons. Even though fewer crimes were being committed, those convicted were facing longer sentences under the harsher sentencing laws.

A women's workshop in Sing Sing Prison, New York, 1877. *(© Corbis)*

Treatment or punishment

Through the years the public has shifted back and forth on how to treat adult prison inmates. From 1890 to 1930 prisons put inmates to work manufacturing various items, like military clothing for World War I. Major industrial prisons included Sing Sing in New York, San Quentin in California, and the Illinois State Penitentiary. In the South chain gangs (convicts chained together to do heavy labor outside the prison) worked on public road projects. In addition to jobs, prisons also provided education, use of a prison library, outdoor recreation, and the opportunity to learn various trades.

Businesses located near prisons often complained of unfair competition from prison factories. Labor unions protested that the low wages paid to inmates caused wages outside prison walls to decline as well.

During the economic crash of the Great Depression in the 1930s, prisons decreased certain operations as the demand for goods dropped sharply. Responding to business, labor, and changing economic conditions, Congress passed the Ashurst-

Summers Act in 1935 prohibiting the interstate or state-to-state transportation of goods produced in prisons. Most states soon followed and passed similar laws prohibiting the sale of prison-made goods within their states.

During the 1930s prisons focused more on strict discipline and punishment rather than treatment. Violence and riots within the prisons resulted from these harsher conditions. In response the prisons turned back to the Wickersham Commission recommendations. They categorized inmates according to their level of security risk and placed less serious offenders in prison farms and forest camps. They also returned to programs of education and vocational training as well as rehabilitation programs. Focus on treatment more than punishment again became the preferred approach toward inmates. Prisoners began receiving individualized rehabilitation plans.

Before long, prison life changed once more. The rising crime rate through the 1960s and 1970s led again to a "get tough" approach on crime. Treatment approaches ended and tougher prison conditions resulted.

Organized crime

America's fear of organized crime grew in the 1950s. The perception of a giant organization of professional criminals, mostly of Sicilian (from Sicily, Italy) origin and referred to as the Mafia or La Cosa Nostra, captured the nation's attention. Many remembered back to the 1920s Prohibition era when crime syndicates (a group of people who work together in a business activity, legal or illegal) led by well-known criminals such as Al Capone (1899–1947) overwhelmed the criminal justice system.

In 1950 and 1951, U.S. senator Estes Kefauver (1903–1963) of Tennessee chaired a special congressional committee to investigate organized crime in America, including racketeering (obtaining money through illegal activities). Based on limited evidence, the Kefauver Committee claimed rich and powerful crime organizations operated in many U.S. cities. Dramatic media coverage of the Kefauver hearings on organized crime increased public concern. Kefauver even wrote a book, *Crime in America* (1951), based on the committee's findings.

In response to hearings, the FBI formed a special racketeering unit and began tracking interstate crime groups. Attorney

Members of the Kefauver Committee, also known as the Senate Crime Investigating Committee, offered many suggestions on how to better tighten the laws surrounding organized crime in the early 1950s.
(AP/Wide World Photos)

General Robert F. Kennedy (1925–1968) made organized crime one of his highest priorities.

In 1967 a presidential task force under President Lyndon B. Johnson (1908–1973; served 1963–69) revealed for the first time the inner workings of organized crime, particularly the Cosa Nostra, which operated an entire network of more than twenty Italian and Sicilian crime families in various U.S. cities. To give law enforcement greater authority to combat organized crime, Congress passed the Racketeer Influenced and Corrupt Organization Act (RICO), also known as the Organized Crime Control Act, in 1970.

RICO led to the successful prosecutions of Cosa Nostra members in the 1980s and 1990s. Owing to the longstanding public fascination with organized crime kept alive by the *The Godfather* movie series, the 1992 trial of mobster hit man John Gotti (1940–2002) in New York attracted considerable public attention. While federal authorities were concentrating on mobsters, other organized crime groups grew in wealth and power involving drug trafficking. These organizations were composed of ethnic gangs, largely from Latin America, East Asia, and Eastern Europe. (See chapter 7 on organized crime for more information.)

Terrorism

By the 1980s domestic and international terrorism began to capture the public's attention. Ted Kaczynski (1942–), known as the Unabomber, began mailing bombs to selected individuals in 1980, killing and maiming a number of people. He continued off and on for over a decade before he was captured. The nation was stunned in June 1995 when Timothy McVeigh (1968–2001) set off a deadly car bomb, destroying a five-story federal building in Oklahoma City, killing 265 men, women, and children.

International terrorism struck American soil in February 1993 with a bombing in the underground parking of the World Trade Center (WTC) in New York City that killed six and injured some one thousand. The cost of security grew, as did the rise of private police and security businesses.

Terrorism struck a deadlier blow, again at the WTC, on September 11, 2001. Two airliners hijacked by Middle Eastern terrorists struck the two high-rise office buildings, bringing them down and killing 2,800 people. Another airliner struck the Pentagon building in Washington, D.C., killing over 180. A fourth hijacked airliner crashed in rural Pennsylvania, killing over forty people while on its way to another planned target, most likely the White House or U.S. Capitol Building.

Fear of international terrorism dramatically increased. In reaction to the 2001 attacks, Congress passed the Patriot Act in 2002 and created a new federal department, the Department of Homeland Security. The new department, working with the Department of Justice, pursued security measures to guard against future terrorist crimes. The Justice Department focused on tracking illegal aliens in the United States and

Enron executives being sworn in prior to testifying before the Senate hearings in 2002. *(AP/Wide World Photos)*

monitoring any suspicious activity brought to its attention. (See chapter 10 on terrorism for more information.)

White-collar crime

White-collar crime refers to a person who uses his position of authority and responsibility in an organization, such as a business, to commit crimes of fraud and deceit. Fraud and deceit are intentionally deceiving a person or persons for one's own economic benefit. White-collar crimes can be carried out in most any business ranging from small automobile repair shops to the healthcare industry, financial institutions, and large corporations.

White-collar crime came to the public's attention in the 1980s with the collapse of the savings and loan industry, banks that primarily loaned money for building construction and home ownership. The collapse affected the financial health of millions of Americans. Other high-profile cases followed, including criminal charges against executives of Worldcom, a communications giant, and Enron, a company that controlled the flow of electrical power to customers, and the insider trading case against celebrity Martha Stewart (1941–) in 2004.

Given the national and international standing of the corporations involved, state courts were not those best equipped to deal with white-collar crime. It has become the concern of the Justice Department and the FBI to coordinate numerous organizations nationwide to track business dealings and irregularities. (See chapter 6 on white-collar crime for more information.)

Crime trends

By the mid-1960s following the assassination of President John F. Kennedy (1917–1963; served 1961–63) violent crime and property crime rates rose to high levels that would carry through the following decade. Police were falling behind. In addition, political crime had become widespread. In 1965 President Lyndon B. Johnson (1908–1973) declared a "war on crime." Congress passed the Law Enforcement Assistance Act (LEAA) that funneled billons of federal dollars to states over the next ten years to fight crime. The federal Crime Commission created by Johnson issued a lengthy report in 1967 warning that crime was greatly affecting the culture and quality of life in the United States. Congress responded with the Crime Control and Safe Streets Act to direct the war on crime.

Since the 1930s local police departments had been fully responsible for the health and safety of their community residents. Since citizens did not really help in community policing, the commission recommended they become more active in protecting themselves, such as installing alarms and improving locks on their properties. Such advice from a presidential commission, however, also served to increase the public's fear of crime. Many people avoided public parks and felt uncomfortable on the streets at night.

To lessen public fear, another national advisory commission in 1973 recommended citizens form local organizations to take a more active part in crime prevention. Such programs as Neighborhood Watch grew out of this idea. Residents banned together to watch for suspicious activities in their

New Technologies, New Crime, New Challenges

During the 1990s increasingly complex communications became available in businesses and homes. New communications networks provided tools for criminals. The growth of the Internet in particular opened new opportunities for criminal activity and created challenges for the criminal justice system.

The first computer-related criminal law in the United States was the Computer Fraud and Abuse Act. It targeted people interfering with computers and computer networks. Soon the focus changed to the kinds of information available over the Internet. New high-speed techniques were available for gathering, processing, and distributing information on almost any topic. A major consequence was that personal information about individuals became easily accessible. Controlling how this information was used and who used it proved a big challenge.

Concerns over privacy became of utmost importance. The explosion of available information affected copyrights, trademarks, and patents. Copyright laws allow

neighborhoods and report any activity to police. The earliest focus was on property crime, but this expanded in high crime areas to include drug activity by the late 1980s. By 2000 some fifty million Americans participated in local Neighborhood Watch programs.

By the late 1970s, the American public wanted a tougher approach to crime, including harsher punishment of criminals. This included a renewed interest in the death penalty and fixed or mandatory sentencing in order to not only discourage crime but make sure criminals paid for their crimes. Local commissions, created to study the crime issue in numerous cities and towns, developed new approaches to fighting crime. These included expanding police departments with money provided in part by federal funding.

Approaches to local policing changed through time as well. For example, the 1980s brought a return to police walking their patrols. Police wanted to reconnect with their communities on a much more personal level than they could while riding in patrol cars. Called community policing, police tried to create stronger ties with the public in fighting crime.

authors or artists the right to determine how their creations may be used, including how their works are reproduced, distributed, or performed. Trademark laws allow manufacturers to assign a specific identifying symbol to their products, meaning no other business can use that particular symbol. Patent laws grant inventors exclusive rights to operate, produce, or sell their products. Enforcement of these laws, if violated by using the Internet, has been virtually impossible. For example, songs have been freely copied off Internet sites instead of buying the music, which prevents artists from receiving proper royalties. The government has tried to penalize these criminals with fines but new "share" music and free music download sites that help conceal the identity of the downloader are launched everyday.

Other issues for criminal justice involving the Internet include the sale and distribution of child pornography (photos and films of children engaged in sex acts) and adults luring kids through Internet chat rooms into meetings and often into sexual relations. These criminal activities have crossed state and national boundaries. New technology has enabled criminals to operate where no boundaries exist. In the twenty-first century, the criminal justice system struggles to keep pace as it must continually redefine crime and criminals. (See chapter 11 on cyber crime for more information.)

Mounted police patrols (officers on horseback) became common sights in public areas such as parks.

Through the 1980s crime rates remained high as almost every basic category of serious crime increased. Youth gangs became a major concern, as did a rise in crack cocaine use. Twenty-two out of every 100,000 males, between the ages of fifteen and twenty-four, died violent deaths in 1987.

In 1990 some 35 million crimes occurred and 2.3 million Americans were victims of violent crime. Fear of violence was a major part of life in the United States affecting millions. This fear was heightened by racial rioting, known as the Rodney King riots, in Los Angeles in 1992. These riots broke out after videotapes of white policemen brutally beating a black man named Rodney King were shown on newscasts across the country.

Gun purchases rose dramatically, and business and home security systems became a very profitable business in the 1990s. Private security firms that provided bodyguards and other security measures, also received many customers. Mace (a chemical spray used to stun criminals) sold briskly and self-defense

Such programs as Neighborhood Watch grew out of a 1973 national advisory commission recommendation that citizens form local organizations to take a more active part in crime prevention. (© Landmann Patrick/Corbis Sygma)

classes became popular. The wide-spread use of cell phones in the 1990s was driven, in part, by concerns over crime and personal safety.

Juvenile justice

How to treat juvenile offenders has received considerable attention throughout the twentieth century. Ideas on how to make juvenile justice more effective changed through the decades. Illinois was the first state to separate juveniles from the regular justice system in 1899 when it passed the Juvenile Court Act. Reformers were dismayed that youths charged with crimes were placed in facilities along with hardened adult criminals. The new juvenile system was for youthful offenders under seventeen years of age. In addition, the justice records of juveniles were kept confidential. By 1925 almost all the states had juvenile systems. Although varying slightly from state to state, teen offenders who had turned eighteen were generally transferred to the adult criminal justice system.

In 1947 Congress passed the federal Juvenile Courts Act establishing a more consistent informal process for juveniles among the states. Emphasizing rehabilitation (treatment) over punishment, judges had considerable flexibility in deciding juvenile cases.

Over the next half century, thoughts on the treatment of juveniles in the criminal justice system changed steadily. With rising concern over juvenile delinquency in the 1950s, the public felt the juvenile system was too lenient or relaxed. Some states changed to more adult-like processes.

By the later 1960s the public was less concerned about juvenile crime. In 1972 Congress passed the Juvenile Delinquency Prevention Act setting out general rules for state juvenile justice systems. States once again kept juveniles separate from adults in jails and prisons, and every juvenile was given a court-appointed guardian. Greater emphasis was also placed on preventing youths from turning to crime.

By 1980 youth gangs and gun violence caught the public's attention. Juveniles were sent in greater numbers to adult courts to face more severe punishment, including the possibility of the death sentence for those over sixteen years of age.

Despite a decline in juvenile crime rates by the mid-1990s, the tougher approach remained. A series of school shootings kept juvenile offenders in the news and fears of crime high. Some states even passed laws making parents legally responsible for their children's criminal acts. In the early twenty-first century, the distinction between the juvenile and adult justice systems remained less than during earlier decades of the twentieth century. (See chapter 19 for more information on juvenile justice.)

A drop in crime, but not fear

During the 1990s the rate of violent crimes decreased significantly. Some claimed community policing, more police officers, and longer prison terms were key factors. Others pointed to the aging population in general and a stronger national economy. Previous studies had shown that most crimes were committed by males between seventeen and thirty-four years of age. By the 1990s, the number of males in this age range was steadily declining. Continuing into the twenty-first century, the homicide rate in the United States, though down from previous years, remained high compared to other industrialized nations. It was seven times greater than Canada and forty times greater than Japan.

Though crime rates declined, people still felt vulnerable. Crime was widely publicized in the media and seemed more random in its victims. Mass or large-scale shootings at schools and businesses as well as terrorist threats made the entire nation feel uneasy. Increased security in public buildings and at airports kept the threat of crime uppermost in people's minds. Despite the changes in criminal justice since the 1920s, citizens have continued to search for the answers to try and eliminate crime or at least to control it.

For More Information

Books

Chase, Anthony. *Law and History: The Evolution of the American Legal System.* New York: The New Press, 1997.

Federal Bureau of Investigation. *Crime in the United States, 2002: Uniform Crime Reports.* Washington, DC: U.S. Department of Justice, 2003.

Friedman, Lawrence M. *Crime and Punishment in American History.* New York: Basic Books, 1993.

Walker, Samuel. *The Police in America: An Introduction.* New York: McGraw-Hill, 1992.

Web Sites

Court TV's Crime Library: Criminal Minds and Methods. http://www.crime library.com (accessed on August 20, 2004).

"Uniform Crime Reports." *Federal Bureau of Investigation (FBI).* http://www. fbi.gov/ucr/ucr.htm (accessed on August 20, 2004).

Violent Crime: Crime Against a Person

On the evening of January 27, 2001, Roxana Verona arrived at the home of Susanne and Half Zantop for dinner. Verona and the Zantops were professors at Dartmouth, an elite Ivy League university in the peaceful wooded town of Hanover, New Hampshire. The Zantops lived in Etna, a village just outside Hanover. When Verona arrived at the Zantop home, she immediately sensed something might be wrong. Although the lights were shining brightly through the windows, it was eerily quiet. Verona entered the house, calling out to let the Zantops know she had arrived. When she came to the study she was greeted by a horrific scene: the Zantops lay in pools of dried blood, murder victims in their own upscale, rural home.

The murderers turned out to be two middle-class, intelligent teenagers—sixteen-year-old Jimmy Parker and seventeen-year-old Robert Tulloch. The boys robbed the Zantops so they could travel the world, and killed their victims to eliminate witnesses. As news of the murders spread through the media, shocked Americans were reminded that violent crime was a very real part of their country, even reaching into its most quiet towns.

Students, parents, and supporters bow their heads at a memorial service one year after the attack by Kip Kinkel. *(AP/Wide World Photos)*

Across the country in another peaceful town, Springfield, Oregon, fifteen-year-old Kip Kinkel had become a murderer. On May 20, 1998, Kinkel murdered his parents, who were both teachers, then went to his high school the next day and opened fire with a semiautomatic rifle. Kinkel killed one student and wounded eight, one of whom later died. The Springfield tragedy was part of an epidemic of school shootings that had escalated in the United States, beginning in late 1995 with the shooting of two high school teachers and one student by another student in Tennessee.

By the early twenty-first century many Americans had either been victimized by violent crime or knew someone who had. Everyone listened to news stories reporting violence on a daily basis. In 2002 one violent crime occurred every 22.1 seconds. Violent crime includes murder, robbery, aggravated assault (a particularly violent attack), and rape (forcing someone to have sexual relations). Sniper attacks, crimes of hate, and stalking also victimize U.S. citizens.

Reliable criminal statistics (compiled figures) on violent crime, recorded since 1930, are kept by the U.S. Department of Justice and the Federal Bureau of Investigations (FBI). Statistics of violent crime are collected from 17,000 local and state law enforcement agencies under the FBI's Uniform Crime Reporting (UCR) Program. Once compiled they are published in a yearly book titled *Crime in the United States*. Statistics in this chapter are from the UCR Program's 2002 publication.

Crimes against individuals

Homicide and murder both mean the killing of one human being by another. While in conversation, Americans commonly use the words murder and homicide as if they were the same, but homicide has a broader definition than murder. Homicide includes both murder and legally "justifiable" killing. The law recognizes that not all killings are criminal. The classic example is killing in war when the victim is part of an enemy force.

The law also recognizes killing in self-defense as justifiable or acceptable homicide. When a person is threatened with serious injury or death but manages to kill the attacker, he or she has killed in self-defense. Likewise if a law enforcement

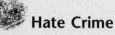

Hate Crime

The UCR Program defines hate crime as "a criminal offense committed against a person, property, or society which is motivated, in whole or in part, by the offender's bias against a race, religion, disability, sexual orientation, or ethnicity/national origin." Bias is another word for prejudice.

About 49.7 percent of the total number of hate crimes against individuals were motivated by racial prejudice; 18 percent by bias against a victim's religion; 16.4 percent against a victim's sexual orientation; and 15.3 percent against a victim's ethnicity or national origin.

Of the offenders whose race was determined, 61.8 percent were white, 21.8 percent were black, 1.2 percent were Asian or Pacific Islander, and 0.6 percent were American Indian or Alaskan Native.

officer should kill an individual who is in the process of committing a felony (serious) crime, the killing is considered justifiable homicide. On the other hand, murder is not justifiable homicide but criminal homicide. Murder is an unlawful or illegal killing of another human being.

Murder and manslaughter

Murder is the most serious violent crime, punishable by long prison sentences, often life in prison, and in some cases by death (capital punishment). Each state has slightly different laws pertaining to murder but it is commonly divided into murder and manslaughter.

Murder is the premeditated intent to kill with no justifiable reason to do so. Premeditation means the killer thought ahead or planned the killing. Without provocation means that a killer had no reasonable explanation for committing the murder and taking someone's life. Murder may also occur under the felony-murder rule. If an individual is in the process of committing a felony, such as rape or robbery, and someone is killed (other than the person committing the crime) the charge is murder even though no actual premeditation of the murder occurred. In such a case, the offender acted in a dangerous manner and this behavior caused another person's death.

The difference between murder and manslaughter is the absence of premeditation in manslaughter. Manslaughter is divided into two categories, voluntary and involuntary. With voluntary manslaughter the intent to kill is present and rises suddenly out of intense emotion, though it is not premeditated. It is often referred to as an action taken in the "heat of passion." The killer is provoked by the victim into an uncontrollable anger or rage. There can be no cooling off period between the provoking action and the killing. A typical situation of voluntary manslaughter would be a bar fight where the people involved have been drinking or are legally drunk. Voluntary manslaughter is also known as non-negligent manslaughter, as defined in the FBI's UCR Program.

With involuntary manslaughter, there is no intention to kill. Instead the killing is accidental and due to negligence (carelessness). Negligence implies that the offender failed to use necessary caution, or was distracted in a possibly danger-ous situation. Examples of involuntary manslaughter are han-dling of a loaded gun that accidentally goes off killing another person in the room, or hunting accidents where the hunter mistakes another human for an animal.

Voluntary manslaughter is a less serious offense than mur-der but still results in prison time, often lengthy depending on the laws of the state where it is committed. Involuntary manslaughter also may carry penalties. Killing in self-defense is the only killing where the offender is released from re-sponsibility. The offender claiming self-defense must prove that he or she acted only when in obvious, direct danger of severe injury or death.

National murder statistics

The UCR Program reported 16,204 murders in the United States in 2002. This number translates into a murder rate of 5.6 crimes per 100,000 residents. One murder occurred every 32.4 minutes in 2002. These figures and all figures in this sec-tion include the crime of murder and voluntary manslaugh-ter together and are from the FBI's UCR records.

In 1933 at the height of the Great Depression (1929–41), America's worst economic slump, murder rates were roughly twice the 2002 rate. By the mid-1950s, during economic pros-perity, the rate was down to 4.5 per 100,000 residents. The rate peaked in 1980 at 10.7 per 100,000 and was at another high point in 1991 at 10.5 per 100,000. The rate has steadily decreased since the early 1990s to 6.8 per 100,000 in 1997 and to 5.6 in 2002. In actual numbers of murders, there were 18,210 in 1997 compared to 16,204 in 2002.

Economic or financial well-being usually contributes to the variation in crime rates. Also widely recognized as a reason for declining rates in the early 1990s is the aging of the baby boom generation. The baby boom population bulge began with an increased U.S. birth rate in 1946 following World War II and did not slow until about 1962. Murder rates, as with all crime rates, are age-dependent with the highest number of offenders in the seventeen to thirty-four-year-old age bracket. By the 1990s most baby boomers were at least thirty years old with most well past the thirty-four-year-old mark. By the early to mid-1990s, there were considerably fewer individuals in the seventeen to thirty-four age bracket than in the 1960s, 1970s, and 1980s, leading to lower murder numbers.

Leading factors

Another important factor in crime rates is the gender or sex of the offender. Over 90.3 percent of those arrested for murder in 2002 were male. Murder victims were 76.8 percent male. Race, too, was another factor as black males accounted for 49.8 percent of murderers, whites and Hispanics accounted for 47.8 percent, and 2.4 percent of murders were committed by other races. The UCR combines white and Hispanic statistics together. Black victims were generally murdered by black offenders and white victims by white offenders. The murder weapon of choice was a firearm—76.6 percent handguns, 5.1 percent rifles, 5.1 percent shotguns, and 13.2 percent other or unknown types.

When the relationship between offender and victim was known, about 25 percent of murders occurred between strangers. These murders tend to be "thrill" killings—done for the immediate thrill and with no personal motive. Examples are random drive by shootings, dropping a rock on a car from an overpass or bridge, or shooting at cars on highways. Roughly 22 percent of murders were between family members. In 53 percent of murders the offender and victim were acquaintances. At the start of the twenty-first century approximately one thousand individuals per year were killed in gang-related activities. The victim may or may not have known his or her murderer. Teenage gangs often operate in a culture where violence and killing is not only expected but encouraged.

Over time, the most common traits of murderers have found them to be male, between the ages of eighteen and thirty-four, and an acquaintance of the victim. The weapon of choice is a firearm.

Serial and mass murder

Serial killers are those who, over a period of time longer than one day, kill a number of victims. In contrast, a mass murderer kills numerous individuals in a single violent episode that may last from a few minutes to a few hours until the attacker is caught, killed, or escapes.

While most serial killers are male, approximately 14 percent are female. Ted Bundy (1946–1989) was an infamous serial killer who killed a confirmed thirty young women across the United States between 1974 and 1978. (The real total of Bundy's victims is suspected to be over one hundred.) Bundy was handsome, well educated, and received intense pleasure from the act of killing. His killings began in Washington State, moved to Utah, then to Florida where his last murders occurred. Bundy was captured in 1976 and convicted of kidnapping. He escaped twice in 1977 and was recaptured for the final time in February 1978. Bundy was convicted of three murders and executed on January 24, 1989.

Confident and attractive, Ted Bundy shattered society's vision of what a serial killer looked like. *(AP/Wide World Photos)*

Beginning in 1996 and moving into the 2000s, a number of mass murders occurred in U.S. schools. Kip Kinkel, described at the beginning of this chapter, killed two students and seriously wounded seven others when he opened fire with a semiautomatic rifle in the lunchroom of Thurston High School in Springfield, Oregon. Other examples of mass murders are a gunman opening fire in a shopping mall or a disgruntled worker firing at a boss and coworkers.

Robbery

The UCR Program defines robbery in *Crime in the United States, 2002* "as the taking or attempting to take anything of value from the care, custody, or control of a person or persons by force or threat of force or violence and/or by putting the victim in fear." The seriousness of a robbery and its punishment is not based on the value of what was stolen, but on how much force was used to frighten the victim. This is why robbery is considered a crime against a person not a crime against property.

Armed robbery in which the robber threatens the victim with a weapon receives the harshest penalties since the victim could be seriously harmed. Robbery is punishable by imprisonment in a state or federal prison. Armed robbery results in a longer prison term than a robbery without the use of a weapon. Unlike murders, most victims of robbery do not know their robber. Robberies often take place in public places, on streets or sidewalks, rather than inside buildings or homes.

The motivation for most robberies is the need for cash to support a lifestyle of gambling and partying, buying drugs, or simply to be the most successful and powerful street hustler. Robbers on the street strike suddenly with a threatening pose that allows the victim no time to think how to escape or stop the robbery. Most victims hand over what is demanded.

Robbers are generally rational or reasonable individuals who commit their crime after deciding what type of person, where, and how they will rob and get away with their crime. Individual targets are often those who do not look like they will fight back such as elderly men or women. People in poor neighborhoods are frequently targeted as they are more likely to carry cash than those in more affluent neighborhoods where credit cards are preferred to cash. Staking out victims at cash machines is common. Convenience stores and gas stations open late at night are also favorite targets. While banks present a more difficult target, the temptation of larger amounts of cash can prove irresistible.

National robbery statistics

The UCR Program reported an estimated 420,637 robberies in 2002. This number translates into an overall U.S. robbery rate of 145.9 offenses per 100,000 residents. One robbery occurred every 1.2 minutes in 2002. Just as murder rates have declined since the early 1990s, so too have robbery rates. The 2002 robbery rate represents an 11.8 percent decline from rates

A still frame from a video produced by the Aryan Republican Army, who recruited young white supremacists for a bank robbery gang that zigzagged across the country for two years. *(AP/Wide World Photos)*

in 1998 and a large 43 percent decline from rates in 1993. A majority of robberies occurred in cities—an overall city rate of 208.1 robberies per 100,000 residents. Cities with populations of 250,000 and above had the highest rate in 2002— 395.2 robberies per 100,000. Cities under 10,000 had only a rate of 54.2 robberies per 100,000. Rural counties had a lower rate of 17.7 per 100,000 residents.

The highest percentage of robberies occurred against people on the street—42.8 percent of the total number of robberies in 2002. Those victims lost an average of $1,045 per robbery. As a group, commercial establishments such as restaurants, bars, and hotels suffered 14.6 percent of robberies, with a $1,676 average loss per robbery. Private residences were close behind at 13.5 percent, recording an average loss of $1,340 per robbery. Convenience stores, gas stations, and banks experienced 6.5 percent, 2.7 percent, and 2.3 percent of robberies, respectively. Convenience stores lost an average of $665 for each robbery, service stations $679, and banks $4,763. Various other locations, such as bars or cafes, make up the remaining 17.7 percent of robbery targets.

Leading factors

Of the individuals arrested for robbery in 2002, 61.4 percent were under the age of twenty-five but most were adults at least eighteen years of age. Males accounted for 89.7 percent of arrests. Blacks accounted for 54.1 percent of arrests while 44.1 percent were whites and Hispanics, and 1.7 percent were other races including Asian, Native American, Alaskan Native, and Pacific Islander. Robbers used firearms 42.1 percent of the time, but 39.9 percent of robbers "strong armed" their victims, using their fists and feet as weapons. Knives were used in 8.7 percent of robberies and various other weapons made up the remaining 9.3 percent.

Aggravated assault

The UCR Program defines aggravated assault as "an unlawful attack by one person upon another for the purpose of inflicting severe or aggravated bodily injury. This type of assault is usually accompanied by the use of a weapon or by means likely to produce death or great bodily harm."

Aggravated assault requires an actual physical attack on the victim that is intended to cause severe harm. Frequently, the only difference between a murder charge and aggravated assault charge is that the victim lives. A charge of assault, not aggravated assault, may not involve actual physical contact but can be brought when the victim experiences an unsuccessful attempted assault or was threatened in some manner by an offender.

Statistics and leading factors

In 2002 the UCR Program reported an estimated 894,348 aggravated assaults in the United States or an estimated 310.1 aggravated assaults per 100,000 residents. One aggravated assault occurred every 35.3 seconds in 2002. Just as with murder and robbery, assault rates have declined since the early 1990s. The 2002 rates were 14.2 percent lower than the 1998 rates, and 29.6 percent lower than the 1993 rates. Cities with populations of 250,000 and above had the highest rate in 2002—577.5 offenses per 100,000 residents. Towns under 10,000 in population had a rate of 219.1 offenses per 100,000, and rural counties had the lowest rate of 186.0 offenses per 100,000 residents.

Of the reported aggravated assaults in 2002, 79.8 percent of arrests were males. Blacks accounted for 63.4 of arrests, whites and Hispanics accounted for 34.2 percent, and all other races accounted for 2.4 percent. The most commonly used weapons were blunt instruments (such as a baseball bat or hammer), fists, and feet. Firearms and knives were used in about 12 percent of aggravated assaults.

Assault in American homes

Assaults within U.S. homes have been getting an increasing amount of attention in recent years; yet the majority of in-home assaults are not reported to law enforcement authorities because they are usually between family members. This means there are far more aggravated assaults than indicated in UCR figures. Two types of assaults occur in the home: spouse, or husband-wife, abuse and child abuse.

Spouse abuse is difficult to estimate but best guesses by law enforcement agencies put the number of families experiencing spouse abuse at sixteen out of one hundred. Agencies estimate that as high as 60 to 70 percent of calls for help in the evening and night hours involve in-home disputes. Spouse abuse involves physically injuring a partner with varying severity or cruelty. Spouse abusers are also called "batterers." Many spouse abusers were abused as children and see it as a part of daily life. Spousal abuse may occur suddenly and violently in a burst of anger or it may occur regularly over time in an attempt to humiliate the partner. Abuse is often driven by resentment over feelings of dependence on the spouse or feelings of deep insecurity. Excessive alcohol use is frequently present in abuse cases.

Child abuse takes three forms: physical abuse, child neglect, and sexual abuse. Physical abuse involves unreasonable

A "Stop Family Violence" stamp put out by the U.S. Post Office in 2003 to raise money for programs working to curtail domestic violence. *(AP/Wide World Photos)*

disciplinary actions such as beatings, burning, or holding a child under water. Neglect is failure to feed, care, or provide shelter for the child. Sexual abuse of children includes rape (forced sexual relations), incest (sexual relations with a parent or caregiver), or molestation (forced physical sexual touching). As in spousal abuse, adults who abuse children were most likely abused themselves in childhood.

Two additional situations seem to increase the chances of child abuse in family. Children who live in blended families where one adult is not biologically related to them seem to be at greater risk for abuse. Parents who are lonely, isolated, or unable to find help at times of crisis in their personal life can also be prone to child abuse.

Forcible rape

The UCR defines forcible rape as "the carnal (bodily) knowledge of a female forcibly against her will. Assaults or attempts to commit rape by force or threat of force are also included; however, statutory rape (without force) . . . are excluded." Carnal knowledge means having sexual relations or intercourse with the female.

Statutory rape, mentioned in the UCR definition as rape without force and not included in UCR statistics, involves an adult and teenager under the age of consent. Each state defines the exact ages and age difference of the partners. Statutory rape occurs when sexual relations are not forced on the teenager, because the individual has apparently agreed to the act. It is a crime, however, because many teenagers are considered too young to make such a decision or to give their consent. Statutory rape cases are very difficult to prosecute since juries do not like to convict if the two individuals seemed to agree to have sex—even if the victim was quite young or there was a large age difference between the victim and adult sexual partner.

Rapes involve the offender's need to feel sexual power and power over the victim. Anger and aggression can also be part of the crime. Some rapes are committed with sudden attacks in public areas such as parks or streets. These generally occur in hidden areas like alleys under the cover of night. Other rapes occur after the offender has befriended the victim with either conversation or by offering a ride in a car. Some of-

Stalking

Stalking is a behavior defined as repeated, unwanted physical closeness or communication from a person that leaves the victim feeling threatened. Often the stalker or offender makes verbal or written threats to the victim.

Media personalities such as singer Madonna (1958–), director Steven Spielberg (1946–), and actress Gwyneth Paltrow (1972–) are well-known victims of stalking, but most victims are not celebrities and are acquainted with their stalkers. The majority of stalkers are men, but some women stalk as well. Women victims are often stalked by former boyfriends or spouses. Stalkers generally become obsessed with their victims, seeking power over them and their lives through frightening incidents and many stalkers believe they have a relationship with their victims (though it is usually imaginary). Stalkers are sometimes motivated by revenge or by rejection. The Internet has made it very easy for stalkers to get information about victims, so they can send threatening emails as well.

By the 1990s states began to realize stalkers were dangerous criminals who often end up doing harm to or even killing their victims. California law classifies stalking as a felony (serious crime) with punishment of up to five years in prison.

fenders are serial rapists, committing the crime again and again with different victims. Rapes occur at a higher rate in summer months, peaking in July since people are out more and later at night making them vulnerable as victims. Besides forcible rape where the offender is completely unknown to the victim, other forcible rapes are called "acquaintance rape," which includes date rape, marital rape (between two people who are legally married to each other), and gang rape (forced sexual relations with more than one person).

Acquaintance rape and gang rape

Date rape occurs when a male and female are dating one another, but one person forces the other to have sex. Date rape may occur at any time during the dating relationship. Some offenders feel that their date owes them sexual relations because they have been dating for a while. Alcohol or drugs are sometimes involved. Date rapes are sometimes common on college campuses; however, few of the rapes are reported if the victim feels partly to blame.

Marital rape was first defined in most states in the 1980s and 1990s. For centuries many believed the crime of rape could not be committed between a man and woman who were married to each other. In the late twentieth century, however, law enforcement and the legal community realized marital rape was often associated with spousal abuse. Marital rape has nothing to do with a loving relationship; instead it tends to be associated with beatings and is so violent the victimized partner is physically injured.

Gang rape involves multiple offenders and a single victim. The victim may or may not be known to the offenders. Like other rapes, the use of alcohol and drugs may be involved. Gang rape generally occurs at night in secluded public or private places. Gang rape involves showing off aggression and power to one's peers through sexual relations.

Difficult prosecutions

Rape, in all but the most blatant or obvious cases, is very difficult to prosecute and to obtain a conviction. Until recently, a conviction almost always demanded proof the victim strongly resisted her attacker, that force was used by the attacker, and proof from an outside source such as a medical exam or a witness that the accused was the actual offender.

If the victim knows the attacker, conviction can be very challenging because the attacker can say the two were dating or had a relationship. Yet by the beginning of the twenty-first century, many states had or were adopting reforms in rape laws, dropping many of the requirements to prove the crime was committed as well as making it easier for victims to prove their cases in court.

In the 1980s and 1990s states and federal lawmakers created "shield laws." These laws excluded the prior sexual history of the rape victims from being part of the court proceedings unless it was somehow directly related to the case at hand. Shield laws vary from state to state allowing trial judges the ability to decide if prior sexual history will or will not be allowed. The use of shield laws was upheld in 1991 by the U.S. Supreme Court in the case *Michigan v. Lucas*. The ruling supported the protection provided to the victims by the shield laws while they pursued prosecution of their attackers. Another attempt to strengthen rape laws came when Congress passed the Violence Against Women Act in 1994. The act allows rape victims to sue their attacker in federal court for violation of their civil rights.

National forcible rape statistics

The UCR Program estimates there were 95,136 rapes on females in 2002. This number means forcible rapes were committed on 64.8 out of every 100,000 females in the United States. One forcible rape occurred every 5.5 minutes in 2002. Although this rate was an increase over the 2001 rate of 62.6, the rate has been declining over the past decade. In 1999 it was 80.4 per 100,000 females. Just as with murder, robbery, and aggravated assaults, rape rates have been declining since the early 1990s. When examining rape rates, it should be kept in mind that the National Crime Victimization Survey (NCVS) estimates that roughly half of attempted rapes are not reported to the police. Victims often feel they will not be believed, that the rape will be difficult to prove causing them humiliation, or they may simply believe their accusation will lead to no corrective results. The NCVS, established in 1973, is maintained by the Bureau of Justice Statistics and provides data on crime incidents, victims, and trends.

Age and race factors

Police estimate they make arrests in one-half of the reported rape cases, with many others not resulting in arrests. According to 2002 figures, 16.7 percent of those arrested for forcible rape were juveniles or youths under eighteen. Adults, eighteen and over, made up 83.3 percent of arrests. Of the juvenile arrests, 62 percent were white and Hispanic youths, 36 percent were black youths, and the

"Three Strikes" Laws

"Three strikes and you're out" laws, also called habitual felony laws, state that a criminal who is convicted of his or her third felony must remain in prison for an extended period of time, sometimes for life. Although various forms of these "get tough" laws for repeat offenders have existed for centuries, twenty-two states and the federal government passed new habitual felony laws between 1993 and 1995. The laws became commonly known as the "three strikes" laws.

Overall crime rates in the United States have been on a steady rise since the late 1960s. By the early 1990s, television news coverage of horrific crimes, often committed by individuals with previous felony convictions or by those out of prison on parole, reached a large segment of the U.S. public. It was reasonable for many to assume that repeat offenders would never reform, would continue to commit felonies, and should be locked up for longer periods of time than a first-time offender. Public pressure to get tough and keep the most violent repeat criminals locked up indefinitely caused state legislatures to pass the "three strikes" laws. After ten years of implementing these penalties, however, some states have encountered negative consequences. The laws remain controversial.

rest were of other races. The juvenile arrest percentages mirrored the overall adult arrest rate percentages of 63.4 percent whites, 34 percent blacks, and 2.6 percent of other races.

For More Information

Books

Allison, June, and Lawrence Wrightsman. *Rape: The Misunderstood Crime.* Newbury Park, CA: Sage, 1993.

Federal Bureau of Investigation. *Crime in the United States, 2002: Uniform Crime Reports.* Washington, DC: U.S. Department of Justice, 2003.

Inglis, Ruth. *Sins of the Fathers: A Study of the Physical and Emotional Abuse of Children.* New York: St. Martin's Press, 1978.

Siegel, Larry J. *Criminology: The Core.* Belmont, CA: Wadsworth/Thomson Learning, 2002.

Wright, Richard, and Scott Decker. *Armed Robbers in Action: Stickups and Street Culture.* Boston: Northeastern University Press, 1997.

Web Sites

Court TV's Crime Library: Criminal Minds and Methods. http://www.crime library.com (accessed on August 20, 2004).

Federal Bureau of Investigation (FBI). http://www.fbi.gov (accessed on August 20, 2004).

"Uniform Crime Reports." *Federal Bureau of Investigation (FBI).* http://www.fbi.gov/ucr/ucr.htm (accessed on August 20, 2004).

Crimes Against Property

Crimes against property are crimes of theft where no force or threat of force is directed toward an individual. According to the Federal Bureau of Investigation's Uniform Crime Reporting (UCR) Program as reported in *Crime in the United States, 2002*, thefts known as property crimes include "the offenses of burglary, larceny-theft, motor vehicle theft, and arson." Burglary involves the unlawful entry into a structure, such as a home or building, to steal something. Larceny-theft is the unlawful taking of property, but does not involve unlawful entry. Motor vehicle theft not only includes stealing automobiles but other vehicles such as motorcycles and snowmobiles. Arson, though not a theft crime, is a crime against property that involves the intentional burning of a structure. All statistics in this chapter are from the UCR Program's *Crime in the United States*.

Crimes against property are usually motivated by financial gain. Going back in history for many centuries, thievery was very common. Travelers on the European continent and in England were often preyed upon by everyone from poor peasants to noblemen down on their luck. Soldiers and warriors took what they pleased as they traveled through rural

While a gentleman kindly bows to two ladies, an elderly woman picks his pocket. *(© Bettmann/Corbis)*

farms and villages. Another form of everyday thievery was killing wild animals in the royal forests or taking livestock that belonged to the royal families.

By the time English and European settlers arrived in America in the seventeenth century, cities in the Old World such as London and Paris were large and crowded with many poor people. In both cities, gangs were organized to carry out planned heists or robberies. Pickpocketing (stealing from someone's pockets) became a skilled career. By the seventeenth and eighteenth centuries, laws against theft were being developed in England and Europe. Those laws defined theft in mostly the same way it is today in the United States.

Crimes of theft remain common throughout the United States in the twenty-first century. The UCR reported 10,450,893 property crimes in 2002, or one every three seconds. In addition, many more property crimes occur but go unreported to law enforcement agencies. Most thieves are not career criminals, they do not think of themselves as part of the criminal element of society. Most have another source of income apart from their occasional acts of theft.

The category of larceny-theft includes shoplifting, stealing credit cards, and knowingly writing "bad" checks (paying by check when there is no money in an account to cover the purchases). Most thieves carry out these criminal actions only occasionally or on the spur of the moment, responding to an opportunity where items are left unsecured, for a thrill, or sometimes because they lack money for a real need. They generally think of their theft as harmless, since in most cases no one is physically harmed. Police often hear a car thief say he was only borrowing the car for a short time. The UCR Program reported in 2002 that approximately 30 percent of property crimes were carried out by youth less than eighteen years of age. A few of these youngsters may become career criminals but most will not.

The United States also has a population of skilled professional thieves who make their livings from burglary, larceny, and car theft. Although much smaller in number than occasional thieves, professional thieves are responsible for considerable financial loss.

Overall in 2002, Americans had $16.6 billion of goods stolen. Burglary accounted for $3.3 billion, larceny-theft $4.9

billion, and motor vehicle theft $8.4 billion. The average dollar loss per reported arson offense was $11,253.

Burglary

The UCR Program defines burglary as "the unlawful entry of a structure to commit a felony (serious crime) or theft." UCR further subdivides burglary into three categories: forcible entry, accounting for about 63 percent of total burglaries; unlawful entry where no force is used, about 30 percent of burglaries; and attempted forcible entry, for about 6.5 percent of burglaries.

Forcible entry, for example, would be getting into a locked house by breaking a window or door. Force is not directed against a victim but against the structure. The fact that an intruder breaks into a private home, however, puts the home's occupants into a threatening, potentially dangerous situation. For this reason burglary is considered a more serious crime than larceny-theft.

Unlawful entry where no force is used could involve walking into an unlocked house or opening an unlocked tool shed for the purpose of stealing items. This middle category of burglary removes force as a required factor for a charge of burglary. An example of attempted forcible entry is simply an unsuccessful attempt to force one's way into a locked structure.

There are different levels of seriousness for a burglary charge. The most serious kind involves forcefully breaking into an occupied home during the night. The least serious burglary offense involves a daytime unlawful and unforced entry into a commercial building or structure that does not have occupants.

Criminal studies show that burglars often have drug habits they support with their activities. Burglars also frequently engage in larceny-theft related activities like shoplifting and may have a history of assault. Approximately one-third of burglaries are carried out by juveniles under the age of eighteen years old. A need for money to buy drugs is the most common motive. These youthful burglars often break into homes and apartment complexes in poor neighborhoods hoping to find cash. While many burglaries are carried out without much planning or forethought, successful, skilled burglars often go through an apprentice-like stage of building their burglary careers.

Professional burglars, those who make a living from burglary, often learn breaking and entering skills from others, such as relatives or friends. They must learn the technical skills of opening locked doors and windows, disarming alarm systems, avoiding video cameras, and opening safes without destroying the contents. These are all techniques learned from experienced burglars. Learning how to pick targets with high-priced goods is also an important part of successful burglaries.

Professionals often work in burglary rings or groups so although they are criminals, they must be able to work together, to organize as a dependable group, and delegate or assign various tasks. Various duties include observing a home or building to learn the habits of its occupants; finding the best locations and times for entry; possibly getting into the target ahead of time to decide which items to steal; the actual break in itself; transporting the stolen goods; and knowing escape routes. Successful professional burglars must also have regular fences for their goods. The term "fence" is frequently used to describe people who buy stolen property at prices below the normal retail price and then sell it for a profit.

There are different levels of seriousness for a burglary charge. The most serious kind involves forcefully breaking into an occupied home during the night.
(© L. Clarke/Corbis)

Favorite commercial targets for professional burglars are retail stores where all preparation can be carried out by simply entering the store during business hours, checking the location of certain items, and finding if any alarms or anti-theft equipment is in use. A burglar may sometimes strike the same store several times. Favorite residential targets are

Neighborhood Watch

From 1930 to the early 1970s the nation's police departments took full responsibility for protecting communities and neighborhoods from crime. Private residents played little role in crime prevention. By the late 1960s, however, property and violent crimes began increasing at a dramatic rate. In 1965 U.S. President Lyndon B. Johnson (1908–1973; served 1963–69) declared a "war on crime" and assembled the Crime Commission to guide the nation.

The commission urged American citizens to take a more active role in protecting themselves, primarily by installing more locks and alarms in their residences. In 1973 a national commission recommended an expanded role for citizens, such as forming citizen groups to organize and prevent crime in their neighborhoods. A well-known program to emerge from this effort was Neighborhood Watch.

Neighborhood Watch programs consist of residents who watch out for suspicious activity in their neighborhoods and notify the police if they spot criminal activity. The participants exchange phone numbers, receive training from local police officers, and learn how to report suspicious activity. Neighborhood Watch signs are posted in the area alerting potential criminals that a neighborhood alert system is in place. Local watch groups will often inspect their neighborhoods for ways to increase security. In some high crime neighborhoods, citizens expanded their vigilance to look for drug trafficking as well as property crimes.

These efforts were so successful nationally that, by the end of the twentieth century, 40 percent of Americans lived in communities with Neighborhood Watch programs. The majority of residents in Watch communities were active participants in their programs. Neighborhood Watch has become the largest crime prevention program in the nation, with more than fifty million people estimated to be involved.

upscale homes when occupants are away. Burglars will often pose as repair or maintenance workers to avoid neighborhood suspicion.

National burglary statistics

The UCR Program reported an estimated 2,151,875 burglaries in 2002, or an overall U.S. burglary rate of 746.2 offenses per 100,000 residents. One burglary occurred every 14.7 seconds in 2002. Although this is a slight increase in the burglary rate of 2001, it represents a 13.5 percent decline from the burglary rate in 1998 and a 32.1 percent decline from the rate in 1993.

The highest burglary rates for 2002 occurred in U.S. cities. The overall city rate was 840.8 burglaries per 100,000 residents. Rural counties had an overall rate of 595.9 per 100,000 people. Large cities with populations between 500,000 and 999,999 recorded a rate of 1,213.6 burglaries per 100,000 residents. Small cities with populations between 10,000 and 24,999 had the lowest city burglary rate of 652.6 offenses per 100,000 residents. Residential home burglaries accounted for 65.8 percent of all burglaries with an average loss valued at $1,549. Commercial areas with stores and offices accounted for 34.2 percent with an average value loss of $1,678 per offense.

In 2002 of those arrested for burglary, 86.7 percent were males and 13.3 were females. Of all males arrested, 30.7 percent were juveniles younger than eighteen years of age. Of all females arrested, 25.3 percent were juveniles. White Americans accounted for 70.4 percent of all burglaries, black Americans 27.5 percent, and 2.1 percent were other races.

Larceny-theft

The UCR Program defines larceny-theft as the "unlawful taking, carrying, leading, or riding away of property from the possession . . . of another. It includes crimes such as shoplifting, picking pockets, purse snatching, thefts from motor vehicles, thefts of motor vehicle parts and accessories, bicycle thefts, etc., in which no use of force, violence, or fraud occurs." Fraud is to misrepresent or lie about facts in order to persuade a victim to give money or other property to the offender. Larceny-theft also includes intentionally writing bad checks and credit card theft.

Most U.S. states divide larceny-theft into two categories of seriousness: petit and grand larceny. Petit, or petty larceny, refers to small amounts of money or goods, usually $100 or less, and is punishable as a misdemeanor (minor crime) with fines or brief jail time. Grand larceny usually involves amounts of money or value over $100 and is punishable as a felony with longer jail or prison sentences. The most frequent larceny-theft crime, which accounts for about 26 percent of larcenies, involves stealing items out of motor vehicles.

A related kind of larceny-theft, making up about 11 percent of the larcenies, is stealing motor vehicle accessories such as air bags or sound systems. Air bags, which cost consumers upwards of $1,000 in 2003 to replace, are sold by thieves for $50 to $200. Another major larceny-theft category, accounting for 12.5 percent of larcenies, is the theft of items from company buildings such as office equipment, communication equipment, cameras, and tools. Picking pockets and purse snatching, while highly frustrating to victims, makes up only about 1 percent of larceny-theft crimes.

Shoplifting

A common form of petty larceny is shoplifting, taking merchandise from a store without paying for it. Shoplifting accounted for about 14 percent of all larceny-thefts early in the twenty-first century. Shoplifting has been on the rise in the United States since the 1980s. Merchants lose an estimated 2 percent of total sales to shoplifting, but the exact dollar loss it difficult to determine. These losses are called "inventory shrinkage."

Only about 10 percent of shoplifters are professional shoplifters who intend to resell stolen goods for profit. Most are amateur shoplifters, known in thievery language as "snitches." Snitches take items such as clothing, cosmetics, jewelry, compact discs (CDs), cigarettes, grocery or pharmacy items, or hardware for their own personal use. Most plan ahead and bring large purses or bags in which to carry the stolen items. Snitches think what they do is harmless and do not consider themselves part of any criminal element in society. They generally shoplift only until they are caught; their first arrest is so traumatic that most snitches never shoplift again. Shoplifting tends to be at its highest levels among teenagers, then gradually lessens with age.

As the amount of money lost due to shoplifting increased for retail stores over the last part of the twentieth century, deterrent or prevention devices were developed. Electronic sensors, small plastic clips attached to clothing, became common in large clothing outlets. If a customer walked out of the store between electronic sensing monitors at door locations, the tag caused a loud beeping to alert store personnel. Sales clerks have special tools to remove the plastic tag when an item is purchased.

Credit Card Theft

In March 2004 the Montgomery, Alabama, police department arrested and charged an eighteen-year-old girl with credit card abuse (theft). The credit card was mistakenly left by a Montgomery woman at a gasoline station on December 21, 2003. She reported the loss to police.

The eighteen-year-old found the card and showed it to her boyfriend. The pair, along with a few other teens, charged more than $1,000 worth of purchases both in Montgomery and Houston, Texas, over the next several weeks.

Following the credit card trail, police pinpointed exact stores where the unlawful purchases were made. At least nine video-tapes from the stores where the teens made purchases were obtained. The eighteen-year-old faced not only a charge of credit card theft (a misdemeanor or minor of-fense), but also a felony charge (major offense) of engaging in organized criminal activity. The felony charge stemmed from the use of the card by a number of individuals known to the teen.

If reported within a reasonable time period, credit card companies such as Visa and MasterCard as well as debit card issuers limit a victim's loss to $50. Losses to credit or debit card companies from credit card theft have been growing every year. In general, credit card thieves are amateurs but even amateurs can cause huge losses—especially if they use the Internet to steal card numbers. Stolen card numbers are usually used for two or three days then abandoned. Police agencies stress that victims must file a police report since most financial agencies, card companies, and credit reporting agencies require a police report to take action.

Some security tagging systems are built into the packaging or item itself during the manufacturing process. Another tactic used to deter shoplifting is physically attaching sample items to counters where the customer may observe them. A retail clerk must retrieve the item from a storage area when the customer is ready to purchase. This approach is used frequently for electronic items such as cameras or cell phones. Many states have a "merchant privilege law," allowing store officials to arrest suspected shoplifters on the spot if they have reasonable grounds. They may hold the offender for a short amount of time while awaiting law enforcement officers.

A security guard watching video monitors of various locations of the mall to prevent shoplifting. *(AP/Wide World Photos)*

National larceny-theft statistics

The UCR Program reported an estimate of over seven million larceny-thefts in 2002. This number translates into an overall national larceny-theft rate of 2,445.8 offenses per 100,000 people. This 2002 rate is 10.4 percent below the 1998 rate and 19.4 percent below the 1993 rate. Collectively cities had a larceny-theft rate of 3,017.1 offenses per 100,000 people. Rural counties reported a rate of only one-third of that of cities. The rural rate was 1,083.3 offenses per 100,000 people.

Total larceny-theft loss was estimated at $419 billion for 2002. Of the stolen property, 39.6 percent was valued at over $200; 22.6 percent was valued between $50 and $200; and 37.8 percent was valued below $50.

Men demonstrating to police how quickly a car can be stripped of valuable parts. *(AP/Wide World Photos)*

For 2002 juveniles, youth under eighteen years of age, accounted for 29.5 percent of larceny-theft arrests. By gender, 63 percent of those arrested were male, 37 percent female. Females made up a considerably larger percentage of arrests for larceny-theft than for burglary. White Americans accounted for 67.9 percent of the arrests, black Americans 29.3 percent, and 2.8 percent were other races.

Motor vehicle theft

The FBI's *Crime in the United States, 2002* defines motor vehicle theft as "the theft, or attempted theft of a motor vehicle. This offense includes the stealing of automobiles, trucks, buses, motorcycles, motor scooters, snowmobiles, etc." *Crime in the United States, 2002* also reveals that every 25.3 seconds a motor vehicle was stolen in the United States in 2002. One in three thefts was carried out by a juvenile. Thieves prefer dark areas or unattended parking areas where no witnesses are near. About one-half of vehicles stolen were unlocked, but it takes an accomplished car thief only seconds to open most locked cars. Younger thieves often steal a car for a few hours of joyriding or to travel short distances. Other motives of car thieves include longer transportation needs or the desire to make a profit by selling the car for its parts.

Some thieves sell cars to illegal theft rings whose members falsify vehicle identification numbers and title documents then resell them. Professional car thieves who make a living from their thievery are usually connected with "chop shops," or strip shops where stolen cars are disassembled and the parts are sold. Other professional car thieves are part of export rings. Cars are stolen and sent to foreign countries where the demand for U.S.-made cars is strong. Owning an illegally exported car has become a status symbol for many individuals in several Eastern European countries.

The National Insurance Crime Bureau (NICB) released a study in June 2003 listing the U.S. cities with the highest motor vehicle theft rates (called "hot" cities). A majority of the cities were close to U.S. borders with Mexico or Canada and major seaports. Phoenix, Arizona, was the number one hot spot followed by several cities in central California—Fresno, Modesto, Stockton, and Sacramento. Port cities in the hottest top ten locations included Oakland, California; Seattle and Tacoma, Washington; and Miami, Florida.

Export of stolen vehicles steadily increased in the first part of the twenty-first century. To combat this trend, the FBI along with the U.S. Customs Office, the NICB, several insurance companies, and state and local law enforcement agencies have joined together to form the North American Export Committee (NAEC). The NAEC encourages x-ray scanning of cargo containers, although by 2003 scanners were used at only a few locations. According to the NICB, illegal exporters simply avoided ports using scanners.

Theft prevention devices

While alarms such as loud warning sounds or flashing lights are widely used on vehicles, studies show they are becoming less effective in deterring thieves. Many go off so frequently, especially in large busy city settings, everyone ignores them. Locking mechanisms, such as steering wheel locks, provide a good deterrent to theft. More effective still are kill switches—which either cut off electrical power needed to start the engine or halt the supply of fuel if a theft is underway.

The most effective high tech devices are electronic tracking systems using hidden transmitters in the car that allow police to track the vehicle. Police often are led directly to the chop shops. Electronic tracking devices are even used on expensive construction equipment so they can be recovered if stolen.

A device called "The Club" locks the steering wheel in place and is a good deterrent to theft. *(© David Butow/Corbis)*

National motor vehicle theft statistics

The UCR Program estimated that 1,246,096 motor vehicle thefts occurred in 2002. This number translates into an overall U.S. rate of 432.1 motor vehicles stolen per 100,000 people. Just as burglary and larceny-theft rates have declined since the early 1990s, so too have motor vehicle thefts. The 2002 rate represents a 6 percent decrease from the 1998 rate and a 28.7 percent decrease from the 1993 rate.

Cities with populations of 250,000 or more inhabitants had the highest vehicle theft rate at 927.8 offenses per 100,000 people. Small cities of less than 10,000 had a rate of 229.9 thefts per 100,000 people. Rural counties had the lowest rate of 143.4 per 100,000 people.

Of the total motor vehicle thefts, 73.6 percent were automobiles. Other vehicles stolen included commercial trucks and buses plus motorcycles and a variety of recreational vehicles such as campers and snowmobiles. The total value of all vehicles stolen was estimated at $8.4 million.

Males accounted for 83.5 percent of arrests for motor vehicle thefts in 2002; of all persons arrested, 30.4 percent were juveniles under the age of eighteen years. White Americans made up 60.4 percent of all motor vehicle theft arrests, black Americans 36.5 percent, and 3.1 percent were other races.

Arson

The UCR Program defines arson as "any willful or malicious [intended to cause harm] burning or attempt to burn, with or without intent to defraud [be deceptive], a dwelling house, public building, motor vehicle or aircraft, personal property of another, etc." The UCR further explains that fires are considered arson only if they have been investigated and proven to have been set on purpose. Other fires of suspicious or unknown cause are not automatically classified as arson. An "intent to defraud" refers to making an arson fire look like an accident so insurance money can be collected.

The crime of arson is generally carried out by one of two categories of individuals, either young males or professional adult arsonists. The UCR Program statistics have found that approximately one-half of all arsons are set by boys under eighteen years of age. While sometimes a teenage-started fire is merely vandalism of property for thrills, or just something to do, chronic (offenders who repeat their crimes) youthful arsonists are the study of psychologists.

Psychologists believe chronic arsons committed by juveniles are usually part of deeper emotional problems. Youths who start fires enjoy the sight of a burning building and the destruction caused. A youthful arsonist will often set a number of fires before being caught. The thrill and excitement they experience watching these fires makes them want to do more. This state of mind is apparently the same for both youthful and adult arsonists. Some exceptions are professional arsonists who are motivated by money and adult arsonists who are seeking revenge against the property owner.

Every city in the United States has expert professional arsonists available for hire. They make a living by burning down buildings or houses and making the fire appear as an accident so the property owner can collect insurance money. There are many reasons why a property owner might hire a professional arsonist. An owner may want to do away with an old house that costs too much to maintain. The owner could collect the insurance on the house then sell the empty lot.

There are a number of reasons why a businessperson might hire an arsonist to destroy a place of business. The owner might have outdated equipment and destroying the equipment would bring in insurance money or low cost government loans to rebuild and start anew. Another reason to hire an arsonist would be to pay off high debts with the insurance money or to destroy records of money mismanagement within the business.

Students in an arson investigation course observe burn patterns in several stages. *(AP/Wide World Photos)*

Another type of arson that appeared in the 1990s and early twenty-first century is environmental arson. Extreme environmental groups on the West Coast started a number of destructive fires to focus public awareness on their concerns. A U.S. Forest Service district headquarters building was burned to the ground in Oakridge, Oregon, in protest over forest logging practices. Other environmentally motivated arson attacks have occurred on car dealership lots in Southern California and Oregon. Environmental arsonists have destroyed a number of new sport utility vehicles, which consume large amounts of gas, to protest their inefficiency and their pollution of the planet.

National arson statistics

Law enforcement agencies reported 74,921 identified arsons in 2002 or an arson rate of 32.4 offenses per 100,000 people. The most frequently reported arsons were structural arsons including residential houses and commercial businesses. Structural arsons accounted for 41.3 percent at an average dollar loss of $20,818. The second most frequent type of burned property, at 33.1 percent of arsons, was mobile properties such as motor vehicles and trailers. The average dollar loss for mobile property offenses was $6,073. Malicious burning of property such as timber and crops made up 25.7 percent of arsons at an average dollar loss of $2,536.

During 2002 approximately half of those persons arrested for arson were under the age of eighteen; of those arrested 84.8 percent were males. By race, 76.8 percent of arrests were white Americans, 21.5 percent were black, and 1.7 percent were of other races.

For More Information

Books

Cromwell, Paul, Lee Parker, and Shawna Mobley. "The Five-Finger Discount." In *In Their Own Words: Criminals on Crime,* edited by Paul Cromwell, 57–70. Los Angeles: Roxbury, 2002.

Federal Bureau of Investigation. *Crime in the United States, 2002: Uniform Crime Reports.* Washington, DC: U.S. Department of Justice, 2003.

Siegel, Larry J. *Criminology: The Core.* Belmont, CA: Wadsworth/Thomson Learning, 2002.

Web Sites

Auto-Theft.Info. http://www.auto-theft.info (accessed on August 20, 2004).

Better Business Bureau. http://www.bbbonline.org (accessed on August 20, 2004).

Federal Bureau of Investigation (FBI). http://www.fbi.gov (accessed on August 20, 2004).

National Insurance Crime Bureau (NICB). http://www.nicb.org (accessed on August 20, 2004).

Securities Industry Association. http://www.sia.com (accessed on August 20, 2004).

"The Who, What, When, and Where of Stolen Vehicles." *Texas Automobile Theft Prevention Association.* http://www.dot.state.tx.us/atpa/index.htm (accessed on August 20, 2004).

White-Collar Crime

Sociologist Edwin Sutherland (1883–1950) first coined the term "white-collar crime" around 1939 and used it for the title of a book published in 1949. White-collar crime is difficult to define because it can be committed by anyone with money and apply to many different activities. White-collar crime is illegal activity carried on within normally legal business transactions. For example, white-collar crime comes from within legal businesses such as banking, stock trading, or insurance claims. It does not include drug trafficking or smuggling, since both activities are illegal. White-collar crime is also nonviolent.

The motive of white-collar crime is personal gain. Individuals or groups may use and abuse their positions within a company to hide or steal money. White-collar crime can be committed by one individual like a car repairman charging for unnecessary work on a vehicle. Or it can involve a number of individuals in a large corporation who deceive investors (those who own stock in the company) while fattening their own bank accounts by millions of dollars.

A common term associated with white-collar crime is fraud. Fraud is the intentional deception of a person, business,

The motive of white-collar crime is personal gain. Individuals or groups may use and abuse their positions within a company to hide or steal money. *(© Ed Bock/Corbis)*

or government agency for the purpose of stealing property or money, or causing financial injury in other ways. This chapter defines and describes many types of white-collar fraud, including healthcare, government, bank, telemarketing, insurance, bankruptcy, securities (stock and bonds), and corporate fraud.

Victims of white-collar crime can be an individual; a group of individuals such as customers of a stock brokerage firm; a local organization whose treasurer secretly spends its money for his own benefit (embezzling); a company like a bank whose officers use its funds for their own gain; the government cheated by the companies who win its contracts; or a large corporation whose officials purposely falsify its financial records.

White-collar crime can be prosecuted by states or by the federal government. Federal law covers a much wider range of criminal misconduct. The federal criminal justice system is better suited to deal with white-collar crimes on a large scale, cases where the crimes often have an interstate, nationwide, or international scope. The Federal Bureau of Investigation (FBI), Department of Justice, U.S. attorney general, and other federal agencies have extensive investigative and prosecuting powers to bring white-collar criminals to justice.

Healthcare fraud

According to the FBI, for many of its fifty-six field offices across the nation healthcare fraud is the number one white-collar crime. During the 1990s and into the twenty-first century the number of healthcare cases under investigation increased rapidly. Defrauding Medicare (the national healthcare insurance plan for U.S. seniors) out of millions of dollars became the primary healthcare fraud problem. Medicare health fraud has unnecessarily increased federal spending. For example, privately-owned home healthcare agencies, hospitals, nursing homes, physicians, and related healthcare professions have been found to bill Medicare for services never performed or to exaggerate expenses for more Medicare funds.

In the late 1990s the largest certified home healthcare agency in Miami, Florida, billed Medicare for services that were not provided, for unnecessary services, and for services to peo-

In 1997 U.S. attorney Jackie Williams, left, and FBI special agent David Tubbs announced a sixty-three-count indictment in a Medicare fraud scheme involving five hospitals in Missouri and Kansas.
(AP/Wide World Photos)

ple not eligible for Medicare, including those who had already died. Medicare paid out $120 million for these services. After five years of investigation, twenty individuals associated with the home care agency were convicted for defrauding Medicare. The federal government estimates that over $100 billion annually in federal healthcare expenditures are for fraudulent claims. Private healthcare insurers are also victims of fraud.

In March 2004 two Orange County, California, residents were convicted of defrauding both Medicare and private health insurance companies. A Garden Grove pharmacy owner gathered patient and doctor identifications from legally filled prescriptions and used the information to submit false claims to insurance companies. He submitted claims of over $5 million. Once insurance companies caught up with him, he transferred his pharmacy to a colleague who opened another pharmacy and proceeded to charge $1 million more in false claims before being caught. Some claims involved up to twenty or more prescriptions for a single patient. Others were fake prescriptions for elderly patients written by pediatricians (children's doctors). Still other prescriptions carried the forged signature of a doctor who saw only prison inmates.

In another pharmacy related incident, millionaire pharmacist Robert R. Courtney of Kansas City, Missouri, pleaded guilty to diluting cancer fighting drugs then delivering the premixed drugs to doctors' offices for patients. Investigators found premixed chemotherapy drugs at Courtney's Research Medical Tower Pharmacy that were diluted to between 13 and 53 percent of the correct strength. A drug representative from Eli Lilly Company discovered the scam after noticing Courtney had billed physicians for much more of the drug Gemzar than Courtney had ever ordered from Lilly. Doctors use Gemzar to treat pancreatic and lung cancer.

Government fraud

Defrauding U.S. government agencies has long been a popular white-collar crime of both companies and individuals. Not only is Medicare a prime target, but much of government spending is susceptible to fraud because of the number of individuals and large sums involved. The federal government spends the nation's tax dollars in procurement (buying supplies), by awarding contracts to companies for a wide variety of needs, and for federally funded programs. The FBI watches over the procurement process to prevent private companies from overcharging the government for ordered items. The massive Departments of Agriculture, Defense, Education, Energy, Housing and Urban Development, Transportation, the General Services Administration, and National Aeronautics and Space Administration, all are aided by the FBI's watchful supervision over purchasing activities.

The government awards billions of dollars in contracts to private companies every year. Contracts range from huge dollar amounts to the relatively small—from military contracts for airplane and shipbuilding to contracts to excavate archaeology sites. Fraud often proves too tempting to pass up. In the late 1990s the government brought charges against Bay Ship Management, Inc. (BSM), which had a contract to maintain U.S. Navy vessels. BSM overcharged the navy millions in excessive fees for repair work, some for work never done. Fraudulently collected money often goes directly to company officials for luxury homes, expensive cars, and vacations.

Financial institution fraud

While armed robberies immediately catch the public's attention, the amount stolen is only a fraction of the total lost to financial institutional fraud on a yearly basis. In an attempt to protect U.S. banking, the FBI assists institutions in the identification of fraudulent schemes and aggressively pursues suspicious activity if it is reported to the agency.

Financial institution fraud, commonly called bank fraud, can range from a one-person operation at one local bank to criminal conspiracies defrauding large U.S. banking institutions. In the 1980s and early 1990s, the FBI reported that 60 percent of bank fraud involved "insider" abuse, from the bank's own employees who used institutional funds for their own use—sometimes to such an extent that the bank collapsed.

A prime example of widespread misuse of bank funds was the savings and loan industry collapse in the 1980s. Savings and loans primarily lent money to the construction and home-building industries, but bank officers at numerous institutions diverted millions of dollars, much of which was never recovered. By the time the savings and loans became aware of the missing funds, so much money had been taken the banks could no longer conduct business and were forced to closed. By the twenty-first century, financial failure cases from insider abuse had been almost entirely replaced by external or outside fraud—mostly check or loan fraud by bank customers, not employees.

Check fraud is the use of fake or doctored checks to illegally receive payment from financial institutions. Major types of check fraud include forgery and counterfeiting. Billions of dollars are lost to check fraud every year.

Check fraud generally begins with the theft of a real check—from a mailbox, the garbage, or from a home or vehicle burglary. After chemically washing out the recipient's name and the signature, the criminal signs the check and

Frank W. Abagnale

Frank Abagnale (1948–) has seen the criminal justice system from both sides—first as a master con (to deceive someone after gaining their confidence) and fraud (to trick someone) artist and later as an expert adviser on fraud prevention. Abagnale was raised in New York and enjoyed a comfortable upbringing. His father owned a profitable stationary store on Madison Avenue in New York City. However at sixteen years of age when his parents suddenly divorced, Frank moved into the city and began a life of sophisticated crime. For the next five years

Abagnale developed numerous scams ranging from fraud such as passing bad checks to impersonating various professionals. The diverse impersonations included airline pilots for Pan Am and Trans World Airlines (TWA), a lawyer working in the Louisiana state attorney general office, a pediatrician (children's doctor) in a Georgia hospital, and a sociology professor at Brigham Young University in Utah. In five years he used eight different identities and passed bad checks in twenty-six countries amounting to over $2.5 million. He was eventually arrested in Mont-

cashes it at a store or bank with false identification. This is an example of forgery. Counterfeiting means reproducing more checks to look like the original stolen check. Counterfeiting has become a criminal art that extends far beyond making fake checks.

Criminals use computer software to produce credit cards, travelers checks, payroll checks, U.S. Department of Agriculture food coupons, U.S. postage stamps, and of course, U.S. currency. Counterfeiting is easily accomplished using computers, copiers, scanners, and laser printers. Simply logging onto the Internet and entering the terms check fraud or counterfeiting into a search engine can lead to information on how to produce fraudulent documents.

Loan fraud

Check fraud is the most common form of bank fraud but the largest loss of money comes from fraudulent loans. Both banks and individuals can be victims of loan fraud. Individuals are victimized by criminals who pretend to be lenders; they often claim to be a person's only chance for obtaining a loan. These loans are written with unusually high interest rates. In-

pellier, France, in 1969 while posing as a Hollywood screenwriter. Abagnale served six months in a notoriously harsh French prison and several more months in a Swedish prison before being extradited (transferred) to the United States. After briefly escaping twice from U.S. authorities, he was found guilty of numerous charges of forgery (making false documents) and sentenced to twelve years in prison.

Abagnale's life took a sudden turn while serving his sentence in a federal corrections facility in Virginia. At twenty-six years of age after only four years of confinement in the federal facility, he was released in 1974 under the condition that he assist at no pay federal law authorities in crime prevention programs to stop frauds and scams. He could teach well on the workings of a criminal mind from his firsthand experiences. Abagnale also established a successful consulting firm, Abagnale and Associates, to advise private businesses such as banks on how to design secure checks. Abagnale also went on extensive lecture tours giving advice on white-collar crime prevention. Abagnale has written numerous articles and books including *Catch Me If You Can* (1980), which was made into a 2002 Hollywood movie directed by Steven Spielberg, and *The Art of the Steal: How to Protect Yourself and Your Business From Fraud—America's #1 Crime* (2001).

terest is a charge by the lender for borrowing money, usually based on a certain percentage of the amount borrowed. If the individual is purchasing property, a lender with criminal intent may include empty blanks in the loan documents that he or she will fill in later after the victim has already signed. The cost or terms of the loan may be much higher than the victim had agreed to and sometimes a lender may offer to arrange for home repairs at inflated prices.

Loan fraud schemes often involve groups of people working together. On March 29, 2004, the FBI field office in Los Angeles, California, reported the arrest of three individuals and the hunt for a fourth who had supposedly masterminded an eight-year loan fraud scheme by using multiple stolen identities. The individuals netted more than $30 million, which they then used to continue the scheme while living extravagant lifestyles.

Those arrested in the Los Angeles fraud case had stolen the identities of real estate agents, mortgage brokers, and deceased individuals. With these identities they applied for loans using fake paycheck stubs, bank statements, income tax forms, and so forth. Once they obtained a loan they "flipped" the

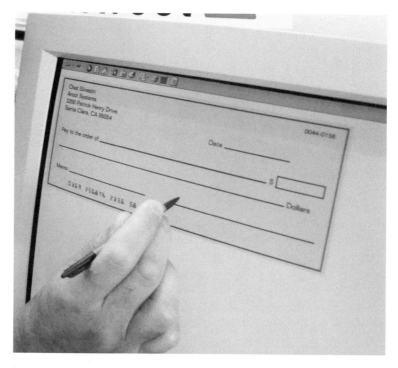

Businessman pointing to a fake check on a computer screen. Counterfeiting is easily accomplished using computers, copiers, scanners, and laser printers. *(AP/Wide World Photos)*

property, selling it at an inflated price to yet another stolen identity to obtain another loan. The criminals also took out additional loans to cash out the value of the home. Eventually, the property would fall into foreclosure (when a lender takes back property or goods after nonpayment) at a large loss to the banks who made the loans.

Telemarketing fraud

In the 1990s and early 2000s, telemarketing (selling items over the phone) fraud cost consumers billions of dollars. The typical telemarketing call would come around dinnertime with a sincere voice promising free gifts and vacations. All a person has to do to receive a prize is purchase an amazing water purifier, vitamins, or other product by credit card or check. Free prizes plus the purchase of a seemingly wonderful item seems like too good of an offer for some to turn down. Neither the purchased item nor the prize, however, would ever arrive since they never existed. The telemarketers would make up a scheme and simply take the purchaser's money. In addition, the buyers would probably end up on a list of susceptible victims passed around to other scam telemarketers. If an individual falls for a scam once, it is possible he or she will do so again.

Individuals committing telemarketing fraud use multiple names, phone numbers, addresses, product lines, and prepared scripts. They can change these overnight, making arrests difficult. The FBI reports that senior citizens are particularly vulnerable and likely to fall for scams.

While telemarketing scams still offer free prizes and vacations frequently, they prey on economic uncertainties. A favorite telemarketing fraud involves credit card loss protection. Although federal law limits an individual's legal responsibility or liability for unauthorized credit card charges to $50, fraudulent telemarketers will tell cardholders they will be held responsible or liable for all unauthorized charges. They claim everyone needs credit card loss insurance should criminals get access to a card number and charge thousands of dollars before the owner realizes it. The scammers offer loss protection insurance for a fee that can be charged to a credit card. If successful, the fraudulent telemarketer has managed to get money from the victim, as well as his or her credit card number.

People making calls in an effort to warn others that they may be targets of fraudulent telemarketers. *(AP/Wide World Photos)*

Another frequently used telemarketing scam is the advance-fee loan. Telemarketers target people with poor credit and offer loans to pay off debt for a small amount of money due immediately. Once the fee is collected the scammer disappears.

Through the 1990s and early 2000s, the FBI carried out a number of successful operations against telemarketing scams. Together with retired FBI agents and volunteers from the American Association of Retired Persons posing as vulnerable elderly citizens, the FBI set up operations to catch fraudulent telemarketers. The marketers would call numbers thinking they were targeting people who had fallen for scams before. The volunteers recorded the solicitations and prosecutors were able to use these recordings to arrest the telemarketers for fraud.

Insurance fraud

Resulting in increased insurance premiums for all Americans, insurance fraud is one of the most common and costly white-collar crimes. Billions of dollars are lost yearly. This section deals with life/disability, auto, homeowners, and business/commercial insurance, but not health insurance (covered under healthcare insurance fraud). Insurance fraud can occur within an insurance company, by its own employees, or outside the company by individuals not associated with the company.

External insurance fraud is committed by policyholders or by professionals who provide assistance to those making claims. A common fraudulent activity is "padding" claims to make the loss appear more than it actually is. By overstating the damage, an individual claimant and an insurance adjuster (one who assesses the damage for the insurance company) receive a higher insurance payment than necessary. The adjuster then receives some of the payment for his or her part in the scam, generally called a "kickback."

Other aggressive schemes involve organized groups such as automobile accident rings. These crime rings file numerous accident claims involving fraudulent damage. Other fake claims involve falsifying or exaggerating disability (being unable to work due to an injury) claims. Fraudulent disability claims cost insurance companies over a billion dollars per year. Insurance scammers are even able to fraudulently collect on life insurance policies, costing hundreds of millions of dollars every year.

Internal fraud comes from within the industry through company officials, employees, and agents. One type of internal fraud is diverting insurance premiums paid by policyholders to the personal accounts of company employees. Agents may also receive policy payments and not pass them to the company. The most aggressive form of insurance fraud is creating an entirely bogus or fake company, often through offshore (not in the United States) banks owned by criminals. A victim is conned into paying premiums to the nonexistent insurance company for nonexistent coverage.

Bankruptcy fraud

The intent of U.S. bankruptcy law is to protect businesses and individuals from the loss of all their belongings and ability to earn a livelihood due to a financial failure. The number of bankruptcy claims increases every year due mostly to how easy it is to declare bankruptcy. Decades ago filing for bankruptcy was considered an extreme measure, but so many people have declared bankruptcies in more recent years that it is almost commonplace.

The FBI estimates 10 percent of filings are fraudulent. Those filing fraudulent bankruptcies do so to hide assets (items of value owned by a person) and submit false statements and documents. Creditors (businesses or individuals owed money) lose billions of dollars yearly, because successful bankruptcies allow the individuals or businesses who filed to pay only a portion of their debts. This nonpayment impacts both local and national economies.

Another bankruptcy scheme involves foreclosure scams. Foreclosure is a legal proceeding begun by a lender to take possession of property when the owner fails to make payments on his or her loan. Foreclosure scammers pursue individuals who are about to lose their homes in foreclosure. The scammers promise to work with lenders and arrange a plan for the owners to keep their home. Scammers often tell homeowners to send their mortgage payments to them instead of the lender; the scammers then take the money and disappear. The homeowners generally do not realize they have been scammed until it is too late.

Securities fraud

Securities are stocks and bonds an investor may purchase. Stocks give the investors an ownership share in the com-

Securities Regulation

Between 1929 and 1941 the people of the United States suffered through the Great Depression, the deepest and most prolonged economic crisis in American history. Although many factors contributed to the economic depression, the crash of the stock market in October 1929 marked its beginning. Investors in securities, stocks, and bonds lost everything in the unregulated market.

Following the leadership of President Franklin D. Roosevelt (1882–1945; served 1933–45), Congress passed new legislation known as the New Deal, designed to protect citizens from economic fluctuations. Two of these legislative remedies were the Securities Act of 1933 and the Securities Exchange Act of 1934. Both laws restored investor confidence in the market by providing more structure and government regulation.

The 1933 Securities Act required both businesses who desired to sell their stock and stockbrokers who sold stock to provide full information about stocks to potential investors. The Securities Exchange Act of 1934 prohibited certain activities in stock market trading and set penalties for violations. It also established the Securities and Exchange Commission (SEC) to oversee stock market trading.

These laws were based on two ideas. First, companies offering stock on the market had to tell the public the truth about their businesses and the risks involved in investing in them. Second, stockbrokers were to put the interests of investors above any other consideration and deal with them fairly and honestly.

The two 1930s acts remain the foundation of securities regulation. The SEC continued to be the top regulatory agency at the beginning of the twenty-first century. The SEC oversees all key participants in the securities market including the stock exchanges, stock brokerage firms, the actions of individual stockbrokers, investment advisors, and mutual funds (groups of stocks in which people may invest). They are the overseer to protect investors against deceptive or illegal activities such as security fraud.

pany. Stock ownership entitles investors to a dividend or payment per share of stock if the company earns a profit (money left over after all expenses are paid). Stock increases in value if the company is growing and profitable. Investment in bonds pays the investor a set amount over a period of time like a bank pays interest in a savings account. Bonds do not grant the investor any ownership in the company. Commodities are economic goods being sold and purchased in large quantities. Securities fraud is committed by an individual or firm intending to influence the price of a stock or commodity by providing misleading information to investors.

As more people invest in securities and business practices become more complex, securities fraud involving company officials, investment bankers, and others operating in the industry also increases. Dealing with millions of dollars everyday, some individuals cannot resist fraudulent schemes to pad their own pockets. A stable securities industry is essential for the nation's economic health and financial growth. By the early twenty-first century, approximately 80 percent of the American population owned some kind of stock, bond, or commodity. Only 20 percent of these citizens bought and sold stocks themselves; the majority were invested in retirement plans or company stock option plans.

The FBI is responsible for uncovering securities and commodities fraud schemes. They work in close cooperation with the Securities and Exchange Commission (SEC), the National Association of Securities Dealers (NASD), the Commodities and Futures Trading Commission (CFTC), the North American Securities Administrators Association (NASAA), and state and local agencies.

The usual types of securities fraud are embezzlement and insider trading. Embezzlement is the unlawful use of money belonging to a company or its investors. Types of embezzlement include brokers (those who buy and sell securities) writing forged checks from investor accounts, illegally transferring funds, or purposely misleading investors with falsified documents.

Insider trading involves the sale or buying of stock by people who have knowledge about a company that is not available to the public. For example, executives from a drug manufacturer learn a new drug their company is marketing will not be approved by the FDA (Federal Drug Administration) for general use. They learn this before any public announcement is made and warn a few investors to sell their stock in the drug company before the news breaks and the stock's value falls sharply, leaving the stocks worthless and making them nearly impossible to sell.

The New York Stock Exchange is the center of stock trading. *(AP/Wide World Photos)*

Kickbacks, or money payouts, are often paid to persons who have advance knowledge about a product or company and are willing to tell others. If the insider uses the information for his or her own gain, it is insider trading; if the person tells someone else and receives money in return after the information has been verified, it is called a kickback.

A well-known case of insider trading that gained national attention in 2003 and 2004 involved celebrity homemaker Martha Stewart (1941–). Stewart was allegedly told privately that stock in ImClone Systems Inc., a biotechnology company, would plunge in the next few days. Stewart sold her stock to avoid a loss. While Stewart was only prosecuted for lying to the FBI about the incident, her actions were a high-profile example of insider trading.

Another type of securities fraud concerns illegal trading referred to as Micro-Cap. Micro means very small and Cap refers to capital, or the money invested in a company. Micro-Cap stocks are low priced shares of new companies with little or no business track record. Securities fraud rings included organized crime, which often used highly persuasive calls to pressure people into investing money in a Micro-Cap. Any money received is generally hidden in foreign bank accounts, and investors rarely see their money again.

Other twenty-first century securities fraud schemes make use of the Internet. Investors often check the Internet daily for information on stocks. Many fake get-rich-quick stocks are offered over the Internet, tricking unsuspecting or inexperienced investors (see chapter 11 on Cyber Crime).

Another example of securities fraud played out between 2000 and 2002 at Merrill Lynch, one of the nation's top securities firms. In 2000 a number of relatively new Internet companies did their banking with Merrill Lynch, whose securities expert, Henry Blodget, gave these companies a high or "buy" rating (meaning it was a good time to buy these stocks), even when he knew they were in trouble and might fail. Trusting Blodget, many investors continued to follow his advice and buy stock in the companies.

By 2001 several of the companies had failed and investors lost millions. New York attorney general Eliot Spitzer investigated and found emails written between other Merrill Lynch analysts describing Blodget's recommended stocks as "junk," and called them "disasters waiting to happen." Spitzer even found company emails from Blodget himself calling the very stocks he continued to rate high to investors as junk.

Merrill Lynch paid a settlement of $100 million to the State of New York on May 21, 2002. The SEC and other regulators added another $100 million. Henry Blodget was banned from the securities industry and fined $4 million dollars.

As a high-profile example of insider trading, celebrity homemaker Martha Stewart was sentenced to five months in prison for her convictions on charges of conspiracy, obstruction of justice, and making false statements to federal investigators about a December 2001 stock sale. *(AP/Wide World Photos)*

Corporate fraud

Investors buy stocks and bonds to make money, therefore they generally invest in companies that appear to be successful. Corporate fraud occurs when a company misleads the public and analysts by manipulating information to make itself look strong and profitable when in reality it is not.

In 2004 one of the largest corporate fraud cases ever involved a Houston, Texas-based energy company, Enron. Enron was formed in 1985 as a merger of Houston Natural Gas and InterNorth. The corporation expanded rapidly both in the

In one of the largest corporate fraud cases ever, the debt of energy company Enron was purposely hidden from stockholders by fraudulent accounting and continually forming new partnerships with other companies through buying and selling stock *(AP/Wide World Photos)*

United States and internationally through complex deals and contracts. Unknown to all but a few top executives and its accountants (from the accounting firm Arthur Anderson), Enron fell billions of dollars into debt.

Enron's growing debt was purposely hidden from stockholders by fraudulent accounting and continually forming new partnerships with other companies through buying and selling stock. Much of the money used in these stock transactions did not go into Enron but into the pockets of its executives. The fraud was revealed in October 2001 when Enron announced it was worth $1.2 billon less than it had been reporting. Enron fell into bankruptcy and many of its officials were charged on multiple fraud counts, including securities fraud. Investors and employees lost millions; many lost their entire life savings.

Other classic types of corporate white-collar crime include price-fixing and antitrust or restraint-of-trade violations. During the late 1880s leaders of several major industries brought their companies together to prevent competition and ruin smaller rivals. The organizations they formed were called "trusts." To stop these trusts from controlling the markets and the American economy, Congress passed the Sherman Antitrust Act in 1890. This act was the cornerstone of U.S. antitrust and price-fixing law.

Price-fixing involves companies with little competition to set high prices for the products they produce. The Antitrust Division of the FBI prosecutes price-fixing and antitrust cases. One successfully prosecuted high profile case of the late 1990s involved Archer Daniels Midland Company (ADM) and seven other companies. The charges against ADM and the others stemmed from the price-fixing of two chemicals, lysine and citric acid.

By fixing the prices of these chemicals, the companies—which were the largest manufacturers of these valuable products—were able to control sales worldwide. Lysine is used by farmers in feed products for poultry and pigs. Citric acid is a flavor additive and preservative used in many items such as soda drinks, processed foods, and cosmetics. Over a billion dollars in sales worldwide were affected by this price-fixing scheme. Eight corporations and six individual defendants admitted to the price-fixing and were fined about $200 million.

For More Information

Books

Frank, Nancy, and Michael Lynch. *Corporate Crime, Corporate Violence*. Albany, NY: Harrow and Heston, 1992.

Siegel, Larry J. *Criminology: The Core*. Belmont, CA: Wadsworth/Thomson Learning, 2002.

Sutherland, Edwin. *White-Collar Crime: The Uncut Version*. New Haven, CT: Yale University Press, 1983.

Web Sites

American Collectors Association International. http://acainternational.org (accessed on August 20, 2004).

"Counterfeit Division." *United States Secret Service.* http://www.secretservice.gov/counterfeit.shtml (accessed on August 20, 2004).

"Don't Be a Victim of Loan Fraud." *U.S. Department of Housing and Urban Development.* http://www.hud.gov/offices/hsg/sfh/buying/loanfraud.cfm (accessed on August 20, 2004).

Federal Bureau of Investigation. http://www.fbi.gov (accessed on August 20, 2004).

International Association of Financial Crimes Investigators. http://www.iafci.org (accessed on August 20, 2004).

International Association of Insurance Fraud Agencies, Inc. http://www.iaifa.org (accessed on August 20, 2004).

National Association of Securities Dealers. http://www.nasd.com (accessed on August 20, 2004).

National Check Fraud Center. http://www.ckfraud.org (accessed on August 20, 2004).

North American Securities Administrators Association. http://www.nasaa.org (accessed on August 20, 2004).

"Telemarketing Fraud: Ditch the Pitch." *Federal Trade Commission.* http://www.ftc.gov/bcp/conline/edcams/telemarketing (accessed on August 20, 2004).

U.S. Department of Justice. http://www.usdoj.gov (accessed on August 20, 2004).

U.S. Securities and Exchange Commission. http://www.sec.gov (accessed on August 20, 2004).

Organized Crime

Some of the most recognizable names associated with U.S. organized crime include "Lucky" Luciano (1892–1962), Meyer Lansky (1902–1983), Al Capone (1899–1947), and "Bugsy" Siegel (1906–1947). Legendary American Mafia or Cosa Nostra crime families include the Colombos, Bonannos, Genoveses, Luccheses, and Gambinos. Famous gangs include the Hell's Angels, the Bloods, the Crips, the Green Light Gangs, the Gangster Disciples, and the Latin Kings. These notable crime bosses, crime families, and street gangs span a time period from the 1920s to the 2000s.

The legends and stories of real life mobsters and street gangs have often captivated our nation's imagination. The entertainment industry fed this fascination with the *The Godfather* (1972–90) movies and the Home Box Office (HBO) cable television series, *The Sopranos*. Both depict the extravagant mob lifestyle of fancy cars, clothes, and ritzy homes. The characters of Don Vito Corleone and Tony Soprano, although fictional, have become the public's perception of what real crime families are like.

By the 1990s a number of organized crime units operating within the United States had home bases far from Amer-

The movie *The Godfather,* starring Marlon Brando, helped glamorize the life of a mobster. *(© Bettmann/Corbis)*

ican soil. Chinese organized crime groups called triads, Hong Kong triads, the Russian Mafia, the Japanese Yakuza, South American drug cartels (organized crime groups growing and selling narcotics), and the Mexican Mafia represent just some of the organized crime groups operating and cooperating with U.S. crime outfits. In 2002 the FBI reported U.S. organized crime activities brought in an annual income of between $50 and $90 billion dollars—more income than any major national industry. Around that time worldwide profits for organized crime were estimated to be approximately one trillion dollars a year.

Organized crime is any group that has an organized structure of bosses, advisors, and working members whose key goal is to obtain money and property through illegal activities. Organized crime groups use extortion (threats of violence) and force to obtain money or property from a person or group. For example, an organized crime group may extort business owners in a neighborhood by making them pay a monthly fee for protection. If an owner refuses, his business may be vandalized or destroyed. Organized crime activities can negatively impact a community, a region, and the whole country.

RICO

In 1970 the U.S. Congress passed the Organized Crime Control Act. A central part of the act is the Racketeer Influenced and Corrupt Organizations (RICO) section. RICO is law enforcement's most powerful tool against organized crime. Defined by RICO, racketeering is the act of participating in a continuing pattern of criminal behavior.

Authorities can charge a wide variety of crimes under RICO. These include murder; kidnapping; gambling; arson (intentionally setting a destructive fire); robbery; bribery (promising a person money or a favor in return for certain action); extortion; dealing in obscene matter (pornography); dealing in controlled substances or chemicals (drug violations); alien smuggling (moving illegal immigrants across the nation's borders); bribery including sports bribery; counterfeiting; embezzlement (to steal money or property, such as a banker using bank funds for his or her own use); mail fraud (fake offers through the mail); murder for hire; prostitution; sexual exploitation of children; theft from the interstate shipping of goods, such as from trucks, trains, or ships; transporting stolen goods across state lines; drug trafficking; and money laundering.

Organized crime offenses

Two of the most profitable racketeering activities of organized crime are drug trafficking and money laundering. Gambling, prostitution, and pornography have also been major moneymakers. In 2002 drug trafficking was the largest illegal organized crime activity both in the United States and worldwide. The three most commonly trafficked illegal drugs were cannabis (marijuana and hashish), cocaine, and heroine. RICO makes growing, smuggling (transporting illegally), receiving, buying, and selling illegal drugs a racketeering activity.

The term "trafficking" means dealing, smuggling, buying with the intent to sell, and selling a substance. For example, once a shipment of illegal drugs enters the United States, a dealer or trafficker pays the smuggler for the drugs. The first trafficker then sells the drugs again to a second trafficker who will transport the drugs to a location where a third trafficker pays the second. Each trafficker is a member of an organized crime group. The amount of money that changes hands goes up with every transaction so each trafficker makes a profit. The money received is called "dirty" money and it needs to be "laundered," or cleaned so it can be passed as legal money.

Money laundering involves specialists within the crime organization who get the dirty money into legitimate financial institutions while concealing where the money came from. Money laundering and global crime usually go together. Financial specialists within organized crime establish a series of bogus companies and deposit dirty money into their bank accounts, usually into banks outside of the United States.

Dirty money is frequently mixed with "clean" or legally obtained money in the bank accounts of legitimate companies, which happen to be owned or run by organized crime groups. This practice is called comingling, or mixing legal and illegal funds together, which makes tracking dirty money difficult. Organized crime money handlers try to completely hide the origins of illegal funds by creating confusing paper (re-

More than seven hundred pounds of marijuana was seized from this Mexican shipment. *(AP/Wide World Photos)*

ceipt) trails and often succeed in making dirty money appear to be legitimate company deposits or laundered money.

Once clean or laundered money is moved into legally run businesses, it can be used freely. The types of legal businesses crime organizations commonly run include garbage disposal, meat and produce distribution, restaurants, garment manufacturing, bars and taverns, real estate, and vending machine companies.

Organized crime supplies goods and services that are illegal but which the public nevertheless demands. Illegal gambling or gaming is available in most states, while prostitution and pornography have been favored activities for hundreds of years. Prostitution rings recruit women who engage in sexual activities for money. Pornography is the business of supplying photography or books about sexual behaviors. Using children in pornographic materials is known as child pornography or the sexual exploitation of children.

Characteristics of organized crime

Organized crime groups, whether traditional mob families or street gangs, have a number of common characteristics:

1. Organized crime thrives on supplying illegal goods and services for which a large number of people are willing to pay. For example, in 1999 an estimated fifteen million Americans used illegal drugs, 75 percent of whom used marijuana.

2. The goal of organized crime groups is to make money; members also gain a sense of pride, power, and protection.

3. Groups have what is called a pyramid power structure like legal businesses. In legitimate businesses, there is a boss called the chief executive officer (CEO), under the CEO are vice presidents, treasurers, advisors, accountants, lawyers, technical staff, and so on. Organized crime has a boss, advisors who work closely with the boss and assign tasks to different crews, captains who run the different crews, soldiers who carry out the physical work and act out tasks from collecting money to killing people, and men with special skills.

4. Members are extremely loyal and committed; they go through initiation rituals, take oaths, and swear to secrecy.

5. Punishment for members who stray might be demotion to a lower rank or, depending on their offense, death.

During the mid-twentieth century, organized crime in the United States was dominated by the American Mafia whose "godfathers," meaning founders, were of Italian and Sicilian descent. In the latter half of the century, other groups appeared and grew in number, including motorcycle gangs, street gangs, and by the 1990s, organized crime units with home bases in other countries. The remaining portions of this chapter describe types of organized crime units doing business in the United States.

Early Las Vegas and the Mafia

Las Vegas in the early 1940s was not an attractive place to do business or live. It was a dirty desert town of rugged, rough residents. Travelers taking U.S. Highway 91 cut right through the city on their way to California. It was not a place for stopping over, until New York City organized crime bosses Meyer Lansky and Frank Costello sent well-known gangster Bugsy Siegel (1906–1947) to Las Vegas. Siegel's mission was to see if Vegas would make a great gambling spot for West Coast gamblers.

Nevada had legalized gambling in 1931 but no one paid much attention except local cowboys and men from nearby military bases. With Siegel's imagination and organizational skills and the Mafia's money, the first gambling palace in Las Vegas opened on December 26, 1946. The Flamingo, located right on Highway 91, was the first of many gangster-financed gambling houses in Las Vegas. The Desert Inn and the Thunderbird were built and along with the Flamingo ushered in a very profitable and legal business for the mob, at least under Nevada law. Highway 91 was transformed into the glitzy Las Vegas "Strip."

By the 1950s the Chicago Outfit had joined New York City gangsters in Las Vegas. The Outfit ran three major casinos—the Stardust, the Desert Inn, and the Riviera. The Hacienda, Sahara, and Fremont casinos were added by Chicago mobsters in the 1960s. The Stardust was home base to the famous "Rat Pack," a group of entertainers including Frank Sinatra (1915–1998), Dean Martin (1917–1995), and Sammy Davis Jr. (1925–1990). Tourists from the West Coast and Southwest flooded into Vegas for an exciting time of gambling, entertainment, and nightlife.

In the 1970s the presence of organized crime diminished in Vegas when the Nevada legislature allowed public corporations (corporations selling stock to the public) to own casinos. Gangsters made millions by selling their casinos. Millionaire Howard Hughes (1905–1976) bought the Desert Inn in 1967.

American Mafia

Prohibition officially became law on January 17, 1920, as the states ratified (voted approval) of the Eighteenth Amendment to the U.S Constitution, banning the manufacture, sale, and distribution of alcoholic beverages in the United States. Those in favor of Prohibition predicted its enforcement would be easy and inexpensive. It soon became apparent, however, that Americans were not prepared to give up alcohol. Beating Prohibition became a national pastime.

Alphonse "Al" Capone, whose brief career as a Chicago mob boss made him into a legendary character, generated an income of more than $100 million per year. *(AP/Wide World Photos)*

Gangs who had limited their activities to gambling and thievery before 1920 transformed into organized groups of "bootleggers," individuals who illegally brought liquor into the country and sold it to thirsty Americans. Bootlegging gangsters became millionaires. Prominent among them was Alphonse "Al" Capone, whose brief career as a Chicago mob boss made him into a legendary character. His income was estimated at over $100 million per year.

Near the end of the 1920s, gangs had become so organized they held a national convention in Cleveland, Ohio, on December 5, 1928. Twenty-three bosses, all of Sicilian families, gathered from New York City, Chicago, Detroit, St. Louis, Tampa, and Philadelphia. Capone could not attend because he was not Sicilian, but he sent representatives.

Although mutually suspicious of one another, they discussed common interests, problems, and explored the idea of establishing a nationwide crime syndicate. A syndicate is an association of individuals or groups who agree to carry out certain activities. In another meeting held in May 1929 in Atlantic City, New Jersey, crime bosses from around the country divided up the United States into territories. Next they established a national "Commission," made up of one representative from each of the country's nine territories.

By September 1931, Charles "Lucky" Luciano and his allies—which included Jewish crime boss Meyer Lansky—were at the top of the New York crime scene. They were the victors of the Castellammarse War, a New York City gangster war between old line Italian and Sicilian Mafia bosses who had migrated to the United States in the late nineteenth and early twentieth centuries.

The older bosses focused on settling old vendettas (bitter prolonged feuds), not on making money. The winning Luciano-Lansky faction concentrated entirely on making money and killed anyone who got in their way. Luciano was also responsible for energizing the nine-member commission. This change in direction and the activation of the commission is referred to as the Americanization of the Mafia.

New York City was divided among five crime families with approximately nineteen more family units around the country. The five New York City families became famous; each was named after their Godfather. The legendary families were the Bonnano, Columbo, Gambino, Genovese, and Lucchese.

When the highly profitable bootlegging period ended in 1933 with the repeal of the Eighteenth Amendment, organized crime syndicates (groups) focused on other criminal activities including gambling, loan sharking (charging very high interest rates on loans, usually very hard to pay back), prostitution, and drug distribution, a natural extension of bootlegging. Labor racketeering was another popular criminal activity. Gangsters worked their way into positions of power in a labor union and then stole from the union's retirement and health funds.

Keeping a relatively low profile, the national organized crime syndicate received little interference from the FBI, headed by J. Edgar Hoover (1895–1972). Fearing a poor showing against the underworld, Hoover chose not to battle orga-

Before their arrest, Charles "Lucky" Luciano and his allies were at the top of the New York crime scene.
(AP/Wide World Photos)

nized crime. Hoover insisted the mob did not exist in the United States. Organized crime grew and prospered across the country.

In 1951 the Kefauver Committee of the U.S. Senate conducted hearings on crime and concluded an organized Mafia did indeed operate nationwide. The Kefauver Committee was a special congressional committee created by Congress to investigate organized crime in America, including racketeering (obtaining money through illegal activities). In 1957 the New York State Police accidentally uncovered a large meeting of sixty organized crime bosses at a rural home in Apalachin, New York. As police moved in the bosses ran into the New York countryside to escape. After this incident, there was no denying the existence of an American Mafia.

The U.S. Senate Subcommittee on Investigations gained considerable information about the mob from a defendant named Joseph Valachi in 1963. A member of New York City's Genovese family, Valachi was the first Mafia insider to give major information about the workings of the Mafia. For the first time, the American public learned about the commission and the internal structure of crime families in New York and across the nation.

During the 1960s, under the direction of U.S. Attorney General Robert Kennedy (1925–1968), the U.S. Department of Justice began a major effort to arrest and prosecute crime family members. At the time, government reports listed twenty-four crime families with five thousand members of Italian and Sicilian ancestry. About this time the American Mafia families became known as the Cosa Nostra. Cosa Nostra means "our thing" in Italian.

Throughout the 1970s crime families warred with each other for power. Members of one family would assassinate another family's boss; then the family of the murdered boss would seek revenge with another killing and so on. Murders were also often committed to prevent a member from testifying in a trial.

The first RICO convictions of mob bosses or heads of families came in 1980. Numerous other gangsters were convicted under RICO for crimes ranging from operating illegal garbage collection associations to loan sharking to murder. In 1985 the bosses of all five Cosa Nostra crime families in New York City received prison terms of at least one hundred years, dealing a major blow to organized crime.

In 1992 Salvatore "Sammy the Bull" Gravano (1945–) broke the mob's code of silence, like Joseph Valachi. Gravano, a high-ranking member of the Gambino crime family, testified against his boss, John Gotti (1940–2002). Gotti was sentenced to life in prison. Gotti's successor was his brother Peter, whose legal business was in trash collecting. Peter Gotti ran the Gambino family, which received monthly cash payments from violent thugs who controlled the Brooklyn waterfront where garbage was collected and transported to landfills. Peter, at age sixty-four, was sentenced to more than nine years in prison in April 2004 on charges related to waterfront payoffs.

Salvatore "Sammy the Bull" Gravano broke the mob's code of silence and testified against his boss, John Gotti. Gotti, seen here, was sentenced to life in prison. *(AP/Wide World Photos)*

Three decades of arrests and convictions of Cosa Nostra family members decreased the American mob's power. RICO proved to be a powerful tool for convicting organized crime members and resulted in long prison sentences. The code of silence, to never testify against another crime member, had been broken. Those who testified received much shorter prison sentences than if they had not cooperated.

Government enforcement had sent many high-ranking mob leaders to prison. A life of crime was no longer as attractive and a considerable number of young people from Cosa Nostra families chose to attend universities and pursue lawful careers. A greater number of crime family recruits came from uneducated kids who had neither leadership skills nor the loyalty of past members. The face of organized crime began to significantly change. New criminal gangs of black Americans, Hispanics, Asians, Chinese, Russians, and South Americans competed with the traditional American Mafia. Motorcycle, or "biker," gangs became a major rival of the mob.

Motorcycle gangs

Beginning as motorbike sporting groups after World War II, the freedom of the road and riding across the country attracted a rebellious, adventurous, tough group of young people. Biker groups became biker gangs proud of living outside the norms of the traditional American family life of the 1950s. Two movies propelled the biker life: *The Wild Ones* in 1954 and *Easy Rider* in 1969. In 1969 the Hell's Angels, an especially tough and violent motorcycle gang at the time, were hired for the security force at a Rolling Stones (a rock group from England) concert in California at Altamont Speedway. A fan was killed by the Hell's Angels during the concert. This murder gained national attention and Americans suddenly realized the violence associated with biker gangs.

During the 1970s outlaw biker gangs numbered about nine hundred. The largest biker gangs were the Hell's Angels, the Outlaws, and the Bandidos. Each improved its organizational structure and learned how to plan and carry out criminal activities for profit. Their most profitable activity was drug trafficking. By the 1980s the FBI ranked bikers right behind the American Mafia as the most serious organized crime groups in the United States.

By the 1990s, the Bandidos, Hell's Angels, and Outlaws all had chapters in other countries. Hell's Angels had organizations in twenty countries and continued to expand rapidly. Biker gangs with U.S. roots were active in Canada, Europe, South America, Australia, and Africa. Sometimes rivals but often partners in criminal activities, these powerful bikers often cooperated with the South American drug cartels and the Italian Mafia. Biker gangs launder their drug money into legitimate businesses and have become very wealthy.

Street gangs

Street gangs in the United States generally begin in the poorest areas of big cities. Racism, prejudice, and high unemployment among young people are the major contributing factors. Young people want status and the respect of their peers just as any middle-class or wealthy youth. Generally a gang is the best way to be respected and protected from other gangs. Gangs form in schools, parks, and on neighborhood streets, wherever groups of friends share similar lifestyles or ethnic backgrounds. Males make up 90 percent of gang membership. Violence and weapons are key components of street gangs. Large U.S. street gangs have become organized and profitable; selling drugs and guns are their chief moneymaking activities.

By 2000 several street gangs had grown large and were very structured and profitable. These so-called Super Gangs had spread nationwide. They include the predominately black American Crips and Bloods, and Hispanic gangs like the Green Light Gangs, Latin Kings, and Gangster Disciples.

Biker gangs were proud of living outside the norms of traditional American family life. Since the 1970s, the Hell's Angels has been one of the largest biker gangs in the United States. (© Ted Soqui/Corbis)

Crips and Bloods: Black American gangs in Los Angeles

Throughout the twentieth century, two distinct periods of black American gang formation occurred in Los Angeles. The first was in the early 1940s until 1965, the second from 1970 continuing into the early 2000s. Between the early 1970s and 2000 black American street gangs steadily increased in numbers and membership.

During World War II, large numbers of black Americans migrated from the southern United States to Los Angeles for

Members of the Crips and Bloods gangs stand together in Los Angeles, California. *(AP/Wide World Photos)*

employment in the war industries, chiefly building aircraft. All-black communities in the central part of Los Angeles expanded. The first black gangs developed in the second half of the 1940s and 1950s in defense from white teenage gangs determined to attack and harass black youth.

By 1960 the black areas of central Los Angeles—Watts, Central Avenue, and West Adams—had grown together. Whites increasingly moved to the suburbs leaving the area predominately black. The interracial violence among black and white gangs turned into black versus black gangs. The western areas of the black communities were economically better off than the eastern half, so eastside gangs resented westside youths and fought west gangs. Most scuffles were hand-to-hand fights or with knives and tire irons. Murders rarely occurred. In 1960 only six gang-related murders occurred in all of Los Angeles County.

In 1965 poverty, unemployment, harsh Los Angeles police treatment of black Americans, and continuing discrimination boiled over into the Watts race riots the summer of 1965, when the police used batons on two black men being arrested. After the riots, the Watts community directed its youth into local clubs, looking for solutions to social injustices including police brutality. In 1965 the Civil Rights movement was gathering strength in Los Angeles. To lend support to civil rights activism, the Black Panther Party, a powerful black political organization, opened a chapter in central Los Angeles.

Viewed as a threat to the security of the nation, the FBI targeted the Panthers and other black organizations. The Los Angeles Panthers were greatly weakened and their political leadership dismantled. By 1970 Los Angeles youth had lost the adult leadership that had kept them working on community issues. Filling the void was a new gang organization period.

In 1969 fifteen-year-old Raymond Washington, a high school student of central Los Angeles, and a few friends formed a gang patterned after a 1960s gang called the Avenues. They named their gang the Baby Avenues and sometimes called themselves the Avenue Cribs, a reference to their young ages. The Cribs wore black leather jackets, earrings in their left ear, and often walked with canes. Before long, stealing and assaulting became the gang's chief activities.

Because of the canes used by gang members, a Los Angeles newspaper reporting on an assault called them the "Crips" for cripples. The Cribs latched onto the name Crips because a slang word crippin' meant robbing and stealing. Gang members lived the crippin' way of life, often stealing black leather jackets. The desire to obtain black leather jackets led to the first Crips murder in 1972. Crips attacked and murdered a sixteen-year-old Los Angeles high school student, a nongang youth and son of an attorney, for the leather jacket he was wearing. The murder, in addition to continuing Crips attacks, received sensational media coverage. To youth living in poverty, the gangs seemed to be a way to attract attention and through gang activity a way to prove manliness and power over others. More and more poor black youths joined Crips.

South Los Angeles schools were soon filled with gang fights and shootings. By the end of 1972 there were eight Crip gangs and ten others, which were responsible for twenty-nine gang-related murders. The Crips and other gangs were rivals, though the Crips outnumbered the others and constantly terrorized them. As a result, the non-Crips met on Piru Street in Compton and formed an alliance that became known as the Bloods. Los Angeles County reported thirty thousand gang members and 355 deaths in 1980.

By 1996 twenty-one communities in Los Angeles County had 274 gangs. Six communities—Los Angeles, Compton, Athens, Inglewood, Carson, and Long Beach—had 225 of the 274 gangs. The gangs were highly structured and focused on making money much like the American Mafia. The business of choice was drugs. By the 1990s the Los Angeles gang epidemic had expanded into urban areas along the West Coast and across the nation. Many of the gangs were extensions of the Bloods and Crips. Wherever unemployment, poverty, and racism existed, gangs could attract members.

Hispanic gangs

Just like black Americans, Hispanics flooded into Southern California during the World War II years in search of war industry jobs. They crowded into the poor Mexican neighborhoods and Hispanic street gangs grew. By the early 1940s gang members had adopted a specific form of dressing, wearing what was called a "zoot suit." Originating in El Paso, Texas, and catching on in Los Angeles, the zoot suit consisted of pleated baggy pants, a long loose fitting coat, highly polished shoes, and a long chain hanging from the belt into a trouser side pocket.

In the late 1940s and throughout the 1950s Hispanics moved into various housing projects in East Los Angeles. Fights between gangs were common, generally over protecting a gang's territory or "turf."

Hispanic gangs continued growing in membership in the 1960s, 1970s, and 1980s. Gangs preyed on gangs, fighting turf battles, and often victimizing innocent residents of their communities. Residents, fearing retaliation, would not help law enforcement investigate gang violence. Around 1980 Hispanic gangs began to sell drugs supplied by the Mexican Mafia to make money. Selling drugs was so profitable for the gangs that even more young Hispanics wanted to join.

Community violence escalated with 452 gang-related murders in Los Angeles County in 1988, with 50,000 reported gang members in 450 different gangs. Seven years later in 1995, there were 1,500 different gangs with 150,000 members located in the Los Angeles area. Although the Crips and Bloods were part of these figures, most of the street gangs were Hispanic.

The Mexican Mafia began requiring a tax on the sale of drugs supposedly to help members in prison. Some street gangs refused to pay the tax and called themselves the "green lighters"—tax free and proud of it. Soon they were known as the Green Light Gangs. By 2000 Hispanic gangs were better organized, operated in cities around the country, and were the fastest growing kind of U.S. gang.

Midwest and East Coast gangs

Chicago in the 1920s was home to Al Capone and his mobsters, most of whom had Italian roots. They grew enormously wealthy during Prohibition by supplying alcohol to the public. The Mafia in Chicago was commonly called the "Outfit." At the start of the twenty-first century, the Outfit was still operating in Chicago and its suburbs. In addition to the Outfit, street gangs organized during the 1940s and 1950s. The Latin Kings, predominately Hispanic, became one of Chicago's most violent gangs.

Arrested members of the Latin Kings often ended up in East Coast prisons in Connecticut and New York, where they formed the Almighty Latin King Nation. By the early 1990s, numerous Latin Kings were in the prison system and also had hundreds of members on the streets of New York and New Jersey. One of the nation's most notorious street gangs, the motto of the Latin Kings was "once a king, always a king." Latin Kings are associated with the People Nations, a loose organization of dangerous gangs including the Vicelords, Bishops, Gaylords, Latin Counts, and Kents.

This member of an Hispanic zoot suit gang was arrested after rioting in Los Angeles in 1943. He wears the distinctive suit after which the gang is named.
(AP/Wide World Photos)

The Gangster Disciples, originating in Chicago in the 1960s and 1970s, also spread to the East Coast. Highly organized and specializing in drug sales, Gangster Disciples were found in most East Coast cities by the end of the 1990s and became the largest Folk Nation gang. The Folk Nation is a collection of gangs who banded together as protection from the Latin Kings. Members of the Folk Nation include the Black Gangster Disciples, Spanish Cobras, Black Disciples, Latin Disciples, Two Sixers, and Internation Posse—made up of many ethnicities but joined together as protection from the Latin Kings.

The Bloods and the Crips also sent gang members to the East Coast. Spreading out into neighborhoods across New York City, the Bloods attracted many members. By 2000 the Bloods were the most violent East Coast gang. Youth affiliated with the Los Angeles Crips traveled east in the 1980s and within a decade had a major presence along the East Coast.

Impacts of global organized crime

At the beginning of the twenty-first century, organized crime in the United States was far different than decades earlier when a few powerful Mafia families dominated the country. Modern organized crime activity still includes the American mob, motorcycle gangs, and street gangs but has an increasing number of gangs based in foreign nations.

A major concern for the FBI has been the worldwide cooperation of organized crime groups, forming international partnerships of mutual interest. Major international crime syndicates who partner with U.S. groups include the Russian Mafia, Japanese Yakuza, Chinese Triads, Mexican Mafia, South American drug cartels, West African and Caribbean groups, as well as the continued cooperation of Italian and Sicilian organized crime. In addition to Chinese and Japanese crime operations, many smaller Asian groups are based in Taiwan, North and South Korea, Thailand, Vietnam, and Laos.

International crime groups still deal in their traditional criminal activities but continue to expand their range of goods and services. Drug trafficking remains a top moneymaker, but weapons, diamonds, luxury cars, and even natural resources such as oil from Russia can all be smuggled and traded illegally. Because of the vast profits involved, money laundering has become the number one crime worldwide. Drug profits alone were close to $100 billion each year in the early 2000s.

Organized crime has also benefited from advances in electronic technology. Information speeds around the world ignoring borders and trade restrictions. Hacking into the computer systems of businesses and financial institutions has become a favored organized crime activity. Criminals can extort a business or a nation with computer viruses. In addition,

LGT Bank in Liechtenstein, Germany, suspected of money laundering for criminal organizations, was raided by police in 2000. Many offshore banks granted anonymity in banking transactions so the money laundering would be hard for authorities to trace back to its source.
(AP/Wide World Photos)

there is identify theft, credit card fraud, bank fraud (see chapter 6, White-Collar Crime), counterfeiting, creating fake identification such as passports, and many more crimes made possible by computer technology.

To deal with organized crime and its worldwide connections, the FBI established its Organized Crime Section. Responsibilities are subdivided into three units: the La Cosa Nostra/Italian Organized Crime/Labor Racketeering Unit; the Eurasian Organized Crime Unit; and the Asian/African Criminal Enterprise Unit. Through these units the FBI attempts to disrupt and shut down international and U.S. organized crime.

For More Information

Books

Lunde, Paul. *Organized Crime: An Inside Guide to the World's Most Successful Industry.* New York: DK Publishing, Inc., 2004.

Lyman, Michael D., and Gary W. Potter. *Organized Crime.* Upper Saddle River, NJ: Pearson Prentice Hall, 2004.

Sanchez, Reymundo. *Once a King, Always a King: The Unmaking of a Latin King.* Chicago, IL: Chicago Review Press, 2003.

Siegel, Dina, Henk von de Bunt, and Damian Zaitch, eds. *Global Organized Crime: Trends and Developments.* Boston: Kluwer Academic, 2004.

Sullivan, Robert, ed. *Mobsters and Gangsters: Organized Crime in America, from Al Capone to Tony Soprano.* New York: Life Books, 2002.

Thompson, Hunter S. *Hell's Angels: A Strange and Terrible Saga.* New York: Modern Library, 1999.

Web Sites

"About Organized Crime." *Federal Bureau of Investigation (FBI).* http://www.fbi.gov/hq/cid/orgcrime/ocshome.htm (accessed on August 20, 2004).

American Foreign Policy Council. http://www.afpc.org (accessed on August 20, 2004).

"Gangsters, Outlaws, and G-Men." *Court TV's Crime Library: Criminal Minds and Methods.* http://www.crimelibrary.com/gangsters-outlaws-gmen.htm (accessed on August 20, 2004).

"International Organized Crime." *Michigan State University School of Criminal Justice.* http://www.cj.msu.edu/outreach/security/orgcrime.html (accessed on August 20, 2004).

National Alliance of Gang Investigators Associations. http://www.nagia.org (accessed on August 20, 2004).

United Nations Office on Drugs and Crime. http://www.unodc.org/unodc/index.html (accessed on August 20, 2004).

Public Order Crimes

Public order crimes are actions that do not conform to society's general ideas of normal social behavior and moral values. Moral values are the commonly accepted standards of what is considered right and wrong. Public order crimes are widely viewed as harmful to the public good or harmful and disruptive to a community's daily life. In this chapter the public order crimes described include prostitution, paraphilia, and pornography, as well as alcohol and drug offenses.

Prostitution is selling or performing sexual acts in return for payment, generally money. Paraphilia is sexual behavior considered bizarre or abnormal, such as voyeurism (spying on another for sexual pleasure) or pedophilia (sexual desire involving children). Pornography includes videos, books, photographs, and other materials focusing on nudity and sexual activities.

While crimes against people and property (see chapters 4 and 5) involve actions considered wrong by any standard, public order crimes are defined by the social and moral rules of the day. For example, prostitution was licensed, legal, and socially acceptable in ancient Greece. Around 500 B.C.E.

Pornographic literature that was confiscated throughout the year was torched by the New York police department, 1936. *(© Bettmann/Corbis)*

prominent men in Greek communities openly went to houses of prostitution. Part of the money paid was applied to the building of Greek temples. Prostitution was considered morally wrong by most Americans in the year 2000. In the United States, prostitution is legal only in Nevada and then only at licensed houses, called brothels, located away from population centers.

Laws against public order crimes, also called "sin" crimes, are highly controversial. What is shameful and immoral is difficult to determine, and public order crimes are often committed by otherwise law-abiding citizens. The activities are carried out between willing participants. Public order crimes are therefore referred to as victimless crimes, except when children are involved.

Some argue that victimless crimes such as prostitution, pornography, and illegal drug sales should be legalized then controlled and taxed like the sale of alcohol and tobacco. Those with a different point of view stress that there is no such thing as victimless crime. They argue that prostitution and pornography are degrading and often dangerous. Drugs destroy individuals and their families, often leading to thievery for drug money, and even death from drug overdoses.

Prostitution

Prostitution has been a part of human societies for many centuries. While for thousands of years prostitutes were generally thought of as female, by 2000 it was recognized that both female and male prostitutes were active in the trade. Both sell their bodies for money. Almost all customers are male and are known as clients. Frequently a third party—called a pimp if male, a madam if female—will set up the sexual encounter and take a portion of the money exchanged.

Studies show that prostitutes generally enter the profession voluntarily rather than being forced. The chief reasons are for money, often much better money than minimum wage jobs, for survival when there appears no other way to make a living, and for drug money. Prostitutes are often drug abusers. Several types of prostitution exist in the United States.

The most dangerous type of prostitution is streetwalking. Streetwalkers, often dressed in revealing clothing and high heels,

A prostitute walking the streets, trying to sell herself for sex. The most dangerous type of prostitution is streetwalking. (© Robert Holmes/Corbis)

stand out as they wait to be picked up by drivers passing by. Streetwalkers are often called hookers. The majority of those arrested for prostitution are streetwalkers. Two other types of prostitutes are bar girls who hang out at bars waiting to be picked up, and call girls. Call girls, who often work for escort services, may have a steady clientele. They are the most highly paid prostitutes often receiving $1,000 or more a night.

The crime of prostitution is a misdemeanor (minor offense) in most states. Those who hire prostitutes may also be arrested on misdemeanor charges. Anyone engaging in promoting prostitution activities, such as a pimp or madam, however, could be charged with felony (major) offenses if arrested. Pimps and madams are charged with felonies because it is likely they have influenced young women or men to engage in prostitution for their own gain.

As previously noted, the only legal prostitution occurs in Nevada in licensed houses of prostitution. These houses or brothels, whether in Nevada or run illegally in other states, are frequently owned and operated by organized crime. Through history these brothels have also been called bordellos, flop houses, cathouses, and "houses of ill repute [reputation]." Madams oversee brothels and the prostitutes who live and work in the house. The money paid for a prostitute's services is split between house owners, the madam, and the prostitute. All other forms of prostitution—streetwalkers, bar girls, and especially call girls—exist in Nevada and elsewhere but are illegal everywhere.

Abnormal sexual behavior

Paraphilia is criminal behavior far outside of what the public considers normal. These include pedophilia, voyeurism, exhibitionism, and sadomasochism. Pedophilia is receiving sexual pleasure from activities that focus on children. Pedophiles, mostly male, prey on unsuspecting children after they win their trust. A pedophile might be a coach, a teacher, or even a religious official. They control the abused children with threats of harm or violence unless the victims keep the sexual activities a secret.

Occasionally there are pedophilia "rings" that consist of a number of active pedophiles. Adult members lure and hold youngsters—the preferred ages being between ten and thirteen—against their will for sexual exploitation and abuse. Many of the victims are runaways who have no home and are not reported missing.

Voyeurism is defined as sexual pleasure derived from watching unsuspecting people undressing or having sexual relations. Exhibitionism is the act of exposing one's genitals or sexual parts to another or to a group for surprise or shock value. Sadomasochism is experiencing pleasure from sexual activities that cause another person pain.

Pornography

Materials such as magazines, books, pictures, and videos showing nudity and sexual acts are considered pornography. Pornography, except when involving minors, is protected by the First Amendment of the U.S. Constitution as free expression and is sold in most cities. It is sold in "adult" stores and is widely available on the Internet.

Pornography becomes a crime when it is considered obscene. Obscene material is so offensive it violates all standards of morality or decency. The production and sale of obscene material is a criminal offense. Law enforcement faces the problem of determining what is obscene in specific cases, since there is no concrete definition to guide them. What may be considered obscene to one person is not necessarily obscene to another.

The one type of pornography that is definitely criminal and a felony offense is child pornography. Child pornography involves minors under the age of eighteen and often very young children being sexually exploited by adults. The most common forms of sexual exploitation are photographing and videotaping nude children or children being sexually abused. The photos and videos are then sold to customers.

Child pornography sex rings exist across the country and generally involve three to eleven children, often runaways. They are recruited by adults who first win over their trust then hold onto them with rewards. Some rings are highly organized and have many regular customers. Other rings are operated by a single individual with a small group of customers.

When law enforcement agencies make a determined effort to halt the sale of obscene material found in adult stores, the effect often drives up prices, which in turn creates higher profits for the pornography business. Determined customers will always find a way to obtain what they desire. Dealers who are being watched by law enforcement often turn to selling their products online.

Congress first attempted to control pornography on the Internet by passing the 1996 Communication Decency Act. The act held online providers criminally liable if their networks were used in the transmission of obscene material. In a 1997 case, *Reno v. ACLU (American Civil Liberties Union)*, the U.S. Supreme Court ruled the act violated the right to free speech, guaranteed in the First Amendment.

In October 1998 Congress passed the Child Online Protection Act (COPA), which was then signed by President Bill Clinton (1946–; served 1993–2001). In March 2003 the Third Circuit Court of Appeals ruled COPA was unconstitutional and in violation of the First Amendment. COPA was still tied up in courts into the early twenty-first century.

Enforcement of online pornography has proven very difficult. As soon as one site is shutdown, others appear. It is not uncommon for people exploring the Internet to accidentally hit on a pornography site. Many pornography sites are "mouse-trapped," which means they are impossible to exit without improperly turning off or crashing the computer. In addition, once someone visits a pornography site endless pornographic pop-ups and emails often invade the computer. Law enforcement agencies have not been able to keep up with the rapidly increasing number of sites.

In spite of efforts by the government to crack down on pornography, it is a booming business. At the start of the twenty-first century, Americans spent as much on pornography as they did on sporting events and live musical shows combined.

Alcohol and crime

Alcohol is the most widely used drug in the United States. Approximately eight out of ten people aged twelve and over consumed alcohol some time in their life and half describe themselves as current drinkers. For those aged twelve to seventeen, 41 percent have used alcohol and 21 percent report being current drinkers. These percentages increase with age, topping out in the twenty-six to thirty-four-year-old age bracket where 90 percent confirmed drinking alcohol and 63 percent were current drinkers.

In the early 1980s, the U.S. government began keeping statistics on the relationship between alcohol and crime. After twenty years, at the start of the twenty-first century, those statistics revealed a clear tie between alcohol and crime. Drinking alcohol does not lead people to commit a crime; the vast majority of those who consume alcohol do not exhibit criminal behavior. Approximately four out of ten crimes, however, involve the use of alcohol. Alcohol also plays a role in four out of ten fatal automobile accidents.

As reported in the National Crime Victimization Survey maintained by the Bureau of Justice Statistics, persons who were victimized by an intimate acquaintance such as a former spouse, boyfriend, or girlfriend, reported alcohol was involved 66 percent of the time. Those victimized by a current spouse listed alcohol as a factor in 75 percent of the offenses. In contrast, about 31 percent of violent stranger-to-stranger criminal acts involved alcohol.

The Department of Justice reports two-thirds of alcohol related crimes are assaults. Seven out of ten crimes associated with alcohol occurred in a private residence, while one in ten occurred in a bar or restaurant. The majority of incidents happened at night, peaking between 11 P.M. and 1 A.M. The fewest occurred between 7 and 9 A.M. Eighty percent of the time, the weapon used in the incident was hands, feet, or fists. Knives were involved in about 7 percent of alcohol related violent incidents and firearms about 4 percent of the time.

Highway patrol officers, checking for drunk drivers at a roadblock in North Carolina, 1997. *(AP/Wide World Photos)*

Driving under the influence (DUI)

A potentially tragic and deadly criminal action involving alcohol is driving a motor vehicle while or after consuming alcohol. The National Highway Traffic Safety Administration (NHTSA) estimated 17,401 deaths in 2003 were due to crashes involving alcohol. This was only 18 deaths fewer than in 2002. The 17,401 figure represented 40 percent of all traffic fatalities in 2003.

In addition to fatalities, over 500,000 people are injured in alcohol related vehicle accidents every year. The NHTSA estimates three in ten Americans will be affected during their lifetime by an alcohol-related crash, involving themselves, a relative, or a friend.

Driving under the influence (DUI) is a public order crime. Organizations such as Mothers Against Drunk Driving (MADD), Students Against Destructive Decisions (SADD), and Remove Intoxicated Drivers (RID) have pressured lawmakers to strengthen DUI laws. Their successes include: (1) passage

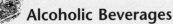

Alcoholic Beverages

Rarely when an individual drinks an alcoholic beverage are they drinking pure alcohol. Only a few ounces of the pure liquid rapidly raises blood alcohol concentrations (BACs) to a very dangerous level leading to unconsciousness and possibly death. The alcohol in drinks is ethanol. The approximate ethanol concentration for the most common alcoholic beverages is as follows:

Beer: 4–6 percent

Malt liquor: 5–8 percent

Wine cooler: 5–10 percent

Wine: 9–13 percent

Champagne: 8–14 percent

Hard liquor (such as vodka, tequila, whiskey, rum): 40–95 percent

Grain alcohol: 95–97.5 percent

Hard liquor and grain alcohol are commonly diluted with various soda, fruit or sweetened juices, or water.

A standard .12-ounce beer, 5-ounce glass of wine, or 1 shot (1.5 ounces) of hard liquor all contain 12 grams of pure ethanol. It takes the human body about one hour to metabolize (absorb and breakdown) 12 grams of ethanol. When drinks are consumed at a pace faster than the body can metabolize, a person begins to feel intoxicated. Intoxication levels will rise as drinking continues. Symptoms of intoxication are slurred speech, bloodshot eyes, a lack of mental clearness, loss of coordination, and often the willingness to take dangerous risks.

(Information from Just Facts.org at http:// www.justfacts.or/jf/alcohol/general.asp)

of state laws raising the minimum legal drinking age to twenty-one; (2) lowering the blood alcohol concentration (BAC) limit for adult drivers (twenty-one and over) to 0.08 in many states; and (3) zero tolerance laws for youth.

The 0.08 figure means a 0.08 percent concentration of ethanol in a person's blood or breath. Zero tolerance laws for youth make it illegal for a driver under twenty-one years of age to have any measurable amount of alcohol in the blood. Some states actually set the limit for those under twenty-one at 0.00 while others allow up to 0.02. Every state makes its own laws.

DUI laws

DUI laws make it a criminal offense to operate a motor vehicle while under the influence of alcohol or drugs. Illegal Per Se laws make it a criminal offense to operate a motor vehicle if the driver has a blood or breath alcohol concentration (BAC) above a specific level. The level for adults over twenty-one years of age is 0.08 in most states and 0.10 in others. Administrative Per Se laws allow driver licensing agencies to suspend or revoke (take away) a driver's license when the driver has a blood or breath alcohol concentration at or above the state's BAC.

Police may seize a driver's license during an alcohol-related arrest. Depending on the laws of each state, limited driving privileges may be restored after a period of time passes. For example, after a specified time period some states may allow work-related driving to and from a place of employment. Other states allow no driving privileges for the entire suspension. The decision to restore privileges is left to a judge.

All states impose monetary fines of varying amounts. License suspensions, fines, and even short jail time depends on the judge's decision in first-time offenses. For second and subsequent DUI arrests states have more severe penalties.

The major federal legislation that impacts drunk driving offenses is the Transportation Equity Act for the Twenty-First Century (TEA-21) passed by Congress and signed by President Clinton in 1998. TEA-21 has been successful in reducing death and injury on highways by aggressively addressing and funding drunk driving prevention measures. Because of TEA-21 and strong lobbying (applying pressure) by MADD and RID, a significant number of states lowered BAC levels to .08, passed open container laws (making it illegal to have open liquor containers in one's vehicle), and strengthened repeat offender laws. TEA-21 expired on September 30, 2003, and was waiting for reauthorization in 2004.

Drugs and crime

Substance abuse or use of illegal drugs is another type of public order crime. Marijuana, cocaine, heroin, and methamphetamines are the four illegal drugs most abused. The U.S. government outlaws drugs they consider most harmful. These include marijuana, cocaine and crack cocaine; narcotics that occur in nature such as heroin, hallucinogens such as LSD, and MDMA/Ecstasy; and the illegal distribution or use of prescription drugs such as Vicodin and OxyContin. Besides health risks, the major reason for outlawing drugs is their close relationship to crime. As drug addiction levels increase or decrease in an area, so does criminal activity.

Drug addictions are expensive habits. A significant percentage of crimes against property are committed for drug money. Drug abuse is a major factor in domestic assaults, or those committed among family members. Over half of all domestic assaults involve use of various combinations of cocaine, marijuana, and alcohol. While drug addictions lead some individuals to criminal activities or to domestic abuse, others become involved in crime as part of drug dealing activities. These activities include transporting drugs, known as drug trafficking, and the manufacture, distribution, and sale or purchase of drugs.

Arrestee Drug Abuse Monitoring Program

The National Institute of Justice (NIJ) under the Department of Justice began a program in 1989 to study trends of drug use across the United States by monitoring the drug use among jail detainees. Drug use among arrestees parallels drug use trends in the general population. The program grew rapidly and in 1997 its name was changed from Drug Use Forecasting to the Arrestee Drug Abuse Monitoring (ADAM) Program.

In 2004 ADAM operated in thirty-eight cities across the United States. ADAM collects urine samples from adults, male and female, awaiting arraignment (where a defendant is charged and enters a plea of innocent or guilty) at central jail booking (processing) facilities. ADAM tests for a wide range of drugs. It most frequently detects marijuana, cocaine, heroin, and methamphetamines.

Middle and High School Drug Abuse Trends

The National Institute on Drug Abuse reports the following key findings on drug trends among eighth, tenth, and twelfth graders for 2003:

- The percentages of 8th- and 10th-graders using any illicit drug continued to decline and were at their lowest levels since 1993 and 1995, respectively.

- MDMA (Ecstasy) use decreased in each grade, continuing a decline begun in 2002.

- Marijuana use decreased significantly among 8th-graders.

- Use of LSD, amphetamines, and tranquilizers was down among 10th- and 12th-graders; use of steroids, crack cocaine, and heroin was down among 10th-graders.

- Use of OxyContin and Vicodin in the past year remained stable but at rates high enough to raise concern; Vicodin was the second most frequently reported drug among seniors, after marijuana.

(From http://www.nida.nih.gov/Infofax/ HSYouthtrends.html)

U.S. customs inspectors examine drugs that were seized in Texas in 2001. The U.S. government continuously attempts to apprehend drug dealers bringing large amounts of illegal drugs into the country.
(AP/Wide World Photos)

In 2000 ADAM reported that 64 percent of the males tested at thirty-five of the thirty-eight sites tested positive for at least one drug. Of females tested at twenty-nine of thirty-eight sites, 63 percent tested positive for at least one drug. Testing reveals marijuana use within the last thirty days, cocaine and heroin use within the last three days, and methamphetamine within the last four days.

ADAM also collects the same information on juvenile defendants, aged twelve to eighteen. At most sites over half of juvenile arrestees tested positive for at least one drug. Of those who tested positive, the largest age group was seventeen. In 2000 marijuana was by far the leading drug among juvenile users, cocaine was a distant second, and the number testing positive for methamphetamine was low.

Drug trafficking in the United States

A strategy traditionally used to deal with drug abuse in the United States is to stop the illegal transportation of drugs into the country. The U.S. government continuously attempts to apprehend drug dealers bringing large amounts of illegal drugs into the country. Despite these efforts, the illegal drug market in the United States is the most profitable in the world. Organized crime groups, both U.S. and foreign, continue to make huge amounts of money from drug trafficking.

Cocaine and crack cocaine. Diverse criminal groups operating out of South America smuggle cocaine into the United States predominately across the U.S.-Mexico border. Wealthy and powerful Colombian drug cartels (organized crime groups growing and selling narcotics) control the worldwide supply of cocaine and see that it is distributed in the United States and elsewhere.

Drug organizations based in the Dominican Republic are also responsible for cocaine in the United States. Use of crack, an inexpensive, smokable, and very dangerous and addictive form of cocaine, has declined in the early 2000s but continues to be available in most U.S. cities. Street gangs such as the Bloods and Crips, Dominicans, Puerto Ricans, and Jamaicans rule the street distribution of crack cocaine.

Heroin. Heroin is grown and moved into the United States from four major areas: Columbia in South America, Mynemar (formerly Burma) in Southeast Asia, Afghanistan in the Middle East, and Mexico. At the start of the twenty-first century heroin arrived in the United States from each of these regions. South American heroin dominates the eastern United States, while "Black Tar" heroin and a brown powdered version from Mexico are the dominate forms in the western United States. Powdered heroin has attracted new, younger users because it can be snorted rather than injected.

Marijuana. Marijuana is the most easily obtained and most widely used illegal drug in the United States. Almost one-third of Americans have tried the drug and there were approximately twelve million current smokers at the beginning of the twenty-first century. Most marijuana is grown in Mexico, Canada, or in the United States. The five leading indoor-growing states are California, Oregon, Washington, Florida, and Wisconsin. Leading outdoor growing states are California, Hawaii, Kentucky, and Tennessee. These sites were determined by the number of plants discovered and destroyed by law enforcement agencies.

Methamphetamine. Methamphetamine distribution and use is concentrated in the western United States. The demand, however, has been increasing in the South, especially in Georgia and Florida. The principle source of methamphetamines is "meth" laboratories located in California and Mexico. In Mexico a majority of the meth laboratories found and dismantled have been in the cities of Tijuana and Mexicali. Points of entry into the United States are along the borders of Southern California and Texas. Increasing numbers of nonprofessional, informal laboratories have been emerging throughout

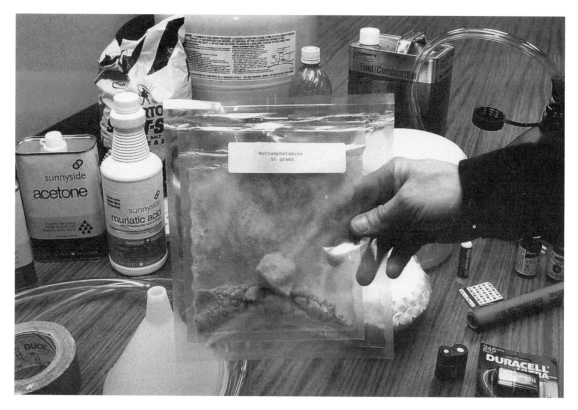

The principle source of methamphetamines is "meth" laboratories located in California and Mexico. *(AP/Wide World Photos)*

the United States as instructions for making highly pure methamphetamine drugs can be found on the Internet.

MDMA/Ecstasy. The drug MDMA, 3, 4—methylenedioxy-methamphetamine, is commonly known as Ecstasy. Ecstasy has both stimulant (making one feel high) and hallucinogen (creating hallucinations or imaginary visions) properties. Among other symptoms are increased heart rate, increased blood pressure, blurred vision, faintness, chills or sweating, and sleeplessness. It is usually taken by teens and young adults attending all night parties called raves.

Ecstasy use skyrocketed among European young people in the late 1990s and in the United States between 1999 and 2001. Use began declining in 2002 and continued in 2003. The majority of MDMA that reaches the United States is produced in Europe, especially in MDMA laboratories in the

Netherlands. It costs as little as 25 to 50 cents to produce a MDMA tablet in Europe, which is sold for between $20 and $30, sometimes up to $40, in the United States. MDMA is transported to the United States by drug dealers, predominately from Russian and Israeli gangs, through Canada, Mexico, and the Caribbean. A small amount of MDMA is produced within the United States.

Operation Candy Box

In August 2003 three laboratories each capable of producing hundreds of thousands of Ecstasy tablets every month were discovered in Canada and dismantled by Canadian law enforcement. At the U.S.-Canadian border city of Burlington, Vermont, $750,000 of U.S. cash was hidden in the fuel tank of a vehicle entering Canada. Both finds contributed important information to a three-year, two-nation investigation called Operation Candy Box.

On March 31, 2004, officials of the U.S. attorney general's office, U.S. Drug Enforcement Administration (DEA), Federal Bureau of Investigation (FBI), and Internal Revenue Service (IRS) announced arrests of more than 130 defendants from across the United States and Canada. All defendants were accused of playing roles in a huge drug trafficking ring that manufactured and distributed Ecstasy pills and marijuana in Canada and the United States. The two ringleaders arrested were Ze Wai Wong, a Chinese national (citizen) in charge of distribution, and Mai Phuong Lee, a Vietnamese national, who channeled the millions in profits into banks.

In the March 31 announcement, DEA administrator Karen Tandy said, "Out of all the dangers of illegal drugs, Ecstasy is of special concern because it is aimed at our teens and youth masquerading as colorful candy. Today we have decimated a criminal organization that has poisoned our neighborhoods with up to a million Ecstasy tablets per month and sent as much as $5 million in proceeds abroad per month over five years."

Operation Candy Box revealed that Ecstasy trafficking had ties to Asian organized crime groups operating in Canada and the United States. Candy Box also revealed how as much as five million illegal dollars could be deposited into the U.S.

An herbal version of the dangerous ecstasy pill. While not calling it a drug, it is marketed as having psychological affects. *(AP/Wide World Photos)*

banking system each month, moved out to worldwide banks including those in Vietnam, and not be detected as suspicious.

Legalization

The U.S. government spends approximately $30 billion every year for drug enforcement. Over the last twenty years of the twentieth century it spent about $500 billion, money that could have been spent on many domestic programs. The government's success in its "War on Drugs" was quite limited, since a plentiful supply of illegal drugs was still available in 2004.

Proponents of drug legalization argue that banning drugs just creates a large network of manufacturers, traffickers, and distributors, all making enormous profits at the expense of U.S. citizens. They argue that the legalization of drugs, then regulating their distribution and sales by the government, is a much wiser approach.

Opponents argue there is evidence in other countries, such as Iran and Thailand, that cheap, available drugs produce an epidemic of drug dependent people whom the government must then care of. Some propose partial legalization, allowing the sale of small quantities of marijuana, as another option. The legalization of drugs in the United States is not likely in the near future since most Americans reject the idea.

For More Information

Books

Abadinsky, Howard. *Drug Abuse: An Introduction.* Chicago, IL: Nelson-Hall Publishers, 1997.

Go Ask Alice. New York: Aladdin Paperbacks, 1998.

Raphael, Jody Ann. *Listen to Olivia: Violence, Poverty, and Prostitution.* Boston, MA: Northeastern University Press, 2004.

Siegel, Larry J. *Criminology: The Core.* Belmont, CA: Wadsworth/Thomson Learning, 2002.

Web Sites

Mothers Against Drunk Driving (MADD). http://www.madd.org (accessed on August 20, 2004).

"Remove Intoxicated Drivers (RID)." *RID-USA, Inc.* http://www.crisny. org/not-for-profit/ridusa (accessed on August 20, 2004.

Students Against Destructive Decisions, Inc. (SADD). http://www.sadd.org/ (accessed on August 20, 2004).

U.S. Department of Health and Human Services, National Institutes of Health, National Institute on Drug Abuse. http://www.nida.nih.gov (accessed on August 20, 2004).

U.S. Drug Enforcement Administration. http://www.dea.gov (accessed on August 20, 2004).

Environmental Crime

In the United States through the first half of the twentieth century little attention was paid to protecting the environment. Americans simply thought the environment and its resources were to be used to build a mighty industrial nation, to build cities, and to create the world's most productive agricultural system. Modern-day environmentalists, those who promote the protection of the environment, often point to the publication in 1962 of the book *Silent Spring,* by Rachel Carson, as a key factor in the start of environmental awareness. Carson, who was a biologist and long-time U.S. Fish and Wildlife Service employee, warned her readers about the destructive properties of pesticides. Pesticides are chemicals used to rid areas or crops of harmful insects and bugs.

Carson researched the effects of pesticides and found that birds, fish, and animals were harmed and that pesticides were also entering the human food chain. *Silent Spring* not only focused global attention on the environment but led to laws restricting the use of pesticides.

Some 270,000 barrels of oil was spilled along the northern coast of Alaska when the *Exxon Valdez* ran ashore in 1989. *(AP/Wide World Photos)*

Growing environmental awareness

Throughout the remainder of the twentieth century a number of major incidents called the public's attention to environmental issues. One of the earliest was at Love Canal. Love Canal, located in Niagara Falls, New York, was an abandoned dry canal used as a legal chemical dumping site by Hooker Chemical Company between 1942 and 1952. The site was then covered with dirt and sold to the Niagara Falls school district for one dollar.

A school was built on top of the Love Canal dumpsite and a neighborhood grew around it. For the next twenty years as children played around the school and in their yards, residents noticed strange smells and holes suddenly opening in the ground when large chemical drums eroded and collapsed. Small fires and explosions sometimes resulted when these drums burst.

Many female residents in the Love Canal area experienced multiple miscarriages (loss of a baby while pregnant), children born with birth defects, and cancer. By 1978 the problems became first local then national news. The Love Canal region was declared a threat to the health and safety of the residents. The school was closed and the state bought hundreds of homes in the area as a massive cleanup began.

In 1969 a large oil spill off the coast of Santa Barbara, California, killed marine wildlife. In 1979 and 1986 two incidents at nuclear power plants left people skeptical of the safety of these plants. The 1979 accident occurred at the Three Mile Island nuclear power plant located in Pennsylvania. While the worst was avoided at Three Mile Island, the 1986 Chernobyl incident was devastating. Chernobyl was a town located in the Soviet Union and home to a large nuclear power plant. The power plant's main radioactive core melted down and thousands of Russians suffered severe and deadly radiation exposure.

In 1989 another massive oil spill occurred in the waters surrounding the United States when an oil tanker, the *Exxon Valdez,* ran ashore on the northern coast of Alaska. In response to growing concerns about the environment, as well as the humans and animals living in it, Congress began passing environmental protection legislation. Major laws were passed during the 1970s, 1980s, and 1990s. Each law defined certain environmental violations, created penalties, and a whole new legal field emerged to deal with the concept of environmental law. The term "environmental crime" also came into use.

Defining environmental crime

At the beginning of the twenty-first century environmentalists, government agencies, and environmental attorneys were still struggling to define exactly what was an environmental crime, what actions should be prosecuted, and what penalties were considered appropriate.

Through the 1980s and 1990s the public usually linked environmental crime with the following actions: contaminating water by dumping chemicals into a stream or river; releasing pollutants into the air; and, improper disposal, storage, or transportation of hazardous wastes such as pesticides, chemicals, and radioactive materials. Legal proceedings focused on actions by corporations or businesses that violated environmental laws. For this reason, early environmental crimes were considered white-collar crime or illegal activity carried on within normally legal businesses.

Yet many environmental crimes did not fit under the white-collar mold. A truck driver who illegally stores gallons of hazardous waste rather than taking them to a proper disposal site could not be considered part of white-collar crime. Likewise a farmer who dumps pesticides into a stream, a hunter who shoots a protected bald eagle, or someone who smuggles exotic birds or animals into the United States have all committed environmental crime but are not part of the white-collar world.

Rather than calling all environmental crime white-collar crime, law professionals tried to develop a better definition. Factors generally considered are: (1) the harm done, whether the action caused harm immediately or was only potentially harmful; (2) the action itself, ranging from littering to major dumping of hazardous wastes; and, (3) the offender, whether individual or corporation.

Despite the attempt to further define environmental crime, it remains confusing. A person who releases chemical waste into a river, causing numerous fish to die has done immediate harm, but a company's storage of hazardous chemical containers in a warehouse is only potentially harmful to wildlife and humans. Scientific uncertainties make it more difficult to prove whether an action is harmful, potentially harmful, or not harmful.

Concerning specific actions, should someone who illegally dumps leftover paint thinner down a street drain be prosecuted as forcefully as a company employee who dumps hazardous wastes into a stream in the middle of the night? Should the employer of the person who committed "midnight dumping" (disposing waste in the middle of the night) be prosecuted along with the employee? If a large company violates environmental law, can a corporation be prosecuted or only individuals within the company? Should only the top officials of a company be prosecuted? Should only those who seek financial gain from environmental crime be prosecuted? These questions show why environmental crime is much more difficult to define than crimes such as assault or robbery.

Mary Clifford proposed a definition of environmental crime in her 1998 book *Environmental Crime,* as "an act committed with intent to harm or with a potential to cause harm to ecological and/or biological systems" as well as with the purpose to increase business or personal gain. According to Clifford, an environmental crime "is any act that violates an environmental protection statute [law]."

Environmental laws

In the second half of the twentieth century, Congress passed numerous environmental laws that included penalties to help guide judges and juries. Both small offenses, with mostly local impact, as well those affecting large areas and many people, have been prosecuted. Environmental laws are constantly being updated, changed, and sometimes abandoned. Following are the major federal laws regulating the environment as of 2000.

Clean Air Act of 1970

The Clean Air Act (CAA) regulates emissions of gases or small particles released into the air. The act authorized the U.S. Environmental Protection Agency (EPA) to set air quality standards to protect public health and the environment. These standards are called the National Ambient (surrounding) Air Quality Standards (NAAQS).

A stream polluted with waste water runoff flowing into the Ohio River in 1972. (© Charles E. Rotkin/Corbis)

The Clean Air Act provides penalties for violating the NAAQS. No individual or business may knowingly violate the standards, make false statements to the EPA, or tamper with EPA monitoring equipment. Penalties involve fines and possible prison sentences. If any offender releases hazardous pollutants into the air knowing they may place humans in immediate danger, the fines and prison sentences are severe.

Federal Water Pollution Control Act Amendments of 1972 (Clean Water Act)

Congress passed the earliest form of the Federal Water Pollution Control Act in 1948. With the growing complexity of

Endangered Species Act

Congress passed the Endangered Species Act in 1973. The act protects certain plants and animals that are struggling to survive. In 2004 approximately 326 species of plants and 306 species of animals were on the endangered list. The act prohibits any activity that is considered harmful to listed species or their habitats. The EPA strictly controls the use of pesticides and makes it a crime to import, export, trap, or harm any listed species.

controlling water pollution and increasing public awareness and concern, Congress passed the Federal Water Pollution Control Act Amendments of 1972. After more amendments in 1977, the act became known as the Clean Water Act (CWA). The CWA's goal is to reduce water pollution.

The act made it illegal for any person or company to release a pollutant into U.S. waters unless a permit carefully controlling the release was obtained. The CWA set four levels of criminal penalties for environmental violations: (1) those considered negligent, where an offender did not realize the release was harmful and prohibited; (2) when the offender knowingly releases a harmful substance; (3) when the offender knows the release will endanger the environment of the water and possibly humans; and, (4) when the offender supplies EPA with false information or tampers with monitoring equipment. Penalties involve fines and sometimes prison sentences. Repeat offenders receive harsher penalties than first time offenders.

Marine Protection, Research and Sanctuaries Act of 1972 (Ocean Dumping Act)

The Ocean Dumping Act controls the dumping of substances into ocean waters. Dumping sewage, industrial waste, or materials that include radioactive, chemical, or biological substances is prohibited. Any kind of high level radioactive waste or medical waste is also illegal.

Resource Conservation and Recovery Act of 1976

The Resource Conservation and Recovery Act (RCRA) controls hazardous waste, including its transportation, treatment, storage, and disposal. A hazardous waste is any solid or liquid substance that because of its quantity, concentration, or physical or chemical properties may cause serious harm to humans or the environment when it is not transported, treated, stored, or disposed of properly.

Sign warning about hazardous waste and toxic substances in the area.
(© Joseph Sohm; Chromo Sohm, Inc./Corbis)

Hazardous waste is often toxic (poisonous), corrosive (damaging to eyes, skin, or surfaces), flammable (easy to set on fire), and explosive. Common examples of hazardous waste are pesticides, asbestos (a material formally used in building and manufacturing now known to be harmful), metals such as lead and arsenic, and automotive antifreeze and gasoline.

Any biological substance with the potential to cause infection is considered a biological hazard, or "biohazard," for short. Blood is a common biohazard, as well as soiled material generated at healthcare facilities, such as bed sheets and surgical dressings contaminated with body fluids. Living organisms such as bacteria and viruses from diagnostic procedures or used in research are also considered biohazards.

Criminal offenses under the RCRA include: (1) transporting hazardous waste without a permit; (2) treating, storing, or disposing of hazardous waste without a permit or in violation of a permit's terms; (3) deliberately making false statements in reports to the EPA; (4) destruction of records or failing to file required reports; and, (5) moving hazardous wastes into a foreign country without the knowledge of the country.

Penalties for RCRA violations include fines and prison sentences. Under the RCRA, EPA officials frequently charge corporate officers for the violations of their companies. The 1986 amendments to the RCRA strengthened EPA enforcement, set stricter waste management standards, and addressed problems of underground storage tanks leaking.

Toxic Substances Control Act of 1976

The Toxic Substances Control Act enables the EPA to track approximately seventy-five thousand industrial chemicals either produced or imported into the United States. Keeping track of these materials means screening, testing, and requiring special reports of chemicals that could be harmful to the environment or cause health risks for humans. The act also supports and helps in the enforcement of other acts like the Clean Water Act and the Clean Air Act.

Comprehensive Environmental Response, Compensation, and Liability Act of 1980 ("Superfund")

The Comprehensive Environmental Response, Compensation, and Liability Act (CERCLA), also known as the Superfund, requires the cleanup of sites contaminated with hazardous waste by those responsible for creating them. The act authorizes the EPA to find those responsible for pollution and require them to cooperate in the cleanup. Once EPA agents locate and identify a site, find the person or group responsible, determine what hazardous substances are present, and verify funds are required to cleanup the site, then criminal penalties are applied.

The Superfund Amendments and Reauthorization Act (SARA) of 1986 added new technical requirements and strengthened enforcement of Superfund cleanup. (Superfund is the fund originally established by CERCLA for private corporations to contribute to, so as to create a singe "superfund" [large fund] to finance the cleanup of toxic sites.) Criminal offenses include failing to notify the EPA of a hazardous waste release and falsifying records related to sites. SARA also authorized the government to pay informers (persons who secretly provide information to authorities) money for any information that leads to the arrest and conviction of a violator of CERCLA.

Oil Pollution Act of 1990

The Oil Pollution Act tries to prevent oil spills by requiring oil storage facilities and oil tanker ships to follow strict regulations for oil storage. They also must submit plans explaining how they will deal with an oil spill. Congress passed the Oil Pollution Act the year after the massive and devastating oil spill of the *Exxon Valdez* in southern Alaska waters.

Occupational Safety and Health Act

Congress passed the Occupational Safety and Health Act in 1970. The Occupational Safety and Health Administration (OSHA) within the U.S. Department of Labor enforces the provisions of the act. The act requires workplaces be safe environments, free of hazards. Exposure to harmful chemicals, unsanitary conditions, excessively hot or cold conditions, and mechanical dangers are all prohibited under the Safety and Health Act. OSHA works closely with the EPA to monitor conditions, investigate, and prosecute anyone responsible for violations.

Federal Insecticide, Fungicide, and Rodenticide Act of 1947 (amended in 1972 and 1996)

This act regulates the manufacture, distribution and sale, and use of insecticides, usually called pesticides, fungicides, and rodenticides. Pesticides are poisons that kill insects harmful to plants and people. Fungicides are poisons that kill mold, mildew, or any fungus harmful to plants. Rodenticides are poisons that kill rodents such as mice and rats.

The act requires users of pesticides and fungicides to register with the EPA. Individuals face criminal penalties if they knowingly misuse a registered poison. Penalties include fines and possible prison sentences.

Environmental enforcement agencies

Congress passes environmental laws to protect the environment. Once a law is passed, it must be put into action. Laws like these do not contain details of how to carry out day-to-day enforcement. For example, a law may prohibit dumping hazardous wastes into rivers, but not specify which wastes,

A hazardous waste team from the EPA takes test samples from storage drums at an abandoned factory.
(© Bettmann/Corbis)

how much, which rivers, and so on. Instead Congress creates and authorizes government agencies to write specific regulations about each of these laws.

The EPA creates regulations for environmental legislation and is responsible for enforcing these regulations. Its criminal enforcement program identifies and apprehends offenders, then assists prosecutors in convicting them. The criminal enforcement program employs federal agents trained in all aspects of environmental crime. EPA agents have full law enforcement authority to investigate and arrest offenders.

Environmental specialists such as attorneys, forensic (applying medical studies to crime investigation) scientists, engineers, and training specialists are all part of the EPA enforcement team. Over forty regional and area offices are located across the nation. The EPA officials at these offices work closely with other federal (Department of Justice and Federal Bureau of Investigation), state, local, and tribal law enforcement agencies to investigate and prosecute environmental crimes.

The EPA maintains training centers in Washington, D.C., and Denver, Colorado, as well as an environmental forensic laboratory in Denver. The U.S. Department of Justice prosecutes cases turned over by the EPA.

The Environmental and Natural Resources Division within the U.S. Department of Justice (DOJ) oversees environmental crime cases. The Environmental Crimes Section prosecutes corporations and individuals who violate environmental laws. Its activities show corporations and the public that environmental crime in the United States at the beginning of the twenty-first century is taken seriously and will be prosecuted.

The Environmental Crimes Section, EPA, and FBI work together to convict environmental criminals.

Three forms of enforcement

There are three forms of environmental law enforcement: administrative, civil, and criminal proceedings. Under administrative enforcement the EPA notifies an offender of a violation and requires the offender halt the activity. If the offender cooperates and a settlement is reached the matter is resolved. If the offender denies a violation has taken place, he or she enters into informal talks with the EPA. Again, if a settlement is reached, the matter ends. If there is no settlement, a formal hearing with a judge is scheduled. The judge listens to all sides and issues a decision. If the offender loses, he or she may appeal the decision by entering the federal court system.

If from the start the EPA either believes the case cannot be settled or the offender is uncooperative, the EPA refers the case to the DOJ. The DOJ looks at five major factors when deciding how to prosecute a case: intent to violate the law; the harm done; the offender's prior environmental record; how much or if the offender will cooperate in the investigation; and media attention the case is or will be receiving.

The DOJ also looks into the possible involvement of organized crime groups. Organized crime, for several decades, had dealt in the illegal disposal of hazardous waste. Proper treatment and disposal of the waste is very expensive. Various organized crime groups with little concern for the environment found dumping waste illegally was far cheaper and simpler than legal disposal.

The DOJ can prosecute environmental crime cases in either civil or criminal proceedings. The goal of a civil proceeding is to force the offender to pay for all damages and injuries experienced by the victimized person or group. The purpose is not to send an offender to prison, but to cover the victim's losses. To win a civil case the government must prove that a "preponderance" (majority or 51 percent) of the evidence supports the claim of the victim.

The goal of a criminal proceeding is to punish the offender with fines and imprisonment. To win a criminal conviction, the government must prove the offender is guilty "beyond a reasonable doubt." Criminal convictions are much more difficult to obtain than civil convictions. The DOJ will often pursue cases in the less demanding civil courts.

State environmental laws

Many federal environmental laws require states to create state implementation (to carry into effect) plans (SIPs). SIPs describe a state's strategy for keeping in line with federal pollution laws. Both the Clean Air Act (CAA) and the Clean Water Act (CWA) require SIPs to stay with their guidelines.

In addition each state may pass its own environmental laws. Most state environmental laws and regulations are patterned after federal legislation. State laws must be at least as strict as federal laws. States may not pass legislation that lowers standards below federal requirements. States create laws to deal with issues unique to their regions. For example, states with beaches pass laws to protect them. Midwestern manufacturing states might pass environmental laws dealing with factory emissions released into the air, waste disposal in rivers, or laws controlling hazardous waste transportation on highways.

States, counties, and local communities generally have environmental quality departments and environmental crime investigation units, but their effectiveness varies depending on funding. They usually work closely with EPA agents, the DOJ, and the FBI.

The most common environmental crimes

Environmental crimes of large corporations often have extensive coverage in the media, but crimes of smaller businesses and individuals are just as common. States and counties deal with several types of environmental crimes. The number one criminal environmental activity is the improper disposal of hazardous wastes, both by companies and individuals. Illegal hazardous waste disposal ranges from unintentional spills in vehicle accidents on highways to planned illegal disposal.

Businesses and industries generate billions of tons of hazardous waste yearly in the United States. Proper disposal is expensive and a majority of the waste is disposed of illegally to

Surveyors from the EPA inspect engines and exhaust systems.

(© Ted Spiegel/Corbis)

avoid these costs. Criminal haulers charge much lower prices than those operating legally.

Typical criminal disposal methods include leaving tank valves open to slowly release a hazardous liquid while driving down a highway; filling 55-gallon drums that are later left in remote areas; renting a truck, filling it with hazardous waste and abandoning it somewhere; renting a storage unit or a whole warehouse, filling it with waste drums, and leaving town; and midnight dumping. Sometimes businesses, thinking they are dealing with a licensed, legitimate hauler, will pay the hauler full price for legal disposal—only to find the hauler illegally disposed of the material and pocketed the money.

Other common state and local environment crimes are the illegal disposal of tires, construction and demolition materials, and household appliances. These crimes are so widespread because offenders are rarely caught. Illegally dumped tires often catch fire and release highly toxic substances into the air. Debris from construction sites and demolition jobs is frequently dumped alongside roads, forcing communities to clean them up. Cancer-causing asbestos fibers from insulation material and lead-based paint pose the greatest health hazard to humans.

Another common local problem is abandoned household appliances. Mercury leaks from appliances and human exposure—by breathing mercury vapors, direct skin contact, or eating or drinking contaminated food or water—can be severe. Exposure leads to nerve system damage in some people. The same is true of freon, the coolant used in refrigerators and older car air conditioners, which contains chlorine and fluorine, both toxic elements. Most states and cities have high fines if tires, building materials, and appliances are dumped illegally rather than taken to a designated landfill site.

Case studies of corporate environmental crime

The type of environmental offender Americans are most familiar with is the large corporation. These crimes are covered on television and in newspapers. The first three case examples involve Wal-Mart, the nation's largest retail sales corporation; General Motors Corporation, an automobile manufacturer; and Exxon Corporation, an oil giant.

Wal-Mart

In May 2004 Wal-Mart agreed to pay a $3.1 million civil penalty to the United States, Tennessee, and Utah for violations of the Clean Water Act. In the early 2000s Wal-Mart was building approximately two hundred new stores each year. Water runoff from construction sites has been a major contributor to the nation's water quality. Wal-Mart was charged with storm water violations at twenty-four construction sites in nine states.

The charges included failure to have a plan in place to control polluted runoff water, failure to install effective controls, and failure to inspect sites that were releasing sediments into sensitive ecosystems (ecological communities, including plants, animals, and microorganisms, together with their environment). The case was investigated and prosecuted by the EPA and DOJ along with the U.S. attorney in the District of Delaware, plus the state attorney generals' offices of Utah and Tennessee.

In the settlement Wal-Mart was required to use aggressive measures to control runoff, setting an example of high standards for other developers and contractors. Wal-Mart was to conduct training on how to deal with runoff, inspect sites frequently, and take immediate corrective action when needed. They were also required to spend $250,000 on wetlands protection projects in at least one of the states where violations were found.

General Motors Corporation

In 1995 General Motors (GM) Corporation settled with the U.S. government for $45 million for violations of the Clean Air Act. The DOJ prosecuted the case, charging General Motors with selling vehicles, specifically the 1991 to 1995 model year Cadillacs, that did not meet Clean Air Act emission standards for carbon monoxide.

The Cadillacs were equipped with illegal devices that caused up to three times the allowed amount of carbon monoxide to be released whenever the vehicle's heating or cooling systems were operating. General Motors added the device after customers complained about stalling engines. The EPA discovered that the Cadillacs failed to meet federal air emission requirements in routine testing in 1993.

GM's $45 million settlement included an $11 million fine, $25 million to recall and fix the Cadillacs, and $8.75 million on projects to help lessen effects of carbon monoxide poisoning. Carbon monoxide poisoning affects a human's ability to work and learn, and can cause headaches and impaired vision.

Exxon Mobil Corporation

At 9:12 P.M. on March 23, 1989, the *Exxon Valdez,* an oil tanker loaded with nearly 54 million gallons of oil, left the Trans-Alaska Pipeline terminal in Valdez, Alaska. The ship ran aground on Bligh Reef at 12:04 A.M. the following day, and 11 million gallons, or 257,000 barrels, of oil spilled into Prince William Sound. Over the next three days the oil spread over the flat calm water.

The oil-covered beach following the *Exxon Valdez* oil spill in 1989. As of 2004 approximately 3.6 miles of shoreline were still contaminated with oil. *(© Natalie Fobes/Corbis)*

Little was skimmed off before it polluted approximately 1,300 miles of Alaskan shoreline, an area filled with wildlife. Approximately 35,000 birds and 1,000 sea otters were confirmed dead. Since most of the dead sank into the water, it was estimated that actually 250,000 seabirds, 2,800 sea otters, 300 harbor seals, 250 bald eagles, 22 killer whales, and billions of salmon and herring eggs were lost.

The DOJ's Environment and Natural Resources Division, the U.S. attorney general's offices in Washington, D.C., and Anchorage, Alaska, as well as the state of Alaska attorney general's office cooperated in the prosecution of Exxon under the Clean Water Act. Congress passed the Oil Pollution Act in 1990.

Settlement was reached on October 9, 1991. Exxon was fined $150 million in the criminal agreement. Since Exxon cooperated in the massive cleanup and also paid private claims, the court forgave $125 million. The remaining $25 million was split between the North American Wetlands Conservation Fund and the national Victims of Crime Fund.

Exxon also paid $100 million to federal and state governments. The federal government spent its share on environmental protection projects, such as shoreline monitoring and oil spill research. The state of Alaska spent its share on improvements for fisheries, wildlife habitats, research, and new recreational facilities.

Exxon agreed to a $900 million settlement in the civil agreement. Exxon paid the entire amount over a ten-year period ending in September 2001. The $900 million went to pay for cleanup, research and monitoring of affected wildlife, habitat protection, restoring the natural landscape, public information, and managing all of the newly established programs.

As of 2004 approximately 3.6 miles of Alaskan shoreline were still contaminated with oil. Wildlife species and the areas affected were categorized as recovered, recovering, or not recovering. Among those listed as "not recovering" are the common loon (a species of duck), harbor seals, Harlequin ducks, and Pacific herring (fish). Although many spills worldwide have been larger, the *Exxon Valdez* spill is still considered the most damaging.

Tyson Foods and Colonial Pipeline Company

The DOJ's Environmental and Natural Resource Division regularly issues reports on its prosecution of environmental crimes. Two examples from 2003 involve Tyson Foods, Inc., and Colonial Pipeline Company.

Tyson Foods, Inc., pled guilty to twenty Clean Water Act violations. During a four-year period Tyson admitted releasing untreated wastewater from a poultry processing plant in Sedalia, Missouri, into storm drains. The drains poured into the Lamine River. Tyson agreed to pay a $5.5 million fine plus $1 million each to the state of Missouri under a separate state civil proceeding and to the Missouri Natural Resources Protection Fund. The company was placed on three-year probation, agreed to an environmental review of its Sedalia facility, and started a new environmental management program.

Colonial Pipeline Company was charged under the Oil Pollution Act of multiple spills along a pipeline that crossed nine states. Its most damaging spill occurred in South Carolina's Reedy River. Approximately 950,000 gallons of diesel fuel went into the Reedy killing 35,000 fish. Prosecuted under civil proceedings, Colonial was required to pay a $34 million civil penalty.

Case studies of small companies and individual environmental crimes

The EPA regularly issues reports of environmental crime cases just like the DOJ. Information on the following two cases was released on May 5, 2004.

Rhodia, Inc., was sentenced on two counts of the Resource Conservation and Recovery Act on April 29, 2004. Rhodia, headquartered in Cranbury, New Jersey, operated a phosphorous manufacturing plant in Silver Bow, Montana. The Silver Bow plant manufactured phosphorous from 1986 until 1996. Following closure of the plant, phosphorous waste was illegally stored at the facility.

Posing a risk to human and environmental health, phosphorous is highly flammable and can catch fire when exposed to air. Rhodia agreed to pay a fine of $16.2 million, plus $1.8 million to the Montana Department of Environmental Quality. It was put on five years of probation and required to cleanup the site.

Illustrating federal and state cooperation, the EPA's agents of the Criminal Investigation Division from the Denver area and the Montana Department of Environmental Quality worked together to investigate the Silver Bow plant. They were assisted with legal and technical support by the EPA's National Enforcement Investigations Center and its offices in Helena, Montana, and Denver. Prosecution was carried out by the DOJ's U.S. attorney's office in Missoula, Montana.

An individual, David E. Ortiz from Grand Junction, Colorado, was convicted under the Clean Water Act and sentenced on April 28, 2004, to one year in prison and payment of a $2,000 fine. Ortiz was associated with Chemical Specialties, a company that produces propylene glycol, an aircraft de-icing chemical. In 2002 Ortiz released industrial wastewater containing propylene glycol into the Colorado River, which killed numerous fish. The EPA's Denver office and the National Enforcement Investigations Center investigated the crime; it was prosecuted by the DOJ's U.S. attorney's office in Denver.

For More Information

Books

Burns, Ronald G., and Michael J. Lynch. *Environmental Crime: A Source Book.* New York: LFB Scholarly Publishing, 2004.

Clifford, Mary. *Environmental Crime: Enforcement, Policy, and Social Responsibility.* Gaithersburg, MD: Aspen Publishers, Inc., 1998.

Jackson, Donna M. *The Wildlife Detectives: How Forensic Scientists Fight Crimes Against Nature.* Boston, MA: Houghton Mifflin, 2002.

Situ, Yingyi, and David Emmons. *Environmental Crime: The Criminal Justice System's Role in Protecting the Environment.* Thousand Oaks, CA: Sage Publications, 2000.

Web Sites

"Criminal Enforcement." *U.S. Environmental Protection Agency.* http://www.epa.gov/compliance/criminal/index.html (accessed on August 20, 2004).

"EPA Newsroom." *U.S. Environmental Protection Agency.* http://www.epa.gov/newsroom (accessed on August 20, 2004).

"Oil Spill Facts." *The Exxon Valdez Oil Spill Trustee Council.* http://www.evostc.state.ak.us/facts (accessed on August 20, 2004).

U.S. Department of Justice, Environment and Natural Resources Division. http://www.usdoj.gov/enrd/components.htm (accessed on August 20, 2004).

10

Terrorism

Terrorism is the preplanned use of force or violence against innocent civilians to make a statement about a cause and influence an audience. Terrorist action is staged for maximum surprise, shock, and destruction. Its goal is to so terrorize or alarm individuals, groups, or governments that they give into the demands of the terrorists.

Terrorists are individuals or groups who plan and carry out violent acts to achieve their goals. While victims see them as murderous criminals, terrorists see themselves as heroes for their cause. The U.S. intelligence community further defines terrorist groups as subnational, not a recognized government or official agency of any country, and as operating in secret. The actions of a country's military or police are not considered terrorist acts.

Global terrorism continually impacted nations in the twentieth century and into the early 2000s. Europe, the United States, the Middle East, South America, Asia, and African countries all experienced violent unexpected terror acts. This chapter describes the different types of terrorism, the techniques used to spread fear by injury, murder, or the destruction of

A plane hijacked by Islamic extremists just before crashing into the south tower of the World Trade Center on September 11, 2001. Seen burning behind it is the north tower, which was hit by a hijacked plane about fifteen minutes before this photo was taken. *(AP/Wide World Photos)*

property, and measures taken by the U.S. government to combat terror and protect American citizens.

Terrorists and terrorist groups differ widely in their behavior and goals. Terrorism can generally be placed into six main categories: nationalistic; religious; state-sponsored; political-social; environmental; and individual.

Nationalistic terrorism

Nationalistic terrorism is an outgrowth of an unwavering devotion and loyalty to a specific group that believes they have been suppressed, treated unfairly, or persecuted by the ruling majority of the country in which they live. Groups are defined by ethnicity (racial or cultural background), language, religion, or customs. Nationalist terrorism calls attention to the plight of the group. The goal is to eventually secure a separate independent homeland or country for the group. The following are examples of groups who engage in terrorism for nationalistic reasons.

Arabs living in the land known as Palestine from which the Jewish nation, Israel, was created in 1948 began nationalistic terrorist activities around 1970. The most active Arab Palestinian terrorist organizations in the early 2000s were HAMAS (Islamic Resistance Movement) and Hezbollah (Party of God). HAMAS cells (small units serving as part of or the center of a larger political movement) are based in the West Bank, Gaza Strip, and Israel. Hezbollah (also spelled Hizbollah) cells are based in Lebanon and worldwide. Other active Arab Palestinian groups include Palestine Islamic Jihad (PIJ), Palestine Liberation Front (PLF), and Popular Front for the Liberation of Palestine (PFLP).

Hoping to convince the Spanish government to create an independent Basque homeland, Basque terrorists of northern Spain carry out activities within Spain. The largest Basque terror group is Basque Fatherland and Liberty, or Euzkadi Ta Askatasuna (ETA). Because their goal is to separate the Basque people from Spain, ETA is also commonly referred to as the Basque Separatists.

Kashmir, an area between India and Pakistan, is populated by people of the Islamic faith. Those who follow the religion of Islam are called Muslims. The predominant religion of India is Hinduism although many Muslims also live there. India has no official religion. Pakistan's population is Muslim, and Islam is its official religion. Both Pakistan and India have long clashed over the control of Kashmir. The people of Kashmir, however, want to be an independent Islamic state.

Major Islamic terrorist groups fighting to create that independent state are Lashkar-e-Tayyaba (LT), meaning "Army of the Pure," Jaish-e-Mohammed (JEM), and Harakat ul-Mujahideen (HUM). Although the terrorists of Kashmir are predominately thought of as nationalistic terrorists, their struggle is an example of a nationalistic cause interlocked with a religious struggle.

The Irish Catholic population of Northern Ireland, ruled by Britain, wants independence from Britain and to be part of the Republic of Ireland. The Protestant population of Northern Ireland resists the movement away from Britain. The major nationalistic terrorist group in 2004 working for separation from England is the Real Irish Republican Army (RIRA). Again, the RIRA's nationalist struggle has religious overtones.

Religious Terrorism

Religious beliefs and the willingness of people to die for these beliefs rather than compromise have led to wars fought in the name of religion for centuries. Modern day devotion to religion follows the same pattern. Many believers are intensely committed to their specific religion. At the beginning of the twenty-first century, Islamic religious terrorism is the most serious form of all terrorism worldwide.

Radical Muslims call for a pan-Islamic Caliphate, which is an ancient government system based entirely on Sharia, Islamic law, and led by one individual, a Prince of Believers. Pan simply means to be located everywhere, throughout the world. The enemy is any Islamic government that does not strictly adhere to the Sharia and all unbelievers—Christians, Jews, and other non-Muslims. The term Christian and non-Muslim describe the majority of the people of the Western world, including western Europeans and the United States. According to Islamic radicals, God wants them to kill the "unbelievers."

The most infamous Islamic terrorist group is Al Qaeda. Its leader, Osama bin Laden, issued a *fatwa* (religious ruling) in

Osama bin Laden, leader of Islamic terrorist group Al Qaeda. In 1998, Bin Laden called for a worldwide Islamic holy war to kill Christians and Jews. *(AP/Wide World Photos)*

February 1998 calling for a worldwide Islamic *jihad* (holy war) to kill Christians and Jews. Bin Laden's key targets appear to be U.S. citizens and U.S. property. He is infuriated by the U.S. military presence in Saudi Arabia and by the influence of Western culture on Islamic nations. The United States is also Israel's strongest supporter, an enemy of bin Laden and his followers who favor the Palestinians.

Al Qaeda, formerly based in Afghanistan until U.S. military forces disrupted their stronghold there in late 2001, has loosely affiliated but independent cells operating in Europe, East Africa, the Middle East, Southeast and Central Asia, and North America. They are financed by bin Laden's inheritance from his wealthy Saudi Arabian family (once estimated by U.S. officials to be between $250 and $300 million), by Islamic charities that funnel donations to Islamic terrorists groups, and by legal and illegal businesses.

Al Qaeda is responsible for the destruction of Khobar Towers residence in Saudi Arabia (1996), the U.S. embassy bombings in Kenya and Tanzania (1998), the bombing of the *USS Cole* in Yemen (2000), the Bali Indonesia nightclub bombing (2002), and the September 11, 2001, (9/11) attacks on New York City's World Trade Center and the Pentagon in Washington, D.C.

Since 9/11 the U.S.-led war on terrorism has resulted in over three thousand Al Qaeda terrorists arrested or killed. Bin Laden, however, had not been captured as of the summer of 2004. Al Qaeda cells remain active and are difficult to detect since they operate independently giving few clues of impending attacks.

Many Islamic groups adhere to the same beliefs as Al Qaeda but there are other modern non-Islamic religious terrorist groups. The Japan-based Aum Shinrikyo is a mixture of Hinduism, Buddhism, and Christianity, and believes its leader to be the "enlightened one." They believe the world will soon come to an end and only their members will go to paradise. Aum Shinrikyo was responsible for the sarin poisonous gas attacks in a Tokyo subway in 1995.

In the United States a militia group known as the Christian Patriots is armed and carefully watched by the FBI. Some believe it was linked to the Oklahoma City bombing on a government building in 1995.

State-sponsored terrorism

Two forms of state-sponsored terrorism exist at the beginning of the twenty-first century: governments that carry out terrorism acts against their own citizens, and government support of groups who carry out terrorism against other governments. Amnesty International, a human rights overseer organization based in London, estimates that about one hundred countries use terrorist activities against their own citizens. These activities include jailing and torturing dissidents (persons with opposing political views to those in power or the government), and sponsoring death squads who seek out, kidnap, and murder dissidents. Countries known to terrorize their own citizens are Brazil, Colombia, Peru, Guatemala, Honduras, and the Sudan. Iraq, when under the leadership of Saddam Hussein, was notorious for such terror tactics.

Genocide, attempting to kill a whole minority population within a country, is the extreme form of state-sponsored terrorism. In addition to the extermination of Jews by Germany in World War II (1939–45; war in which Great Britain, France, the Soviet Union, the United States, and their allied forces defeated Germany, Italy, and Japan), genocides have taken place in the Southeastern Asian nation of Cambodia, Rwanda in Africa, and Bosnia (part of the former Yugoslavia).

According to the U.S. State Department's official list, the second form of state-sponsored terrorism was practiced in 2003 by Cuba, Iran, Iraq, Libya, North Korea, Sudan, and Syria. For example, Iran has long supported HAMAS and Hezbollah, Arab Palestinian groups who have carried out terrorist attacks on Israel. The Sudan has allowed terrorist group members to hide within its country.

The most famous terrorist to spend time in the Sudan was Al Qaeda's Osama bin Laden following his expulsion from his native Saudi Arabia for activities against his own government. Terrorist leaders are also allowed to live within Cuba by its longtime leader Fidel Castro (1926–). Following the U.S.–Iraq war of 2003–04, Iraq will presumably be coming off the state-sponsored terrorism list.

Political-social terrorism

Terrorist acts have long been used to call attention to political and social causes. Political terrorists attempt to make their views known by violent actions in an effort to influence others. Terrorists with social causes seek to change a specific policy or behavior. Social terrorists attempt to force their beliefs on the general population.

One of the most violent American political terrorist organizations of the second half of the twentieth century was the Weather Underground, active between 1969 and 1975. The Weather Underground, whose members were called Weathermen, split off from a larger organization called Students for a Democratic Society (SDS).

The SDS, made up of mostly college students, first formed in 1960 to help with the nonviolent Civil Rights movement of black Americans in the United States. As more and more young people were sent off to fight in the unpopular Vietnam War (1954–75; a controversial war in which the United States aided South Vietnam in its fight against a takeover by Communist North Vietnam) in the 1960s, SDS became active in protests hoping to halt the war. SDS was considered part of the "New Left," or liberal, element of the American political scene that strongly supported civil rights and peaceful solutions to conflict.

Some SDS members believed their actions were making no difference as the United States continued to escalate the war. A small group formed the Weathermen and declared a "State of War" on the U.S. government. They were responsible for about twenty-four bombings, including those at the New York City police headquarters (1970), a U.S. army base and courthouse in San Francisco (1970), and a New York City Bank of America and courthouse (1970). They planted bombs in the

Members of the organization Students for a Democratic Society during a 1968 demonstration. *(© Bettmann/Corbis)*

U.S. Capitol (1971) and inside the Pentagon (1972). As the Vietnam War wound down in the mid-1970s, the Weathermen who had escaped arrest went into hiding and the Weather Underground dissolved.

On the other side of the political spectrum are groups on the far right, known as ultraconservatives. They too oppose the U.S. government but for different reasons. Called the "militia movement," they began to form in the early 1970s and remain active into the 2000s. Members generally hate the U.S. government believing it is too big and powerful. They oppose taxes and arm themselves against the perceived risk that the U.S. government will take away their possessions.

Another major element of their philosophy is white supremacy, which insists those of white or Caucasian background are superior to minorities such as Jews, black

Americans, and more recently homosexuals. The Aryan Nation, Posse Comitatus, and Christian Patriots are examples of heavily armed groups capable of terrorist activities in the American homeland. These groups tend to be located in the Midwest and western states.

The worst terrorist action carried out in the United States prior to 9/11 was the bombing of a federal building in Oklahoma City, Oklahoma, by Timothy McVeigh and Terry Nichols. McVeigh, although not a member of a militia group, strongly agreed with their beliefs and was considered a political terrorist. McVeigh was convicted on eleven counts of murder, conspiracy, and using a weapon of mass destruction. He was later sentenced to death and executed in June 2001. Nichols was convicted first in federal court, then again in state court but was spared the death penalty in 2004. He received life in prison for his role in the bombing.

An ongoing example of a social terrorist group in the United States is the Ku Klux Klan (KKK). First formed in 1866, the KKK remains active in the early 2000s. The KKK is a white supremacy group associated with brutal activities against black Americans for almost 150 years. The Klan also expresses hatred of Jews and Catholics. The KKK's most recent major period of activity occurred against black Americans during the Civil Rights movement of the 1950s and 1960s.

The most radical and violent social terrorism to occur in the United States from the 1970s into the 2000s involves antiabortion or "Pro-Life" activists. Abortion is the ending of a pregnancy by a medical procedure. The U.S. Supreme Court ruled in the 1973 case *Roe v. Wade* that any woman could choose to end a pregnancy by abortion performed by medical doctors at abortion clinics.

This ruling sparked intense debate over when a fetus (unborn child) becomes a child able to sustain life outside the mother's body, thus having the right to live. Abortion is considered the murder of an unborn child by many Americans. Pro-Life terrorist groups have used bombs, arson, and murder to target abortion clinics and their personnel. Starting in the early 1980s, abortion clinics and staff were the targets of about two thousand violent actions in a twenty-year period. In the 1990s at least eight people—doctors, receptionists, a guard, and a policeman—were killed in abortion terrorist actions.

The ruins of the Alfred P. Murrah Federal Building in Oklahoma City, Oklahoma, after a 1995 bombing by Timothy McVeigh. *(AP/Wide World Photos)*

Environmental terrorism

Environmental terrorism is commonly referred to as "ecoterrorism," a combination of the terms ecology and terrorism. An environmental protection movement began in the 1970s when Congress passed a number of environmental protection laws (see chapter 9, Environmental Crime). By 1980 some environmentalists believed little progress was being made to halt developers and industries destroying wilderness areas for profit.

Some environmentalists decided to take action and used ideas from two books, *The Monkey Wrench Gang* (1975) by Edward Abbey, a former forest ranger, and *Ecodefense: A Field Guide to Monkeywrenching* (1985) by Dave Foreman. These books discussed environmental protection "techniques" such as driving large stakes into trees scheduled for logging (which can destroy logging equipment) or setting fire to construction equipment and property. These techniques became environmental terrorist tools.

Foreman founded the terrorist group Earth First! in 1979. Its members successfully used the tree stake method, which does not hurt the trees, in California and the Pacific Northwest to slow logging. Earth First! members also set fires and cut livestock fences in protest of overgrazed grassland. Another ecoterrorist group, the Earth Liberation Front (ELF), formed in the late 1990s when Earth First! began backing away from violent activities. The FBI considers ELF one of the major terrorist groups within the United States.

ELF's terror act of choice is setting fires. Claiming a Vail, Colorado, ski resort negatively impacted the habitat of the lynx (a type of wild cat), ELF set fire to a portion of the resort on October 18, 1998, resulting in $12 million damage. In the 2000s ELF was responsible for burning sport utility vehicles (SUVs) on car lots as well as mansions under construction in Southern California.

The Animal Liberation Front (ALF) carries out terrorist activities directed at university research centers that use animals in experiments. They also target industries that they believe harm animals. Examples of businesses hit by ALF are mink breeders, trapping supply companies, and biological supply companies that provide dead animals for research and biology classes.

The FBI reported that environmental and animal rights terrorists groups committed fifty-nine criminal acts in the United States in 2003. It also reported that ELF openly claimed that it caused about $55 million in damages to industries in 2003.

Individual terrorism

Occasionally individuals acting on their own undertake terrorist activities. Their goal may be tied to causes of other terrorist groups even though they do not belong to the group. Although generally considered a political terrorist, some put Timothy McVeigh in this category. Another example of an individual terrorist in the United States is Theodore "Ted" Kaczynski (1942–), known as the "Unabomber."

Between 1978 and 1995 Kaczynski sent sixteen bombs through the mail. They went mostly to science professors and businessmen dealing in computers. Kaczynski believed modern technology, especially computers, were ruining the world. In all, three people were killed and twenty-nine injured. On a tip from his brother, the FBI arrested Kaczynski in April 1996 at the tiny cabin in Montana where he had lived since 1979. In January 1998, Kaczynski pled guilty to being the Unabomber and was sentenced to four consecutive life sentences in prison.

Terrorist tools

Always unexpected, terrorist attacks are meant to instill fear. Since such acts usually attract media attention, details of an attack can reach millions, which is exactly what the terrorists desire. Actions used by terrorists in the twentieth century and into the twenty-first century included kidnapping and assassination, bombings, and airline hijackings. The U.S. government treats all of the actions as criminal activities.

Theodore "Ted" Kaczynski, also known as the "Unabomber," eluded capture for seventeen years, during which he sent sixteen mail bombs that killed three people and injured twenty-nine others.
(AP/Wide World Photos)

Kidnapping and assassination

Kidnappings and assassinations have always been tools for terrorist groups. Historically, the assassination of a country's leader has been a way to gain maximum notoriety and attention. Assassination of a country's leader, however, rarely brings about the kinds of change terrorists seek. Someone else takes over in the government, and problems carry on.

In the 1970s and 1980s terrorists turned to the kidnapping and assassination of diplomats or government officials.

U.S. diplomats were kidnapped and assassinated in Guatemala (1968), Brazil (1969), Uruguay (1970), Sudan (1972), Cyprus (1974), Afghanistan (1979), and Lebanon (1984). By the end of the 1980s and into the 1990s U.S. victims abroad were more likely to be military personnel, agency workers, business executives, and missionaries than diplomats.

On January 23, 2002, protesting Pakistan's cooperation with the United States, terrorists kidnapped and later killed Daniel Pearl (1963–2002), a reporter for the *Wall Street Journal.* In February, Pakistani officials received a videotape of Pearl's murder. Four suspects in the murder, including Saeed Sheikh, were apprehended and tried. Sheikh had belonged to Jaish-e-Muhammad, a Kashmir separatist group. Sheikh was sentenced to death and the others received life imprisonment.

Another form of kidnapping and assassination involves taking hostages. One of the most infamous hostage dramas occurred in Iran on November 4, 1979. Iranian terrorists seized sixty-six American hostages from the U.S. embassy in Tehran. Thirteen were released quickly but fifty-three were held until January 20, 1981. The hostages were taken in protest of the United States admitting the former shah of Iran into the United States for medical treatment.

Another famous hostage incident occurred on October 7, 1985, aboard an Italian cruise ship, the *Achille Lauro,* in the eastern Mediterranean Sea. Four Palestinian Liberation Front terrorists took more than seven hundred passengers hostage and killed one wheelchair-bound U.S. tourist before the Egyptian government negotiated the release of the passengers.

Bombings

Many types of bombing incidents have been used by terrorist groups during the second half of the twentieth century and into the twenty-first. Every year bombing incidents account for the most lives lost and property destroyed at the hands of terrorists. Types of bombings include planting bombs in structures such as embassies, government office buildings, and hotels. Cars and trucks with bombs planted inside are frequently used to kill and destroy property. Beginning in the 1990s, suicide bombings—individuals with bombs strapped to their bodies—became common in the Middle East.

The following are examples of major structural bombings impacting the United States. On April 15, 1983, members of Islamic Jihad terrorist organization drove a truck holding a 440-pound bomb into the U.S. embassy in Beirut, Lebanon. The suicide truck bombing killed 63 people, including the U.S. Central Intelligence Agency's director of Middle East operations, and injured 120. Another Islamic Jihad attack in Beirut came on October 23, 1983, when a suicide truck bomber armed with a 12,000-pound bomb blew up a marine barracks within a U.S. compound. The attack killed 242 Americans.

A car bomb planted by Islamic terrorists detonated in the underground parking garage of the World Trade Center in New York City on February 26, 1993. Six people were killed and one thousand injured. The deadliest terrorist attack on U.S. soil, up to that point, occurred in April 1995 when extremists Timothy McVeigh and Terry Nichols blew up the U.S. federal building in Oklahoma City. The attack killed 166, many of them young children at a daycare center, and injured hundreds more.

On June 25, 1996, a bomb-rigged fuel truck exploded at the Khobar Towers housing facility in Dhahran, Saudi Arabia, killing 19 U.S. service personnel and injuring 515 others, including 240 U.S. citizens. Several Islamic terrorists groups claimed responsibility.

Two bombings of U.S. embassies took place at approximately the same time on August 7, 1998, in Nairobi, Kenya, and Dar es Salaam, Tanzania. In Nairobi, 291 people including 12 U.S. citizens were killed and over 5,000 were injured. In Dar es Salaam, eighty-seven people including one U.S. citizen were killed. Both U.S. embassies were severely damaged. Osama bin Laden's Islamic terror organization, Al Qaeda, was responsible.

A new twist on bombing occurred on October 12, 2000, when a small boat full of explosives ran into the *USS Cole* docked in Aden, Yemen. Seventeen sailors were killed and thirty-nine injured. Al Qaeda was also responsible for the *USS Cole* bombing.

Suicide bombings. Reports of suicide bombings began about 1996 and were frequent in the early 2000s. At first they were a specialty terrorist action of the Arab-Palestinian terror group HAMAS. By 2002 in addition to HAMAS, the Popular Front

Chemical and Biological Terrorism

In 2004 the Centers for Disease Control (CDC) listed chemical and biological agents that could potentially be used to harm whoever comes into contact with them. The CDC has an emergency preparedness and response plan in place so it can coordinate effective actions to counter a chemical or biological attack.

Chemical agents

Two chemicals associated with terrorist activity that were in the news worldwide in the late 1990s and early 2000s were sarin and ricin. Sarin is a manmade chemical warfare agent that acts rapidly against the nervous system, making breathing difficult or impossible. Sarin is a clear, colorless, tasteless liquid that does not smell and tiny amounts are deadly. It can be evaporated to a poisonous gas that will spread rapidly when released. Sarin nerve gas was used in a Tokyo, Japan, subway station on March 20, 1995, killing 12 people and injuring 5,700. Japanese terrorist group Aum Shinrikyo claimed responsibility.

Ricin is a natural poison found in castor beans. Ricin can be used in a variety of ways to harm people. It can be breathed as a mist or powder, be swallowed when placed in water or food, and can be injected in liquid form into a person's body. Tiny amounts of ricin can kill an adult. On October 15, 2003, an envelope with a sealed container and a note was found at a Greenville, South Carolina, mail processing and distribution facility.

The author of the note threatened to contaminate water supplies if his or her demands were not met. The CDC confirmed the container held ricin. No ricin-associated poisoning cases developed and no further environmental contamination was found. The FBI and local law enforcement officials were investigating to find the source of the ricin.

Biological agents

By the early twenty-first century governments feared that terrorist groups would find a way to obtain deadly biological

for the Liberation of Palestine (PFLP), the al-Aqsa Martyrs Brigade, and the Palestinian Islamic Jihad all regularly claimed responsibility for suicide bombings in Israel. Killing themselves and those around them, suicide bombers strap bombs to their bodies and detonate them in crowded shopping areas, cafés, or on buses.

Arab-Palestinian youngsters are taught from an early age that dying for the cause of eliminating Israelis from Palestine is an honorable action. Suicide bombers are generally young

FBI agents in biohazard suits at the American Media building in Boca Raton, Florida, after a man who worked in the building died of inhalation anthrax. *(AP/Wide World Photos)*

agents. Three biological agents of concern are anthrax (a disease caused by the bacteria *Bacillus anthracis*), smallpox (a viral disease), and botulism (a deadly poison made by the bacteria *Clostridium botulinum*).

Very small amounts of anthrax can be spread in the air and produce upper respiratory problems and even death if inhaled. Inhaled anthrax is the deadliest form of the disease. For example, the U.S. Congress estimates that if two hundred pounds of anthrax was sprayed over Washington, D.C., up to three million people could die.

In October and November 2001 anthrax was used in terrorist activities. Following two deaths in October in Florida, anthrax was sent though the mail to a New York network news journalist and to the Washington, D.C., office of Senate majority leader Tom Daschle. The U.S. Senate building where Daschle's office was located was closed for weeks. Post office machinery used to sort mail was also contaminated. Post offices were closed for inspection and cleaning.

In all, twenty-three people fell ill and five died, including postal workers and individuals whose mail had been contaminated. As of the summer of 2004, the individual or group responsible for the anthrax deaths had not been apprehended.

adults, either male or female. By carrying out a suicide bombing the terrorists believe they become martyrs, a person who suffers death for a cause and is rewarded in heaven or paradise.

By the middle of 2004, the United States had not experienced any suicide bombings by an individual terrorist. The 9/11 attacks, however, involved nineteen suicide bombers who boarded and hijacked four U.S. commercial airplanes and crashed them into the World Trade Center, the Pentagon, and the Pennsylvania countryside.

Terrorist activities involving airlines

Using various approaches, terrorists have commandeered commercial airplanes full of passengers. The earliest form of terrorist use was to merely hijack (to take control of by using force, especially in order to reach a different destination) an airline and have it fly to a country the hijacker wanted to go. Individuals desiring to go to Cuba from the United States were responsible for a number of these hijackings in the 1960s. At the time, there were no regular airline flights between the United States and Cuba. The first U.S. aircraft hijacked was on May 1, 1961, when Antuilo Ramirez Ortiz, a Puerto Rican, forced pilots at gunpoint to fly to Havana, Cuba. As with subsequent hijackings, hijackers would leave the plane once in Cuba and the airliner would return to the United States without injury to passengers.

By the middle and late 1980s, several dramatic terrorist attacks involved blowing up loaded airliners. Kashmiri were blamed for the 1985 destruction of an Air India Boeing 747 over the Atlantic Ocean, killing all 329 people on board. In December 1988 Pan American Airlines Flight 103 blew up over Lockerbie, Scotland, killing all 259 on board and 11 people on the ground. In 1991 two intelligence agents from Libya were charged with the act (one was later found guilty and sentenced to life in prison while the other was found not guilty). Yet another bombing by Libyans in September 1989 killed all 170 on board UTA Flight 772 over the Sahara Desert.

The most deadly air hijacking involved the nineteen Al Qaeda terrorists who hijacked four U.S. airliners on September 11, 2001. They then used the fully-fueled airplanes as bombs when two were flown into the twin towers of the World Trade Center in New York City and one into the Pentagon in Washington, D.C. The fourth crashed in Pennsylvania after passengers fought the hijackers. The fourth plane was on course for Washington, D.C. A total of 3,047 people died in the attacks—2,823 at the World Trade Center including law enforcement officers and firemen responding to the attack, 184 at the Pentagon, and 40 aboard the airliner that went down in Somerset County, Pennsylvania.

The attack led President George W. Bush (1946–; served 2001–) to declare a "War on Terror." He first ordered attacks on Afghanistan where Al Qaeda and its leader Osama bin Laden were headquartered. They were supported and hidden by Afghanistan's Taliban government. The Taliban government fell within weeks but bin Laden was not captured. He was still at large in 2004. President Bush next sent American troops into Iraq in March 2003 to remove Saddam Hussein (1937–) from power and stop Iraq's support of terrorist groups.

Countering terrorism

The term "counterterrorism" as used by government law enforcement agencies means to fight and stop terrorism. Countering terrorism in the United States post-9/11 falls to many government agencies that must coordinate their efforts and intelligence information, much like putting together the pieces of a large jigsaw puzzle. To oversee homeland security coordination President Bush established the Department of Homeland Security (DHS) in October 2001. The president directed DHS to produce the first National Strategy for Homeland Security, which was finished and presented in July 2002. It serves as an overall policy statement for the U.S. government's counterterrorism efforts.

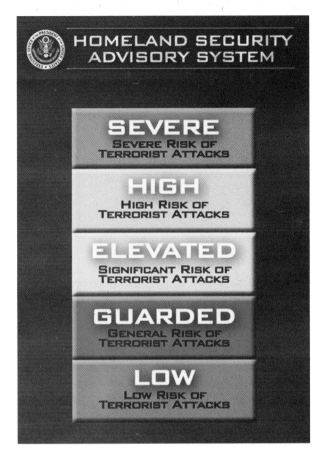

The Homeland Security Advisory System is a means to disseminate information regarding the risk of terrorist acts to federal, state, and local authorities and to the American people. *(AP/Wide World Photos)*

The DHS has the tremendous responsibility of ensuring that the U.S. government's protection and response policies for future terrorist activities are coordinated and effective. In the early 2000s more than one hundred different government organizations had various responsibilities for homeland security and reported to the DHS. The names of only a few of those agencies are the FBI Counter-Intelligence Division, the Central Intelligence Agency (CIA), the National Security Agency (NSA), the Nuclear Regulatory Commission (NRC), the National Security Council, the Defense Intelligence Agency (DIA), and the intelligence departments of the Department of Energy, Department of Transportation, army, navy, air force, and marines. In addition, states and local law enforcement agencies have special counterterrorism units that work together with federal agents to identify and neutralize ongoing national security threats.

Terrorist Threat Integration Center

On May 1, 2003, the Terrorist Threat Integration Center (TTIC) began operation in northern Virginia. The entire national counterterrorism divisions of the FBI and CIA relocated to the single facility. FBI and CIA agents and analysts from every major agency in the U.S. intelligence community work side by side, twenty-four hours a day, seven days a week analyzing intelligence data. These analysts receive a steady stream of intelligence data gathered in states and cities across the nation and from worldwide sources.

The FBI maintains fifty-six field offices and many smaller offices across the nation. In 2004 sixty-six of these offices had Joint Terrorism Task Forces (JTTFs). JTTFs are teams of FBI special agents and state and local law enforcement officers who work together to investigate potential terrorist activity. Local law agencies are considered the "eyes and ears" of intelligence gathering. All leads are funneled immediately to the TTIC for analysis.

The TTIC also receives and sends out continuous information to U.S. intelligence offices worldwide. For example, the FBI maintains forty-five Legal Attaché, or "Legat," offices and four sub-Legat offices around the world. FBI special agents, experts in the foreign country to which they are assigned, help prevent terrorism across international borders that might impact the U.S. homeland.

After one year of operation the TTIC reported in 2004 that another prime source of intelligence information came from questioning captured terrorists. The TTIC gives direction to those sessions and analyzes the information gained. Everyday the TTIC analyzes five to six thousand pieces of information and produces a daily report for the CIA and FBI directors, the president, and senior policymakers. TTIC also sends daily analysis reports to the 2,600 specialists in every major federal agency responsible for counterterrorism activities.

Terrorism lists

In fall of 2001 following the 9/11 attacks, the U.S. government established four lists of terrorists and terrorist-related groups. The goal of the lists is to prevent terrorism and halt support of terrorists. The lists are: (1) State Sponsors of Terrorism; (2) Executive Order 13224—Terrorist Financing; (3) Terrorist Exclusion List (TEL) within the USA Patriot Act; and, (4) Foreign Terrorist Organizations (FTOs).

The State Sponsors of Terrorism list includes any government that consistently supports groups who carry out international terrorism. Restrictions are placed on these countries for as long as they remain on the list. Restrictions can include a ban on sales of arms to the listed countries, no U.S. economic assistance, and trade restrictions. In 2003 seven countries were on the list: Cuba, Iran, Iraq, Libya, North Korea, Sudan, and Syria.

Executive Order 13224 issued on September 23, 2001, enables the U.S. government to block any assets (money) held in any U.S. financial institution that supports designated terrorist groups. Tens of millions of dollars headed for terrorist support have been blocked by the United States and other countries worldwide. The complete Executive Order 13224 list can be found on the U.S. Treasury Web site.

The U.S. Department of State offers rewards in the millions of dollars for information that leads to the arrest and/or conviction of individuals responsible for acts of terrorism. (AP/Wide World Photos)

The Terrorist Exclusion List was created within the USA Patriot Act. President Bush signed the Patriot Act, or Public Law 107-56, into law on October 26, 2001. The Patriot Act is the first comprehensive counterterrorism bill since the Antiterrorism and Effective Death Penalty Act of 1996. The TEL lists organizations known to provide material assistance (money or supplies) to or solicit funds for the Foreign Terrorist Organizations (FTOs) identified by the U.S. State Department.

The secretary of state compiles a FTO list each year. The FTO list has existed since 1997 but took on a new sense of urgency since the 9/11 attacks. The FTO list provides legal authority for the U.S. government to prosecute U.S. citizens or foreign persons within the United States who financially, materially, or physically aid any FTO. The U.S. government may freeze any FTO assets in U.S. financial institutions, and it may deny entry into the United States to any member of a FTO.

The May 2004 FTO list included thirty-six terrorist organizations and forty-one organizations under Other Terrorist Groups. Those under Other Terrorist Groups are assumed to be less active in terrorist activities than the thirty-six FTOs. The FTOs, including their base country of operation and type of terrorist group, were:

> Abu Nidal Organization (ANO)—Iraq, religious
> Abu Sayyaf Group (ASG)—Philippines, nationalistic
> Al Qaeda (The Base)—cells worldwide, formerly Afghanistan until fall 2001, religious
> Al-Aqsa Martyrs Brigade—West Bank, Gaza Strip, and Israel, nationalistic
> Al-Jihad (Egyptian Islamic Jihad)—originally Egypt, religious
> Ansar al-Islam—northern Iraq near Iran border, religious
> Armed Islamic Group (GIA)—Algeria, religious
> Asbat al-Ansar—Lebanon, religious
> Aum Shinrikyo—Japan and Russia, religious
> Basque Fatherland and Liberty (ETA), Northern Spain and southwest France, nationalistic
> Communist Party of Philippines/New People's Army (CPP/NPA)—Philippines, political
> Al-Gama'a al-Islamiyya (Islamic Group)—Egypt, religious
> HAMAS (Islamic Resistance Movement)—West Bank, Gaza Strip, Israel, nationalistic
> Harakat ul-Mujahidin (HUM)—Pakistan, nationalistic
> Hezbollah (Party of God)—Lebanon and cells worldwide, religious
> Islamic Movement of Uzbekistan (IMU)—South Asia, Iran, Tajikistan, religious
> Jaish-e-Mohammed (JEM)—Pakistan, nationalistic

Jemaah Islamiah (JI)—Southeast Asia, religious

Kahane Chai (Kach)—West Bank, Israel (Jewish group), religious

Lashkar-e-Tayyiba (LT)—Pakistan-Kashmir, nationalistic

Lashkar I Jhangvi (LJ)—Pakistan, religious

Liberation Tamil Tigers of Eelam (LTTE)—Sri Lanka, nationalistic

Mujahedin-e Khalq Organization (MEK or MKO)—Iraq near Iran, political

National Liberation Army (ELN-Columbia)—Columbia, Venezuela, political

Palestine Islamic Jihad (PIJ)—West Bank, Gaza Strip, Israel, nationalistic and religious

Palestine Liberation Front (PLF)—Iran, Lebanon, West Bank, nationalistic

Popular Front for the Liberation of Palestine (PFLP)—Syria, West Bank, Gaza Strip, Lebanon, Israel, nationalistic

Popular Front for the Liberation of Palestine-General Command (PFLP-GC)—Syria, nationalistic

Real IRA (RIRA)—Northern Ireland, United Kingdom, Irish Republic, nationalistic

Revolutionary Armed Forces of Columbia (FARC)—Colombia, political

Revolutionary Nuclei—Athens, Greece, political

Revolutionary Organization 17 November (17 November)—Athens, Greece, political

Revolutionary People's Liberation Party/Front (RPLP/F)—Turkey, political

Salafist Group for Call and Combat (GSPC)—Algeria, religious

Sendero Luminoso (Shining Path or SL)—Peru, political

United Self-Defense Forces/Group of Columbia (AUC)—Columbia, political and economic

(Note: many groups have elements of several types of terrorism such as religious, nationalistic, and political.)

For a complete up-to-date FTO list and more information about each terrorist group, go to the U.S. State Department Web site at http://www.state.gov or Center for Defense Information (CDI) Web site at http://www.cdi.org/terrorism/terrorist.cfm.

For More Information

Periodicals

McGeary, Johanna. "Who's the Enemy Now?" *Time,* March 29, 2004.

Web Sites

Center for Defense Information (CDI). http://www.cdi.org (accessed on August 19, 2004).

Department of Health and Human Services, Centers for Disease Control. http://www.cdc.gov (accessed on August 19, 2004).

"Significant Terrorist Incidents, 1961–2003: A Brief Chronology." *U.S. Department of State.* http://www.state.gov/r/pa/ho/pubs/fs/5902.htm (accessed on August 19, 2004).

"Terrorism." *Federal Bureau of Investigation (FBI).* http://www.fbi.gov/terrorinfo/terrorism.htm (accessed on August 19, 2004).

U.S. Department of Homeland Security. http://www.dhs.gov (accessed on August 19, 2004).

U.S. Department of the Treasury. http://www.ustreas.gov/offices/enforcement/ofac/sanctions/terrorism.html (accessed on September 1, 2004).

Cyber Crime

The Internet is a worldwide electronic computer network that connects people and information. It has changed the way Americans communicate, purchase goods and services, educate, and entertain themselves. Possibilities for Internet use seem unlimited. Communication anywhere in the world takes only seconds with electronic mail, or email. Pictures and sound files are easily sent by email. People in areas far from cities can buy as many goods off the Internet as are available in shopping malls. Those who live far from colleges can take courses through the Internet or do research without going to a library. Searching databases such as encyclopedias or directories takes only minutes. News is available online almost as soon as it happens.

Anyone can set up a Web site and post information for the whole world to see. The Internet has also become a major way for companies and the government to conduct business and provide information. By 2004 a serious disruption of computer systems in either a business or government agency can virtually stop all transactions until the problem is corrected. In 1998 65 million Americans at work and at home used the Internet. This figure grew to 149 million by 2001 and

PEW INTERNET & AMERICAN LIFE PROJECT SURVEY "MOST FEARED INTERNET CRIMES" AS OF FEBRUARY 2001*

The percentage of all Americans who say they are most concerned about...

Type of Internet Crime	Percent
Child pornography	50%
Credit card theft	10
Organized terrorism	10
Destructive computer viruses	5
Hackers attacking the government	5
Wide-scale fraud	2
Hackers attacking business	1
Another crime not listed as a choice	13

Source: Pew Internet & American Life Project. "Fear of Online Crime: Americans Support FBI Interception of Criminal Suspects' Email and New Laws to Protect Online Privacy," p. 8. Information available online at http://www.pewinternet.org/reports/toc.asp?Report=32 (cited April 26, 2002).

* Margin of error is ± 2 percent.

(The Gale Group)

530 million worldwide. With the number of Internet users expected to keep climbing, the prospects for electronic commerce (buying and selling of goods) looked bright as sales topped $56 billion by U.S. firms in 2003.

Criminalizing the Internet

While there are many benefits from the Internet, it has also become a powerful tool in the hands of those wishing to engage in criminal activities. Each time an advance in technology becomes available to the public—the telegraph, telephone, automobile, airplane, or the Internet—criminal opportunities increase as well. The Internet provides worldwide, rapid, inexpensive connections, and can be used without revealing one's identity.

Internet crime is also referred to as cyber crime. Existing federal laws that apply to criminal activities committed by traditional means apply to those same activities committed with use of the Internet. For example, existing federal laws for identity theft, credit card theft, securities fraud, and gambling apply to both online and offline activities. Internet crime, however, presents major challenges to law enforcement agencies. Internet criminals not only can hide their identities but can use numerous Internet pathways to make tracking their activities very difficult.

Collecting evidence and prosecuting a cyber criminal requires highly skilled computer sleuths, who must be well equipped and trained. Cooperation is essential between local, state, federal, and international officials since Internet communication moves across many traditional law enforcement regions or geographic areas. The speed of an investigation is also very important since tracing anonymous emails that contain threats of violence can save innocent lives. At the beginning of the twenty-first century, the U.S. government made keeping the Internet safe and secure a top priority.

Computers as targets or criminal tools

Computers can be the target of a criminal activity, a storage place for data about a criminal activity and/or the actual tool used to commit a crime (planning criminal activity). One of the most publicized crimes targeting computers involves

U.S. Attorney General John Ashcroft announcing the results of "Operations Cyber Sweep," an international effort to crack down on Internet fraud and cyber crime.
(AP/Wide World Photos)

unleashing a virus through email. A virus is a computer program that disrupts or destroys existing computer systems. A virus spreads rapidly around the world destroying computer files and costing companies and individuals millions in downtime (time when the computers or networks are shutdown). Most viruses are released by hackers as pranks. A hacker is someone who gains unauthorized access to a specific system. Sometimes hackers may target law enforcement or military computers and read or copy sensitive (secret or private) information. Some are concerned that terrorists will unleash viruses to cripple computer systems that control vital transportation networks.

Computers are also targets for thieves to steal important information. Theft of information takes many forms. A frequent hacking crime involves accessing databanks where credit card numbers are stored. The hacker then uses the credit card numbers for purchases or to charge fake services. Hackers also commit theft-of-service crimes, like accessing telephone equipment systems to get free long distance calling.

Some individuals hack into systems to obtain specific information about another person. Medical records or credit history are favored targets. Using the stolen information, a hacker may attempt to extort or threaten the victim with the release of the information. To keep information quiet the hacker demands a monetary payment.

Another common offense involves illegally using copyrighted materials. A copyright gives an author or publisher the sole right to publish, sell, or distribute original material like computer software programs. Copyrighted material is copied from the computer then offered for sale at a low price to anyone willing to pay. Yet another crime targeting computers is known as "denial of service" or in computer language, "mailbombing." Mailbombing was on the increase in the early 2000s and occurs when a targeted site is flooded with massive amounts of email so the site becomes overloaded and crashes. Popular Web sites such as Yahoo.com, eBay.com, and Amazon.com have all been victims.

The second general type of criminal computer use is the storage of unlawfully obtained data such as stolen credit card numbers. Names and addresses of illegal drug purchasers, pornographic files, and stolen information from corporations are just a few examples of the many types of information stored in computers that involve criminal activities. Even if an offender has deleted his illegal computer files, a trained law enforcement computer expert can usually still obtain the deleted information.

Page-Jacking

Page-jacking is another cyber crime that came into common use in the late 1990s and early twenty-first century. Page-jacking involves using the same key words or Web site descriptions of a legitimate site on a fake site. Search engines like Yahoo or Dogpile use these words to categorize and display sites on a specific topic requested by online users. When users type key words into a search engine, the legitimate site appears on a list along with the bogus site. If users click on the bogus site, they are frequently led to a pornographic site. To make matters worse, when users try to close the window or use the "back" or "forward" keys, they are sent to another pornographic site. Users are "trapped," which is why this kind of online rigging is called "mouse-trapping." Users usually have to crash their computers to get out of the page-jacked sites.

The third general way a computer is used in cyber crime is as a tool used to plan or commit an offense. Most any kind of unlawful act can be planned by way of email. Internet criminal activities include fraud, online child pornography, sale of prescription drugs and controlled substances, sale of firearms, gambling, securities (stocks and bonds) fraud, and stealing or copying software and intellectual property.

Internet fraud

The electronic marketplace allows consumers to purchase a wide variety of goods without ever leaving their homes. Just about anything available in stores is available online. The e-market allows businesses, at low or no cost, to reach consumers worldwide. By the early 2000s people with Internet

A woman sits in front of piles of unauthorized credit card bills that were charged to her name. In one week, thieves had charged more than $30,000 worth of merchandise on credit cards obtained using her identity. *(AP/Wide World Photos)*

access were becoming more and more comfortable purchasing items online. At first, many online customers were afraid to give out their name, address, telephone number, email address, and a credit card number to the Internet seller.

As the number of Internet transactions increased, the Federal Trade Commission (FTC), which is in charge of recording consumer complaints, received complaints of fraud. Fraud is the intentional deception of a person or group for the purpose of stealing property or money. Internet fraud includes any scheme using Web sites, chat rooms, and email to offer nonexistent goods and services to consumers or to communicate false information to consumers. Customers then pay for the fraudulent goods over the Internet with their credit cards. Internet fraud involves a wide variety of schemes limited only by the imagination and creativity of a seller intent on deceiving a buyer. Bogus products such as magnets for pain therapy and weight loss products can be purchased over the Internet.

Online auction fraud is one of the most common complaints received by the FTC. Online auction schemes get thousands of consumers to bid on items, then notifies them that they have the winning bid and should send their money to the seller. The item they bid on and paid for never arrives.

Identity theft has also become a growing concern for Americans as more and more give out their credit card numbers to purchase items from the Internet. There are frequent news reports about people falling prey to online identity theft. Electronic thieves, or e-thieves, access an individual's personal information including credit card numbers. The e-thief then uses the stolen card numbers for services or purchases. Valid credit card holders are responsible for only $50 of unauthorized charges, so the merchant or company selling the products or services becomes the victim.

Online child pornography

Child pornography, images of children involved in sexual activities, is traded on the Internet around the clock. Child pornographers use the Internet's ease of distribution to sell their material to pedophiles (adults who are sexually attracted to children). In addition to purchasing child pornography, pedophiles also visit online chat rooms hoping to lure children into situations for sex. Luring or tricking a minor into sexual activity is prohibited. For example, chatting with a fifteen-year-old girl over the Internet, then suggesting a meeting is illegal conduct. Traveling to a minor's home to engage in sex after meeting by way of Internet chat rooms is also criminal activity that will be prosecuted.

The U.S. Department of Justice prosecuted an increasing number of people for Internet child pornography. The existing federal laws against child pornography are extensive and apply to all kinds of child pornography and the luring of minors (persons under the age of eighteen) online and offline. They prohibit the production, interstate transportation, receiving or distribution of visual images of a minor engaged in sexual conduct, and luring a minor into sexual encounters.

During a child pornography investigation, the FBI, the Criminal Division of the Department of Justice, and the U.S. Attorney General's Office have authority to gain access to subscriber information from an Internet service provider (ISP), such as America Online (AOL), MSN, or Hotmail. If an ISP becomes aware of violations, they must report them to the National Center for Missing and Exploited Children, who then notifies federal law enforcement agencies.

The biggest challenge to law enforcement in child pornography cases is the anonymous nature of Internet communication. The offenses also occur at high speeds across the entire nation crossing many law enforcement jurisdictions. Generally seller and buyer are in different states or could be anywhere worldwide. As in other Internet criminal activities, the coordination between state, local, and federal law enforcement officials is essential.

Sale of prescription drugs and controlled substances

The Internet is used to sell legal prescription drugs and controlled substances such as various narcotic painkillers or steroids used in bodybuilding. Increasingly, dealers of illegal drugs or controlled chemicals such as steroids that only a licensed pharmacy may dispense are using the Internet for their transactions. Three types of online pharmacies exist on the Internet:

The owner of a business that uses the Internet to order lower-cost prescription drugs through an online pharmacy. *(AP/Wide World Photos)*

1. Legitimate online pharmacies—they operate in a traditional manner by requiring a valid prescription from a licensed physician. These pharmacies employ state licensed pharmacists.

2. Diagnose and prescribe pharmacies—they ask customers to fill out online medical questionnaires and prescribe medications based on the questionnaire.

3. Illegitimate pharmacies—they allow customers to purchase prescription drugs without any prescriptions at all.

The first type of online pharmacy legally dispenses drugs. Various forms of criminal intent may possibly exist in the second and third types. Consumers may not be able to confirm whether or not the pharmacy is legitimate. Some of these pharmacies are scams, taking customer names and credit card numbers but never sending any products. Some dispense mislabeled, diluted (watered down), or fake drugs.

The Federal Food, Drug, and Cosmetic Act (FDCA) prohibits the manufacture and distribution of mislabeled or altered drugs. Keeping Americans safe from fraudulent online pharmacies is a challenge to law enforcement since both federal and state officials have jurisdiction over the sale of prescription drugs. In addition to federal laws, each state has its own set of laws and legal requirements for prescription drug sales. Online pharmacies sell in all states but what may be legal in one state may not be legal in another. Further complicating an already complicated situation, many pharmacy Web sites are based outside the United States and offer drugs, both legal and illegal, to customers living in the United States.

Online sale of firearms

The Gun Control Act of 1968 requires whoever imports, manufactures, or deals in firearms to obtain a federal firearms license. The Brady Act of 1993 requires all federal firearms licensees (FFLs) who sell firearms to perform background checks on customers and maintain careful records of gun sales. A criminal, fugitive from the law, or drug addict would not pass the background check. Under the Brady Act, the U.S. government estimates 400,000 such individuals have been turned down for gun purchase since 1993.

The Internet provides an easy alternative to a gun store for acquiring a firearm. Unlicensed dealers, however, may advertise and sell guns over the Internet without keeping records. Anyone willing to pay can obtain a gun online without a background check. If the gun is later used to commit a crime, it usually cannot be traced to the purchaser—who is most likely the offender or directly associated with the offender.

A violation of the Gun Control Act occurs when a gun offered online is sold to an individual in another state from where the online advertisement originates. The act prohibits selling a handgun to a resident of another state. Shipping across state lines is also banned. Yet guns for sale online reach people across the country. Online state to state sales and shipping occurs continuously in violation of federal law.

Online gambling

Federal law prohibits individuals from betting on sports or gambling contests using a "wire communication facility," which includes the Internet. Yet the Internet allows immedi-

Online Encryption

Encryption is the use of secret codes that can be translated into meaningful communications only by authorized persons who have knowledge of the code. Encryption has been studied and employed for decades by governments and militaries. For example, a primary function of U.S. intelligence agencies during World War II (1939–45; war in which Great Britain, France, the Soviet Union, the United States, and their allied forces defeated Germany, Italy, and Japan) involved deciphering German military codes that had information about the movements and missions of German submarines.

The Internet has opened up new uses for encryption, many of which are designed to deter online criminal activity. Companies add encryption into important files like trade secrets. If a hacker gets into their network, the files will be meaningless to him. Companies can encrypt important data such as credit card numbers to protect their customers. This tactic is being used on an increasing basis to reduce Internet fraud and identity theft.

Just as encryption is beneficial to Internet users, its features attract cyber criminals. Cyber criminals encrypt communication and the stored files of their activities. Law enforcement agencies cannot usually obtain wiretaps for a criminal's phone, so encryption often keeps the secrets of cyber criminals safe. Public safety is at risk when criminals including terrorists encrypt communication. Should a code be broken by a law enforcement agency, the criminal can easily and quickly switch to another coding system. In 2004 U.S. law enforcement agencies, including the FBI, constantly asked Congress to designate more and more money for technology to fight cyber criminal encryption.

ate and anonymous communication that makes it difficult to trace gambling activity. Internet sites can be altered or removed in a matter of minutes. For these reasons organized crime operates Internet gambling sites.

Operators alter gambling software to be in their favor so the customer always loses. Unlike real casinos that are highly regulated, Internet gambling is unregulated and dangerous. Individuals gambling on the Internet risk providing credit card numbers and money to criminal gambling operators. Further, minors can gamble on the sites since the Internet is unaware of the age of its users. All a minor needs is access to a credit card number. Internet gambling also lures compulsive gamblers who may suffer devastating financial losses.

Internet securities fraud

Investors consider the Internet a primary tool for researching and trading securities. Securities are stocks and bonds, both financial investments. The number of individuals opening online investment accounts increases every year. With a few mouse clicks investors can gather a great deal of information about a company's stock and decide what to buy and sell. Online they can buy or sell quickly and cheaply.

The same benefits investors enjoy can be used by those intent on committing securities fraud. Easy access, speed, and operating anonymously all create a favorable atmosphere for securities fraud. Law enforcement must deal with three basic types of security fraud:

1. Market manipulation—the most common fraud scheme, involves creating fake or misleading information on a particular stock to run the price up. For example, the owner of a lower priced stock puts fake highly positive announcements about the stock in online newsletters, message boards, and other Internet securities information sites. Investors read this information and begin buying the stock, which in turn makes its price go up rapidly. The owner who made up the phony information sells his stock as soon as the price goes up and makes a large profit. The information is discovered to be false, the stock price falls, and everyone who bought the stock loses money. This scheme is referred to as "pump and dump."

2. Bogus stock—this involves offering stock that does not really exist. For example an unregistered criminal stock dealer may offer phony stock in eel farms in Oregon, pineapple plantations in Hawaii, or most anything else the dealer imaginatively creates. To hundreds of people cruising the Internet looking for investments, they invest their money only to lose it all. The bogus dealer deposits the money in a foreign bank account and leaves the country.

3. Touting—this occurs when a certain individual or group, often a stock investment advisor known and trusted in the investment community, is paid to "tout," or highly recommend, a particular stock as an excellent investment. The touters, however, do not reveal that they are being paid to tout the stock. Investors think they are receiving

honest information when in fact they are victims of a scheme called "bought and paid for," meaning the advisor was paid to put out the positive information resulting in an increase or run-up of the stock price.

The Securities and Exchange Commission (SEC) is charged with overseeing stock transactions and brings criminal charges against violators. The Securities Act of 1933 and Securities Exchange Act of 1934 are the primary laws governing securities fraud. Federal laws also require anyone acting as a stockbroker or dealer, either online or offline, to register with the SEC. The biggest challenge for the SEC is keeping up with rapid growth of the Internet. SEC staff investigators find it difficult to keep pace with the many securities scams that originate not only in the United States but from anywhere in the world. Many Internet fraud criminals target U.S. investors without ever coming into the United States.

Intellectual property theft

Intellectual property (IP) theft is defined as theft of material that is copyrighted, the theft of trade secrets, and trademark violations. A copyright is the legal right of an author, publisher, composer, or other person who creates a work to exclusively print, publish, distribute, or perform the work in public. The United States leads the world in the creation and selling of IP products to buyers nationwide and internationally. Examples of copyrighted material commonly stolen online are computer software, recorded music, movies, and electronic games.

Theft of trade secrets means the theft of ideas, plans, methods, technologies, or any sensitive information from all types of industries including manufacturers, financial service institutions, and the computer industry. Trade secrets are plans for a higher speed computer, designs for a highly fuel-efficient car, a company's manufacturing procedures, or the recipe for a popular salad dressing, cookie mix, or barbeque sauce. These secrets are owned by the company and give it a competitive edge. Theft of trade secrets damages the competitive edge and therefore the economic base of a business.

A trademark is the registered name or identifying symbol of a product that can be used only by the product's owner. A trademark violation involves counterfeiting or copying brand name products such as well-known types of shoes, clothing, and electronics equipment and selling them as the genuine or original product.

The two forms of IP most frequently involved in cyber crime are copyrighted material and trade secrets. Piracy is a term used to describe IP theft—piracy of software, piracy of music, etc. Theft of IP affects the entire U.S. economy. Billions of dollars are lost every year to IP pirates. For example, thieves sell pirated computer software for games or programs to millions of Internet users. The company that actually produced the real product loses these sales and royalties rightfully due to the original creator.

Historically, when there were no computers, IP crimes involved a lot of time and labor. Movie or music tapes had to be copied, physically produced, and transported for sale. An individual had to make the sale in person. To steal a trade secret, actual paper plans, files, or blueprints would have to be physically taken from a company's building and likewise sold in person.

The owner of Napster at a 2001 news conference following a court ruling that the company must stop allowing users to share copyrighted music. *(AP/Wide World Photos)*

In the twenty-first century software, music, and trade secret pirates operate through the Internet. Anything that can be digitized—reduced to a series of zeroes and ones—can be transmitted rapidly from one computer to another. There is no reduction of quality in second, third, or fourth generation copies. Pirated digital copies of copyrighted work transmitted over the Internet are known as "warez." Warez groups are responsible for illegally copying and distributing hundreds of millions of dollars of copyrighted material.

Pirated trade secrets are sold to other companies or illegal groups. Trade secrets no longer have to be physically stolen from a company. Instead, corporate plans and secrets are

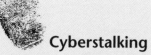

Cyberstalking

Cyberstalking is use of the Internet and email to "stalk" another individual. The crime of stalking has existed for decades; stalking refers to repeated harassment of someone where the stalker acts in a threatening behavior toward the victim. Threatening behaviors include following the victim, appearing at the victim's place of work or near his or her home, then making eye contact so the victim knows someone is following, and leaving threatening messages on paper or the telephone. Stalking leaves its victims fearful of bodily harm or death.

The use of the Internet provides easy pathways for stalking. In 2000 the Working Group on Unlawful Conduct Involving the Use of the Internet, an agency appointed by President Bill Clinton (1946–; served 1993–2001) reported on a recent example of Internet stalking: a fifty-year-old security guard used the Internet to stalk a woman who had rejected his sexual advances. He retaliated to her rejection by posting her personal details to the Internet. These included her physical description, address and telephone number, and even included details about how one could bypass her home security system. As a result of the posted message, at least six men came to her house and knocked on her door. The security guard was arrested, pled guilty, and sentenced to prison for Internet stalking.

downloaded by pirates onto a computer disc. The stolen information can be transmitted worldwide in minutes. Trade secret pirates find pathways into a company's computer systems and download the items to be copied. Companies keep almost everything in their computer files. Pirated copies are sold over the Internet to customers who provide their credit card numbers then download the copy.

Intellectual property pirates use the computer to steal vast amounts of copyrighted material and cause severe damage to the victimized companies. IP pirates never have to make sales in person or travel, their costs are minimal, and profits are huge. Internet pirates target the online shoppers who look for discounted, but legitimate, products. They do so by emails and Internet advertisements that seem to be the real thing. Not just individuals, but companies, educational institutions, and even government agencies have been tricked by IP pirates into buying stolen goods.

Arrest and prosecution of IP crimes is difficult for U.S. law enforcement agencies. U.S. laws combating this new type of crime were only beginning to be written by the early twenty-first century. Very little stops IP pirates, and organized crime groups have become involved as well. The profits they generate from IP crimes finances many other criminal activities such as drug trafficking, illegal gun sales, gambling, and prostitution (see chapter 7, Organized Crime).

Intellectual property pirates also come from many foreign countries such as China, South Korea, Vietnam (Southeast Asia), and Russia. International IP law is practically nonexistent. While offline IP violations can be investigated by the traditional law enforcement tactics such as using undercover agents, cyber IP criminals operate only in cyberspace and can disappear in seconds.

Challenges for law enforcement

As lawful use of the Internet expands, so does cyber crime. Law enforcement agencies must deal with crime unheard of a decade earlier. Online crimes range from chat room threats of violence against a person or property to organized, complicated schemes by those who know their way around cyberspace. While a chat room threat made by someone making no effort to hide their identity is generally easy to trace, highly organized schemes can be nearly impossible to track. Two major challenges to law enforcement include jurisdiction issues and discovering the identity of a cyber criminal.

Jurisdiction

Traditional offline crimes are committed at a particular geographic location by a person with a street address at a precise point in the United States or in another country. Which law enforcement agency investigates the crime is easily determined by jurisdictional or geographical boundaries—city, state, or country. Internet crimes are committed in cyberspace, on worldwide computer linkages. Local, state, national, or international boundaries do not exist for cyber crime.

A phony online pharmacy in New York, for example, might sell prescription drugs to residents in a number of states such as Florida, Alabama, and Georgia. Each state would have to subpoena (call for) records from New York,

A Pennsylvanian police officer demonstrates Global Positioning System technology, which incorporates satellites and cell phone technology to track movements of various suspects. *(AP/Wide World Photos)*

and New York would have to agree to help each state investigate the scam. One state might refer its case to New York, but if no one was victimized in New York, the case might never be investigated.

Jurisdictional problems are more severe when they involve international cyber crime. A group selling nonexistent items might be based in India or Thailand but targets buyers in the United States. It is possible to route communication through several countries before reaching the United States. State law enforcement agencies would have to get assistance from the Department of Justice's international affairs officers who in turn would contact each foreign country involved. All of this is made more difficult because a criminal's trail ends as soon as he or she disconnects from the Internet.

Identity

Another problem facing cyber investigators is identification of the cyber criminal. Cyberspace is considered an anonymous medium where someone's identity is unknown and cyber criminals can completely hide their real identities. They can change origination sites almost instantaneously or proceed through many sites before targeting a victim. Experienced cyber criminals alter both the source and destination of their communications. Further transmission information may be kept by Internet providers like AOL and MSN for only a short period of time.

Cyber criminals can easily hide their identities; they create false personal information and work on the Internet under many screen names, or aliases. With billions of people using the Internet, it can be nearly impossible to trace a skilled cyber criminal.

In 2004 the FBI and Computer Criminal Intellectual Property Section (CCIPS), both in the Department of Justice, had become the lead law enforcement agencies dealing with cyber crime. The FBI Investigative Programs, Cyber Investigations Unit is charged with protecting the nation from cyber crime. It investigates terrorist activities on the Internet as well as cyber criminals, including sexual predators. The FBI provides training to local, state, and federal law enforcement agencies at its headquarters in Quantico, Virginia, and other locations nationwide.

The CCIPS has a team of about forty lawyers who concentrate on all types of cyber crime. CCIPS prosecutes cases and advises and trains prosecutors and law enforcement agents in combating cyber crime. They also advise on and propose needed legislation to help control cyber crime and coordinate international efforts to deal with computer crime. The CCIPS oversees the National Cybercrime Training Partnership (NCTP), composed of local, state, and federal law enforcement agencies. The NCTP provides education in the latest law enforcement techniques for fighting cyber crime.

The FBI and National White-Collar Crime Center (NW3C) together established the Internet Crime Complaint Center

(IC3) to receive, develop, and refer complaints of cyber crime to the proper law enforcement agency. The IC3 receives complaints of all types of cyber criminal activities.

For More Information

Books

Clifford, Ralph D., ed. *Cybercrime: The Investigation, Prosecution, and Defense of a Computer-Related Crime.* Durham, NC: Carolina Academic Press, 2001.

Sherman, Mark. *Introduction to Cyber Crime.* Washington, DC: Federal Judicial Center, 2000.

Wallace, Jonathan, and Mark Mangan. *Sex, Laws, and Cyberspace.* New York: M&T Books, 1996.

Web Sites

Computer Crime and Intellectual Property Section (CCIPS) of the Criminal Division of the U.S. Department of Justice. http://www.cybercrime.gov (accessed on August 19, 2004).

"Cyber Education Letter." *Investigative Programs: Cyber Investigations. Federal Bureau of Investigation.* http://www.fbi.gov/cyberinvest/ cyberedletter.htm (accessed on August 19, 2004).

"The Electronic Frontier: The Challenge of Unlawful Conduct Involving the Use of the Internet." *U.S. Department of Justice.* http://www.usdoj. gov/criminal/cybercrime/unlawful.htm (accessed on August 19, 2004).

Internet Crime Complaint Center. http://www.ic3.gov (accessed on August 19, 2004).

Investigative Programs: Cyber Investigations. Federal Bureau of Investigation. http://www.fbi.gov/cyberinvest/cyberhome.htm (accessed on August 19, 2004).

"Online Child Pornography Innocent Images National Initiative." *Investigative Programs: Crimes against Children. Federal Bureau of Investigation.* http://www.fbi.gov/hq/cid/cac/innocent.htm (accessed on August 19, 2004).

12

Causes of Crime

How do some people decide to commit a crime? Do they think about the benefits and the risks? Why do some people commit crimes regardless of the consequences? Why do others never commit a crime, no matter how desperate their circumstances? Criminology is the study of crime and criminals by specialists called criminologists. Criminologists study what causes crime and how it might be prevented.

Throughout history people have tried to explain what causes abnormal social behavior, including crime. Efforts to control "bad" behavior go back to ancient Babylon's Code of Hammurabi some 3,700 years ago. Later in the seventeenth century European colonists in North America considered crime and sin the same thing. They believed evil spirits possessed those who did not conform to social norms or follow rules. To maintain social order in the settlements, persons who exhibited antisocial behavior had to be dealt with swiftly and often harshly.

By the twenty-first century criminologists looked to a wide range of factors to explain why a person would commit crimes. These included biological, psychological, social, and economic

Throughout history people have tried to explain why a person would commit crimes. Some consider a life of crime better than a regular job—at least until they are caught. *(© Bettmann/Corbis)*

factors. Usually a combination of these factors is behind a person who commits a crime.

Reasons for committing a crime include greed, anger, jealously, revenge, or pride. Some people decide to commit a crime and carefully plan everything in advance to increase gain and decrease risk. These people are making choices about their behavior; some even consider a life of crime better than a regular job—believing crime brings in greater rewards, admiration, and excitement—at least until they are caught. Others get an adrenaline rush when successfully carrying out a dangerous crime. Others commit crimes on impulse, out of rage or fear.

The desire for material gain (money or expensive belongings) leads to property crimes such as robberies, burglaries, white-collar crimes, and auto thefts. The desire for control, revenge, or power leads to violent crimes such as murders, assaults, and rapes. These violent crimes usually occur on impulse or the spur of the moment when emotions run high. Property crimes are usually planned in advance.

Explaining crime

Modern criminology began in Europe and America in the late eighteenth century. During this time people began to accept scientific explanations for occurrences in the world around them and rule out supernatural influences. People increasingly believed individuals had control over their own actions. The idea that people were driven by reason and influenced by their social environment began to dominate explanations about why people behaved the way they did. Naturally, such ideas changed how people thought about criminal behavior as well.

The belief that individuals could be rehabilitated or treated gained more acceptance since crime involved weaknesses in the individual and not mysterious supernatural forces. In addition, special treatment was given to children, the insane, and the mentally disabled in the judicial system since they were less capable of understanding right and wrong.

Explanations about how people became criminals varied for the next two centuries. In the nineteenth century it was

Italian criminologist Cesare Lombroso believed that some people were simply born criminals. *(The Library of Congress)*

believed that people with certain physical abnormalities, insanity, or the excessively poor were considered more likely to be criminals. Late in the twentieth century other factors such as peer pressure, substance abuse, family or school problems, lack of money, and body chemistry figured into the mix.

Throughout time various explanations for criminal behavior fell into two basic categories—individual abnormalities, both physical and psychological; and social environment, which included financial matters, such as whether a person was rich, poor, or in between.

Physical abnormalities

In the nineteenth century criminologists focused on the physical characteristics and sanity of an individual. They believed it was "predetermined" or that people had no control over whether they would lead a life of crime. For example, criminologists believed people with smaller heads, sloping foreheads, large jaws and ears, and certain heights and weights had a greater chance to be criminals. Race was also a determining factor. Some criminologists believed criminals were more like savages or primitive humans, and somehow less human than law-abiding citizens.

Italian criminologist Cesare Lombroso (1835–1909), who believed some people were simply born criminals, published a book in 1906 called *Crime: Its Causes and Remedies*. Though many of his theories about visible physical traits were not supported by other criminologists, Lombroso did identify some traits still considered important in the twenty-first century such as the occurrence of head injuries. Later research showed head injuries often limited a person's ability to control violent outbursts.

Psychological disorders

As late as the 1950s researchers continued to investigate the relationship of body types to delinquency and crime. Aside from biological traits indicating a natural tendency toward criminal activity by some individuals, Lombroso and other early twentieth century researchers also reasoned that criminal behavior could be a direct result of psychological disorders. They believed these mental disorders could be diagnosed and possibly cured. If this was true, then criminal activity could be considered a disease and the offender could be "cured" through psychiatric treatment. Research by Lombroso and others also led to the use of expert medical witnesses in the courtroom during criminal trials.

In 1941 American psychiatrist Herve Cleckley (1903–1984) used the term psychopathy, or sociopathy, in the book *The Mask of Sanity* to describe a form of mental illness. People showing sociopathic traits were antisocial, often destructive, and showed little emotion. Such personality disturbances, he believed, could lead to criminal behavior.

Social and economic factors

In addition to studying the biological and psychological causes of criminal behavior, others looked toward society in general for possible causes. In the early 1900s researchers believed social changes occurring in the United States, such as an industrial economy replacing the earlier agricultural economy (industrialization) and the growth of cities (urbanization), as well as the steady flow of immigrants from eastern Europe affected crime levels. A reform movement, known as the Progressive Movement, attempted to solve increasing crime stemming from social causes.

As part of the growing concern, the University of Chicago's Department of Sociology, the first of its kind formed in 1892, focused on how city problems could lead to criminal behavior. By the 1930s and 1940s its pioneering research efforts became known as the "Chicago School" of thought, and influenced research across the nation and abroad. The researchers claimed criminals were ordinary people of all racial backgrounds who were profoundly influenced by the poverty and the social instability of their neighborhoods. They claimed

Broken Windows

In the 1990s a new idea spread through the criminal justice field concerning the influence of a person's social environment on crime rates. The idea was that general disorder in the neighborhood leads to increased antisocial behavior and eventually to serious crime. For most of the twentieth century, police primarily reacted to serious crimes such as rape, murder, and robbery often with little overall success in curbing crime rates. "Broken Windows," referring to a neighborhood of abandoned vehicles, vacant buildings with actual broken windows, and litter scattered around, is an idea that contends much of serious crime comes from civil disorder. So, the thinking went, if authorities eliminated disorder, then serious crimes would drop.

Disorder creates fear among citizens of unsafe streets; they avoid public areas allowing criminals to gain a foothold. The neighborhood goes into a downward spiral because as crime increases, then disorder increases further. Back and forth the spiral such a poor social and economic environment could produce all types of crime.

Other researchers looked at various ways society can influence crime. Criminologist Edwin Sutherland (1883–1950), influenced by the Chicago School, first published *Principles of Criminology* in 1939. Sutherland argued that criminal behavior was learned, not an inherited trait. Exposure to crime, either through relatives or peers, gave a youth frustrated with his or her social status a choice to pursue crime. These bad influences could be lessened by good relationships with parents, teachers, an employer, or the community.

Income and education

Another theory from 1930s criminologists was that unemployment could be a major cause of crime. In the United States, employment opportunities have been directly related to education. In 1938 sociologist Robert K. Merton (1910–) offered a social theory that crime occurs when society sets goals for its members, such as making money to buy a variety of material goods, but creates barriers to these goes. During the 1990s New York police commissioner William Bratton aggressively applied Broken Windows theory to New York City neighborhoods. His department attacked minor crimes such as public drinking, panhandling (begging for money), prostitution (selling sex for money), and various other kinds of disorderly conduct.

Once minor offenses were significantly reduced in an area, the number of serious crimes decreased as well. Felonies decreased by 27 percent after only two years. One factor they found was that many people committing minor crimes were also the ones committing more serious offenses. For ex-

ample, by cracking down on people evading subway fares, police found many offenders carried illegal weapons and had outstanding arrest warrants. Subway crimes of all types dropped dramatically after enforcing collection of fares.

Police found Broken Windows a convenient way to control serious crime at less cost. As some critics also pointed out, it was simpler for the city to crack down on minor crimes than address social problems like poverty and limited education opportunities —which probably caused much of the criminal behavior in the Broken Window communities in the first place.

achievements. Society teaches that persistence and hard work lead to personal financial rewards; however, educational opportunities are often limited to those who can afford to attend college. People who do not receive higher education or college degrees are often forced to take lower paying jobs. Some attempt to achieve material success through illegal means; in this sense social forces can lead a person into crime.

The belief that education plays an enormous role in deterring crime led to educational programs and job training in prisons. Many correctional systems require inmates to attend classes to gain a basic education. Education and job training not only provide a way to find a job and make a legal living, but potentially places the person into a better social environment once he or she is back in society.

Criminologists believe a good job creates social and personal attachments to a person's community that in turn influence whether or not to commit a crime. A person is less likely to commit a crime, even if there will be substantial rewards, if he or she is tied to the community and is respected by its members.

Inmates at an Oregon state penitentiary work at getting their General Education Diploma (GED) while in prison. *(AP/Wide World Photos)*

A matter of choice

In the 1960s some criminologists decided their studies and the U.S. judicial system were biased against minorities, the poor, and women. As a result they broadened their focus from the poor and working classes to other crime settings, such as white-collar crime in corporations and governments. Street crime, they asserted, cost society $15 billion annually while white-collar crime could reach over $200 billion annually. Researchers believed it was time to look at why someone who already had a good job and comfortable life might choose a life of crime.

Just as Sutherland believed criminal behavior was learned like other social behavior, some researchers believed the process a person went through in deciding to commit a crime was not much different than how someone made other decisions. Like Merton and Sutherland, they claimed it was not personal inborn traits causing crime but social influences affecting the decision to commit a crime. A person weighed the possible penalty against the anticipated benefits or gains of performing a crime. This is particularly true for white-collar crimes where wealth is the basis for the criminal act.

People vary in how much risk they are willing to accept, in general life or in the commission of a crime; so certain biological and psychological personal factors do enter into the decision. One major factor influencing the willingness of a person to accept the risk of committing a crime is the stability of their employment. People who lose their jobs are often faced with desperate financial situations. Historical research clearly shows that as unemployment increases, so does crime.

People who are unemployed or working for minimum wage obviously feel a greater need to take risks to support themselves and their families. Studies have shown, however, that once a person begins criminal activity, they may still continue to commit crimes even after getting a good job. Past criminal behavior, it seems, especially if the person was never caught or punished, also influences whether someone will commit more crimes.

In the late twentieth century criminologists studied various factors that may influence a person's decision to commit a crime. These included the risk of arrest and punishment (deterrence), parental relations, peer pressure, education, brain function, body chemistry, substance abuse, and the availability of weapons.

Discouraging the choice of crime

The purpose of punishment is to discourage a person from committing a crime. Punishment is supposed to make criminal behavior less attractive and more risky. Imprisonment and loss of income is a major hardship to many people. Another way of influencing choice is to make crime more difficult or to reduce the opportunities. This can be as simple as better lighting, locking bars on auto steering wheels, the presence of guard dogs, or high technology improvements such as security systems and photographs on credit cards.

A person weighing the risks of crime considers factors like how many police officers are in sight where the crime will take

Home security consultant conferring with client. Security systems and guard dogs can make crime more difficult or reduce the opportunities for it to occur. *(Ms. Martha Tabor/Working Images Photographs)*

place. Studies of New York City records between 1970 and 1999 showed that as the police force in the city grew, less crime was committed. A change in a city's police force, however, is usually tied to its economic health. Normally as unemployment rises, city revenues decrease because fewer people are paying taxes. This causes cutbacks in city services including the police force. So a rise in criminal activity may not be due to fewer police, but rather rising unemployment.

Another means of discouraging people from choosing criminal activity is the length of imprisonment. After the 1960s many believed more prisons and longer sentences would deter crime. Despite the dramatic increase in number of prisons and imposing mandatory lengthy sentences, however, the number of crimes continued to rise. The number of violent crimes doubled from 1970 to 1998. Property crimes rose from 7.4 million to 11 million, while the number of people placed in state and federal prisons grew from 290,000 in 1977 to over 1.2 million in 1998. Apparently longer prison sentences had little effect on discouraging criminal behavior.

Parental relations

Cleckley's ideas on sociopathy were adopted in the 1980s to describe a "cycle of violence" or pattern found in family histories. A "cycle of violence" is where people who grow up with abuse or antisocial behavior in the home will be much more likely to mistreat their own children, who in turn will often follow the same pattern.

Children who are neglected or abused are more likely to commit crimes later in life than others. Similarly, sexual abuse in childhood often leads these victims to become sexual predators as adults. Many inmates on death row have histories of some kind of severe abuse. The neglect and abuse of children often progresses through several generations. The cycle of abuse, crime, and sociopathy keeps repeating itself.

The cycle of violence concept, based on the quality of early life relationships, has its positive counterpart. Supportive and loving parents who respond to the basic needs of their child instill self-confidence and an interest in social environments. These children are generally well-adjusted in relating to others and are far less likely to commit crimes.

By the late twentieth century the general public had not accepted that criminal behavior is a psychological disorder but rather a willful action. The public cry for more prisons and tougher sentences outweighed rehabilitation and the treatment of criminals. Researchers in the twenty-first century, however, continued to look at psychological stress as a driving force behind some crimes.

Children who are neglected or abused commit substantially more crimes later in life than others.
(© Roy Morsch/Corbis)

Heredity and brain activity

Searching for the origins of antisocial personality disorders and their influence over crime led to studies of twins and adopted children in the 1980s. Identical twins have the exact same genetic makeup. Researchers found that identical twins were twice as likely to have similar criminal behavior than fraternal twins who have similar but not identical genes, just like any two siblings. Other research indicated that adopted children had greater similarities of crime rates to their biological parents than to their adoptive parents. These studies suggested a genetic basis for some criminal behavior.

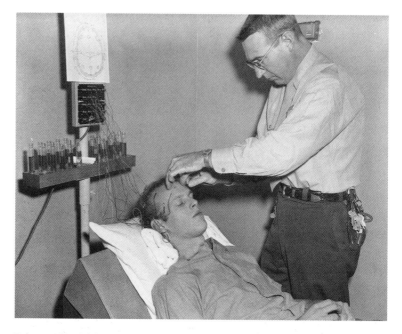

Prisoner in California being prepared for a lobotomy in 1961. At the time, many psychiatrists believed that criminal behavior was lodged in certain parts of the brain, and lobotomies were frequently done on prisoners. *(© Ted Streshinsky/Corbis)*

With new advances in medical technology, the search for biological causes of criminal behavior became more sophisticated. In 1986 psychologist Robert Hare identified a connection between certain brain activity and antisocial behavior. He found that criminals experienced less brain reaction to dangerous situations than most people. Such a brain function, he believed, could lead to greater risk-taking in life, with some criminals not fearing punishment as much as others.

Studies related to brain activity and crime continued into the early twenty-first century. Testing with advanced instruments probed the inner workings of the brain. With techniques called computerized tomography (CT scans), magnetic resonance imaging (MRI), and positron emission tomography (PET), researchers searched for links between brain activity and a tendency to commit crime. Each of these tests can reveal brain activity.

Research on brain activity investigated the role of neurochemicals, substances the brain releases to trigger body activity, and hormones in influencing criminal behavior. Studies indicated that increased levels of some neurochemicals, such as serotonin, decreases aggression. Serotonin is a substance produced by the central nervous system that has broad sweeping effects on the emotional state of the individual. In contrast higher levels of others, such as dopamine, increased aggression. Dopamine is produced by the brain and affects heart rate and blood pressure. Researchers expected to find that persons who committed violent crimes have reduced levels of serotonin and higher levels of dopamine. This condition would have led to periods of greater activity including aggression if the person is prone towards aggression.

In the early twenty-first century researchers continued investigating the relationship between neurochemicals and antisocial behavior, yet connections proved complicated. Studies showed, for example, that even body size could influence the effects of neurochemicals and behavior.

Hormones

Hormones are bodily substances that affect how organs in the body function. Researchers also looked at the relationship between hormones, such as testosterone and cortisol, and criminal behavior. Testosterone is a sex hormone produced by male sexual organs that cause development of masculine body traits. Cortisol is a hormone produced by adrenal glands located next to the kidneys that effects how quickly food is processed by the digestive system. Higher cortisol levels leads to more glucose to the brain for greater energy, such as in times of stress or danger. Animal studies showed a strong link between high levels of testosterone and aggressive behavior. Testosterone measurements in prison populations also showed relatively high levels in the inmates as compared to the U.S. adult male population in general.

Studies of sex offenders in Germany showed that those who were treated to remove testosterone as part of their sentencing became repeat offenders only 3 percent of the time. This rate was in stark contrast to the usual 46 percent repeat rate. These and similar studies indicate testosterone can have a strong bearing on criminal behavior.

Cortisol is another hormone linked to criminal behavior. Research suggested that when the cortisol level is high a person's attention is sharp and he or she is physically active. In contrast, researchers found low levels of cortisol were associated with short attention spans, lower activity levels, and often linked to antisocial behavior including crime. Studies of violent adults have shown lower levels of cortisol; some believe this low level serves to numb an offender to the usual fear associated with committing a crime and possibly getting caught.

It is difficult to isolate brain activity from social and psychological factors, as well as the effects of substance abuse, parental relations, and education. Yet since some criminals are driven by factors largely out of their control, punishment will not be an effective deterrent. Help and treatment become the primary responses.

Education

Conforming to Merton's earlier sociological theories, a survey of inmates in state prisons in the late 1990s showed very low education levels. Many could not read or write above elementary school levels, if at all. The most common crimes committed by these inmates were robbery, burglary, automobile theft, drug trafficking, and shoplifting. Because of their poor educational backgrounds, their employment histories consisted of mostly low wage jobs with frequent periods of unemployment.

Employment at minimum wage or below living wage does not help deter criminal activity. Even with government social services, such as public housing, food stamps, and medical care, the income of a minimum wage household still falls short of providing basic needs. People must make a choice between continued long-term low income and the prospect of profitable crime. Gaining further education, of course, is another option, but classes can be expensive and time consuming. While education can provide the chance to get a better job, it does not always overcome the effects of abuse, poverty, or other limiting factors.

Peer influence

A person's peer group strongly influences a decision to commit crime. For example, young boys and girls who do not fit into expected standards of academic achievement or participate in sports or social programs can sometimes become

Crack cocaine pipe displayed by police. Drugs and alcohol impair judgment and reduce inhibitions, giving a person greater courage to commit a crime. *(© Bettmann/Corbis)*

lost in the competition. Children of families who cannot afford adequate clothing or school supplies can also fall into the same trap. Researchers believe these youth may abandon schoolmates in favor of criminal gangs, since membership in a gang earns respect and status in a different manner. In gangs, antisocial behavior and criminal activity earns respect and street credibility.

Like society in general, criminal gangs are usually focused on material gain. Gangs, however, resort to extortion, fraud, and theft as a means of achieving it. The fear of young people, mostly boys, joining gangs influenced many government projects in the last half of the twentieth century including President Lyndon Johnson's (1908–1973; served 1963–69) "War on Crime" programs.

Drugs and alcohol

Some social factors pose an especially strong influence over a person's ability to make choices. Drug and alcohol abuse is one such factor. The urge to commit crime to support a drug habit definitely influences the decision process. Both drugs and alcohol impair judgment and reduce inhibitions (socially defined rules of behavior), giving a person greater courage to commit a crime. Deterrents such as long prison sentences have little meaning when a person is high or drunk.

Substance abuse, commonly involving alcohol, triggers "stranger violence," a crime in which the victim has no relationship whatsoever with his or her attacker. Such an occurrence could involve a confrontation in a bar or some other public place where the attacker and victim happen to be at the same time. Criminologists estimate that alcohol or drug use by the attacker is behind 30 to 50 percent of violent crime, such as murder, sexual assault, and robbery. In addition drugs or alcohol may make the victim a more vulnerable target for a criminal by being less attentive to activities around and perhaps visiting a poorly lighted or secluded area not normally frequented perhaps to purchase drugs.

The idea that drug and alcohol abuse can be a major factor in a person's life is why there are numerous treatment programs for young people addicted to these substances. Treatment focuses on positive support to influence a person's future decision making and to reduce the tendency for anti-social and criminal behavior.

Easy access

Another factor many criminologists consider key to making a life of crime easier is the availability of handguns in U.S. society. Many firearms used in crimes are stolen or purchased illegally (bought on what is called the "black market"). Firearms provide a simple means of committing a crime while allowing offenders some distance or detachment from their victims. Of the 400,000 violent crimes involving firearms in 1998, over 330,000 involved handguns. By the beginning of the twenty-first century firearm use was the eighth leading cause of death in the United States.

Similarly, the increased availability of free information on the Internet also makes it easy to commit certain kinds of

At the beginning of the twenty-first century, firearm use was the eighth leading cause of death in the United States. *(AP/Wide World Photos)*

crime. Web sites provide instructions on how to make bombs and buy poisons; all this information is easily available from the comfort of a person's home. Easy access, however, will not be the primary factor in a person's decision to commit a crime. Other factors—biological, psychological, or social—will also come into play.

The complexities of crime

Explaining the cause of crime is difficult; two people living in the same circumstances—such as poverty, family problems, or unemployment—may take entirely different paths in life. A related question to what leads people to commit crimes, is what causes some criminals to quit? Some juvenile delinquents stop committing crimes when they become adults; others stop later in adulthood. Leading factors may include changing body chemistry such as lowering of testosterone, improved employment, or growing family responsibilities like becoming a parent.

Aging is definitely a factor in crime trends. Some attribute the crime drop in the 1990s not just to more prisons or lower unemployment rates, but to the aging of the population. Statistics show most criminals are males between seventeen and thirty-four years of age. In the 1970s, this segment of society was quite large; by the 1990s it had substantially declined.

Despite aging some people commit criminal acts throughout their lives, sometimes becoming even more violent. Others do not turn to crime until their later years. Both of these patterns argue against internal causes of crime. Some criminologists insist the tendency to commit a crime remains constant in a person throughout his or her life, that only the opportunities change with time.

By the early twenty-first century the prevailing thought among criminologists was that criminal behavior comes from a combination of factors. People are complex and influenced by social, biological, psychological, and economic conditions in different ways. The links between crime and employment, education, and family life remain extremely hard to predict and difficult to define.

For More Information

Books

Arrigo, Bruce A., ed. *Social Justice, Criminal Justice.* Belmont, CA: Wadsworth, 1999.

Bowlby, John. *A Secure Base: Parent-Child Attachment and Healthy Human Development.* New York: Basic Books, 1988.

Cleckely, Hervey. *The Mask of Sanity.* New York: New American Library, 1982.

Cohen, Albert K. *Delinquent Boys: The Culture of the Gang.* New York: Free Press, 1955.

Curran, Daniel J., and Claire M. Renzetti. *Theories of Crime.* Boston, MA: Allyn & Bacon, 2001.

Fleisher, Mark S. *Beggars and Thieves: Lives of Urban Street Criminals.* Madison, WI: University of Wisconsin Press, 1995.

Karr-Morse, Robin, and Meredith S. Wiley. *Ghosts from the Nursery: Tracing the Roots of Violence.* New York: Atlantic Monthly Press, 1997.

Lombroso, Cesare. *Crime: Its Causes and Remedies.* Montclair, NJ: Patterson Smith, 1968.

Renzetti, Claire M., and Lynne Goodstein, eds. *Women, Crime, and Criminal Justice.* Los Angeles: Roxbury, 2001.

Web Site

Criminal Justice. http://www.wadsworth.com/criminaljustice_d/ (accessed on August 19, 2004).

Where to Learn More

Books

Abadinsky, Howard. *Drug Abuse: An Introduction.* Chicago, IL: Nelson-Hall Publishers, 1997.

Acker, James R., Robert M. Bohm, and Charles S. Lanier, eds. *America's Experiment with Capital Punishment: Reflections on the Past, Present, and Future of the Ultimate Penal Sanction.* Durham, NC: Carolina Academic Press, 1998.

Anderson, Elijah. *Streetwise: Race, Class and Change in an Urban Community.* Chicago, IL: University of Chicago Press, 1990.

Arrigo, Bruce A., ed. *Social Justice, Criminal Justice.* Belmont, CA: Wadsworth, 1999.

Austern, David. *The Crime Victims Handbook: Your Rights and Role in the Criminal Justice System.* New York: Viking, 1987.

Bachman-Prehn, Ronet D. *Death and Violence on the Reservation: Homicide, Violence, and Suicide in American Indian Populations.* New York: Auburn House, 1992.

Baum, Lawrence. *American Courts.* 5th ed. Boston: Houghton Mifflin, 2001.

Belknap, Joanne. *The Invisible Woman: Gender, Crime, and Justice.* Toronto: Wadsworth Thomson Learning, 2001.

Benjamin, William P. *African Americans in the Criminal Justice System.* New York: Vantage Press, 1996.

Besharov, Douglas J. *Recognizing Child Abuse: A Guide for the Concerned.* New York: Free Press, 1990.

Burns, Ronald G., and Michael J. Lynch. *Environmental Crime: A Source Book.* New York: LFB Scholarly Publishing, 2004.

Burrough, Bryan. *Public Enemies: America's Greatest Crime Wave and the Birth of the FBI, 1933–34.* New York: Penguin Press, 2004.

Buzawa, Eve, and Carl Buzawa. *Domestic Violence: The Criminal Justice Response.* Thousand Oaks, CA: Sage, 1996.

Carp, Robert A., and Ronald Stidham. *Judicial Process in America.* 5th ed. Washington, DC: CQ Press, 2001.

Chase, Anthony. *Law and History: The Evolution of the American Legal System.* New York: The New Press, 1997.

Clement, Mary. *The Juvenile Justice System.* 3rd ed. Woburn, MA: Butterworth Heinemann, 2002.

Clifford, Mary. *Environmental Crime: Enforcement, Policy, and Social Responsibility.* Gaithersburg, MD: Aspen Publishers, Inc., 1998.

Clifford, Ralph D., ed. *Cybercrime: The Investigation, Prosecution, and Defense of a Computer-Related Crime.* Durham, NC: Carolina Academic Press, 2001.

Cohn, Marjorie, and David Dow. *Cameras in the Courtroom: Television and the Pursuit of Justice.* New York: McFarland & Company, 1998.

Coloroso, Barbara. *The Bully, the Bullied, and the Bystander: From Pre-School to High School, How Parents and Teachers Can Help Break the Cycle of Violence.* New York: HarperResource, 2003.

Conser, James A., and Gregory D. Russell. *Law Enforcement in the United States.* Gaithersburg, MD: Aspen, 2000.

Cromwell, Paul, Lee Parker, and Shawna Mobley. "The Five-Finger Discount." In *In Their Own Words: Criminals on Crime,* edited by Paul Cromwell. Los Angeles, CA: Roxbury, pp. 57–70.

Curran, Daniel J., and Claire M. Renzetti. *Theories of Crime.* Boston: Allyn & Bacon, 2001.

Davidson, Michael J. *A Guide to Military Criminal Law.* Annapolis, MD: Naval Institute Press, 1999.

Dummer, Harry R. *Religion in Corrections.* Lanham, MD: American Correctional Associates, 2000.

Dunne, Dominick. *Justice: Crimes, Trials, and Punishment.* New York: Three Rivers Press, 2002.

Federal Bureau of Investigation. *Crime in the United States, 2002: Uniform Crime Reports.* Washington, DC: U.S. Department of Justice, 2003.

Felson, Marcus. *Crime and Everyday Life*. 2nd ed. Thousand Oaks, CA: Pine Forge Press, 1998.

Frank, Nancy, and Michael Lynch. *Corporate Crime, Corporate Violence*. Albany, NY: Harrow and Heston, 1992.

Friedman, Lawrence M. *Crime and Punishment in American History*. New York: Basic Books, 1993.

Garbarino, James. *Lost Boys: Why Our Sons Turn Violent and How We Can Save Them*. New York: Free Press, 1999.

Gordon, Margaret, and Stephanie Riger. *The Female Fear*. New York: Free Press, 1989.

Hirsch, Adam Jay. *The Rise of the Penitentiary: Prisons and Punishment in Early America*. New Haven, CT: Yale University Press, 1992.

Hoffer, Peter C. *Law and People in Colonial America*. Baltimore: Johns Hopkins University Press, 1998.

Jones-Brown, Delores. *Race, Crime, and Punishment*. Philadelphia: Chelsea House, 2000.

Karmen, Andrew. *Crime Victims: An Introduction to Victimology*. 4th ed. Belmont, CA: Wadsworth, 2001.

Lane, Brian. *Crime and Detection*. New York: Alfred A. Knopf, 1998.

Levin, Jack. *The Violence of Hate: Confronting Racism, Anti-Semitism, and Other Forms of Bigotry*. Boston: Allyn and Bacon, 2002.

Lunde, Paul. *Organized Crime: An Inside Guide to the World's Most Successful Industry*. New York: DK Publishing, Inc., 2004.

Lyman, Michael D., and Gary W. Potter. *Organized Crime*. Upper Saddle River, NJ: Pearson Prentice Hall, 2004.

Mones, Paul. *When a Child Kills*. New York: Simon & Schuster, 1991.

Oliver, Willard M. *Community-Oriented Policing: A Systematic Approach to Policing*. Upper Saddle River, NJ: Prentice Hall, 2001.

Patrick, John J. *The Young Oxford Companion to the Supreme Court of the United States*. New York: Oxford University Press, 1998.

Ramsey, Sarah H., and Douglas E. Adams. *Children and the Law in a Nutshell*. 2nd ed. St. Paul, MN: Thomson/West, 2003.

Renzetti, Claire M., and Lynne Goodstein, eds. *Women, Crime, and Criminal Justice*. Los Angeles: Roxbury, 2001.

Russell, Katheryn. *The Color of Crime*. New York: New York University Press, 1998.

Sherman, Mark. *Introduction to Cyber Crime*. Washington, DC: Federal Judicial Center, 2000.

Siegel, Larry J. *Criminology: The Core*. Belmont, CA: Wadsworth/Thomson Learning, 2002.

Silverman, Ira. *Corrections: A Comprehensive View.* 2nd ed. Belmont, CA: Wadsworth, 2001.

Situ, Yingyi, and David Emmons. *Environmental Crime: The Criminal Justice System's Role in Protecting the Environment.* Thousand Oaks, CA: Sage Publications, 2000.

Smith, Helen. *The Scarred Heart: Understanding and Identifying Kids Who Kill.* Knoxville, TN: Callisto, 2000.

Stark, Rodney, and Williams Sims Bainbridge. *Religion, Deviance, and Social Control.* New York: Routledge, 1997.

Sullivan, Robert, ed. *Mobsters and Gangsters: Organized Crime in America, from Al Capone to Tony Soprano.* New York: Life Books, 2002.

Sutherland, Edwin H. *White-Collar Crime: The Uncut Version.* New Haven, CT: Yale University Press, 1983.

Walker, Samuel. *The Police in America: An Introduction.* New York: McGraw-Hill, 1992.

Wilkinson, Charles F. *American Indians, Time, and the Law: Native Societies in a Modern Constitutional Democracy.* New Haven, CN: Yale University Press, 1987.

Wright, Richard, and Scott Decker. *Armed Robbers in Action: Stickups and Street Culture.* Boston: Northeastern University Press, 1997.

Yalof, David A., and Kenneth Dautrich. *The First Amendment and the Media in the Court of Public Opinion.* Cambridge: Cambridge University Press, 2002.

Web Sites

"Arrest the Racism: Racial Profiling in America." *American Civil Liberties Union (ACLU).* http://www.aclu.org/profiling (accessed on September 20, 2004).

Center for the Prevention of School Violence. http://www.ncdjjdp.org/cpsv/ (accessed on September 20, 2004).

"Computer Crime and Intellectual Property Section (CCIPS) of the Criminal Division." *U.S. Department of Justice.* http://www.cybercrime.gov (accessed on September 20, 2004).

"Counterfeit Division." *United States Secret Service.* http://www.secretservice.gov/counterfeit.shtml (accessed on September 20, 2004).

Court TV's Crime Library. http://www.crimelibrary.com (accessed on September 20, 2004).

"Criminal Enforcement." *U.S. Environmental Protection Agency.* http://www.epa.gov/compliance/criminal/index.html (accessed on September 20, 2004).

Death Penalty Information Center. http://www.deathpenaltyinfo.org (accessed on September 20, 2004).

Department of Homeland Security. http://www.dhs.gov (accessed on September 20, 2004).

Federal Bureau of Investigation (FBI). http://www.fbi.gov (accessed on September 20, 2004).

McGeary, Johanna. "Who's the Enemy Now?" *Time,* March 29, 2004. http://www.time.com/time/classroom/glenfall2004/pg28.html (accessed on September 20, 2004).

Mothers Against Drunk Driving (MADD). http://www.madd.org (accessed on September 20, 2004).

National Alliance of Crime Investigators Associations. http://www.nagia.org (accessed on September 20, 2004).

National Center for Juvenile Justice. http://www.ncjj.org (accessed on September 20, 2004).

National Center for Victims of Crime. http://www.ncvc.org (accessed on September 20, 2004).

National Child Abuse and Neglect Data System (NCANDS). http://nccanch. acf.hhs.gov/index.cfm (accessed on September 20, 2004).

"National Institute of Corrections (NIC)." *U.S. Department of Justice.* http://www.nicic.org (accessed on September 20, 2004).

National Institute of Military Justice. http://www.nimj.com/Home.asp (accessed on September 20, 2004).

National Organization for Victim Assistance (NOVA). http://www.try-nova. org (accessed on September 20, 2004).

Uniform Crime Reporting Program. http://www.fbi.gov/ucr/ucr.htm (accessed on September 20, 2004).

United Nations Office for Drug Control and Crime Prevention, Organized Crime. http://www.undcp.org/organized_crime.html (accessed on September 20, 2004).

U.S. Courts. http://www.uscourts.gov (accessed on September 20, 2004).

U.S. Department of Justice. http://www.usdoj.gov (accessed on September 20, 2004).

U.S. Drug Enforcement Administration. http://www.dea.gov (accessed on September 20, 2004).

U.S. Securities and Exchange Commission. http://www.sec.gov (accessed on September 20, 2004).

Index

Biological hazards, *1:* 155

Biological terrorism, *1:* 182–83

Black Americans
arrest statistics, *2:* 423
"Black Codes," *1:* 5, 36; *2:* 421
capital punishment, *2:* 403, 428–29
Civil Rights Movement, *2:* 257
crime and, *2:* 416–17, 422–24
Crips and Bloods, *1:* 123–26, 124 (ill.)
incarceration rates, *2:* 429
Jim Crow laws, *2:* 422
juvenile crime, *2:* 345
legal protections, *1:* 36
police, *1:* 36
racial profiling, *2:* 425–27
"three strikes" laws, *2:* 433
victims, *2:* 423–24

"Black Codes," *1:* 5, 36; *2:* 421

Black Panther Party, *1:* 124

Blasphemy, *1:* 15–16

Blodget, Henry, *1:* 107

Bloods and Crips, *1:* 123–26, 124 (ill.), 128–29

"Bobbies," *2:* 249

Bogus stock, *1:* 201

BOI (Bureau of Investigation), *1:* 41; *2:* 255

Bombings
bomb response units, *2:* 273–74
Oklahoma City bombing, *1:* 51, 176, 177 (ill.), 181
terrorist, *1:* 51, 180–83
Weathermen, *1:* 174

Bonaparte, Napoleon, *2:* 249

Bond system, *1:* 18

Boot camp prisons, *2:* 310, 410 (ill.)

Booth, John Wilkes, *2:* 280

Booth, Maude Ballington, *2:* 398

Bootlegging, *1:* 118

Boston Archdiocese, *2:* 371–73

Boston police strike, *2:* 252

Bow Street Runners, *2:* 266–67

Bowling for Columbine (film), *2:* 385

Brady Act, *1:* 199

Bratton, William, *1:* 215

Breaking and entering, *1:* 79

Breath alcohol contraction (BAC), *1:* 139–40

Breed v. Jones, 2: 347

British loyalists, *1:* 25

Broken Windows theory of crime, *1:* 214–15; *2:* 262

Brown, William H., *2:* 444

Bryant, Kobe, *2:* 447–48

Bullying, *2:* 382, 388

Bundy, Ted, *1:* 65, 65 (ill.)

Bureau of Federal Prisons, *1:* 47

Bureau of Indian Affairs (BIA), *2:* 335 (ill.), 336, 338

Bureau of Investigation (BOI), *1:* 41; *2:* 255

Bureau of Justice Statistics, *2:* 413

Burglary, *1:* 75, 78–81

Burns National Detective Agency, *2:* 252

Burns, William J., *2:* 252

Burr, Aaron, *2:* 439

Bush, George W., *1:* 184–85; *2:* 311 (ill.)

Bush, Jeb, *2:* 407

Businesses
organized crime, *1:* 115
theft of equipment, *1:* 82

C

Cable news, *2:* 444, 450

Cadillacs, *1:* 163

California
"three strikes" laws, *2:* 433
victims' compensation program, *2:* 234–35

Calley, William, *2:* 329

Cameras in the courtroom, *2:* 442–44, 449–50

Canada, *1:* 145–46

Capital punishment. *See also* Death row; Executions
abolition of, *1:* 31
colonial period, *1:* 16–17; *2:* 400
as cruel and unusual punishment, *1:* 29
exclusions, *2:* 403–4
federal capital crimes, *2:* 403, 405
morality of, *2:* 401
race/ethnicity, *2:* 428–29
sentencing, *2:* 404–5
statistics, *2:* 400

Internet
child pornography, *1:* 197–98
crime and access to information, *1:* 224–25
cyber crime, *1:* 54–55
encryption, *1:* 200
fraud, *1:* 195–97
Internet service providers (ISPs), *1:* 197
overview, *1:* 191, 193
pornography, *1:* 136
protection of children, *2:* 376
securities fraud, *1:* 106–7
Internet Crime Complain Center (IC3), *1:* 207–8
Interstate crime, *1:* 45–46
Investigations
cyber crime, *1:* 193
MDMA trafficking, *1:* 145–46
Investigative and Prosecutive Graphics Unit, FBI, *2:* 279, 282
Involuntary manslaughter, *1:* 63
IPS (Intensive Probation Supervision), *2:* 317–18
Iran, *1:* 180
IRS (International Revenue Service), *2:* 254
Islamic religious terrorism, *1:* 171–72
ISPs (Internet service providers), *1:* 197
Israel, *1:* 182–83

J

Jackson, Michael, *2:* 447
Jails, *1:* 18, 31; *2:* 308–9, 338
Jamestown, Virginia, *1:* 6–8, 7 (ill.)
Japanese Americans, *2:* 431
Jefferson, Thomas, *1:* 26 (ill.)
Jim Crow laws, *2:* 422
Job training, *1:* 215
Johnson, Lyndon B., *1:* 53, 80; *2:* 257
Johnson, Mitchell, *2:* 383
Judge Advocate General (JAG), *2:* 326, 332, 333, 334
Judges
cameras in the courtroom, *2:* 444, 450

colonial period, *1:* 11–12
federal courts, *2:* 289
juvenile courts, *2:* 349
military, *2:* 332–33
state courts, *2:* 292–94
Judiciary Act, *1:* 26; *2:* 287
Juries
colonial period, *1:* 12
eighteenth century, *1:* 19
Jurisdiction
cyber crime, *1:* 205–7
federal courts, *2:* 288
juvenile courts, *2:* 294, 340, 342
military justice, *2:* 328
Native Americans, *2:* 334–35, 336
state courts, *2:* 287
Jury awards, *2:* 411–12
Jury trials, *1:* 12; *2:* 295
Justices of the peace. *See* Magistrates
Justifiable homicide, *1:* 62
Juvenile Court Act (Illinois), *1:* 56
Juvenile courts
case transfers to adult courts, *2:* 295, 345, 353–54, 354 (ill.)
civil liberties, *2:* 346–47
establishment of, *2:* 294–95
judges, *2:* 349
jurisdiction, *2:* 340, 342
overview, *2:* 343–46
proceedings, *2:* 349–51
rights of juveniles, *2:* 349–51, 375–76
sentencing, *2:* 351–52
Juvenile Courts Act, *2:* 345
Juvenile crime
arson, *1:* 88–89
causes, *2:* 355
delinquents, *2:* 341 (ill.)
Juvenile Delinquency Prevention Act, *1:* 56; *2:* 347
rates of, *2:* 356
statistics, *2:* 344–45
Juvenile justice system
future of, *2:* 355–56
get-tough policies, *1:* 57
Juvenile Court Act (Illinois), *1:* 56
juvenile prisons, *2:* 348 (ill.)

P

Trusts, *1:* 109

TTIC (Terrorist Threat Integration Center), *1:* 186

Tubbs, David, *1:* 95 (ill.)

Tulloch, Robert, *1:* 59

"Two strikes" rule, *2:* 365

Two-way radios, *2:* 254 (ill.), 255

Tyson Foods, *1:* 165

U

UCMJ (Uniform Code of Military Justice), *2:* 328, 333

UCR (Uniform Crime Report), *1:* 43; *2:* 242

"Unabomber," *1:* 51, 179, 179 (ill.); *2:* 279

Unemployment and crime, *1:* 214–15, 217

Uniform Child Custody Jurisdiction Act, *2:* 364

Uniform Code of Military Justice (UCMJ), *2:* 328, 333

Uniform Crime Report (UCR), *1:* 43; *2:* 242

Uniform Interstate Family Support Act, *2:* 374

Uniforms, police, *1:* 34

United Nations, *2:* 297

Unlawful entry, *1:* 78

Unreasonable searches and seizures. *See* Searches and seizures

Unreformed death row prisoners, *2:* 314

The Untouchables (TV show), *2:* 446

Urban decay, *2:* 414 (ill.)

U.S. attorneys, *2:* 287, 290

U.S. Embassy bombings, *1:* 181

U.S. marshals, *1:* 35, 35 (ill.); *2:* 248, 250, 255, 287, 290

U.S. Supreme Court, *1:* 26

USA Patriot Act, *1:* 51, 187–88; *2:* 253

V

Valley State Prison for Women, *2:* 305 (ill.)

Verona, Roxana, *1:* 59

Victim Assistance Legal Organization, *2:* 241

Victim Rights Clarification Act, *2:* 238

Victim and Witness Protection Act, *2:* 238–40

Victimless crimes. *See* Public order crimes

Victims
assistance programs, *2:* 233–34
bill of rights, *2:* 236–38
Black Americans, *2:* 423–24
colonial period, *2:* 231–32
compensation programs, *2:* 234–35
English common law, *1:* 9
Federal victims' rights legislation, *2:* 238
mediation, *2:* 237
murder, *1:* 64
protection, *2:* 238–40
rape, *1:* 72–73
right to sue, *2:* 232–33
rights of, *2:* 235–38
robbery, *1:* 67
role, *2:* 242–43
statistics, *2:* 229
studies of, *2:* 241–43
victim advocates, *2:* 240–41
white-collar crime, *1:* 94

Victims of Child Abuse Act, *2:* 238

Victims of Child Abuse Laws, *2:* 369

Victims of Crime Act (VOCA), *2:* 235, 236

Victims of Trafficking and Violence Protection Act, *2:* 366

Victims' Rights and Restitution Act, *2:* 238

Vietnam War, *1:* 174–75; *2:* 329

Vigilantes, *1:* 34–35; *2:* 249

Violence
black American communities, *2:* 424
drop in rates of, *1:* 57
fear of, *1:* 55
media, *2:* 388
minority communities, *2:* 432
motorcycle gangs, *1:* 122
Native Americans, *2:* 336–37
police and, *2:* 256
rates of, *1:* 53, 61
women victims, *2:* 232

Violence Against Women Act, *1:* 73; *2:* 232, 297